100 THINGS
WILDCATS FANS
SHOULD KNOW & DO
BEFORE THEY DIE

100 THINGS WILDCATS FANS SHOULD KNOW & DO BEFORE THEY DIE

Ryan Clark and Joe Cox

TRIUMPH
BOOKS

Library of Congress Cataloging-in-Publication Data

Clark, Ryan, 1979–
    100 things Wildcats fans should know & do before they die / Ryan Clark and Joe Cox.
        p. cm.
    Includes bibliographical references.
    ISBN 978-1-60078-730-0
    1. University of Kentucky—Basketball—History. 2. University of Kentucky—Basketball—Miscellanea. 3. Kentucky Wildcats (Basketball team)—History. 4. Kentucky Wildcats (Basketball team)—Miscellanea. I. Cox, Joe, 1980– II. Title. III. Title: One hundred things Wildcats fans should know and do before they die.
    GV885.42.U53C53 2012
    796.323'630976947—dc23
                                                    2012028870

This book is available in quantity at special discounts for your group or organization. For further information, contact:

Triumph Books LLC
814 North Franklin Street
Suite 303
Chicago, Illinois 60610
(312) 337-0747
Fax (312) 280-5470
www.triumphbooks.com

Printed in U.S.A.
ISBN: 978-1-60078-730-0
Design by Patricia Frey
Photos courtesy of AP Images unless otherwise indicated

Ryan:
To one of the greatest players in UK history
(and my Granddad's favorite), Ralph Beard.
If only more people could have seen him play.

Joe:
To my wife, Julie, and our children,
Natalie and Ryan—my other favorite team!

Contents

Foreword

Through the years I have had the pleasure to view the development of the Kentucky basketball faithful, watching it transform from a strong state to what it is now known as—the Big Blue Nation. My view has been from a recruit and player back in the day to a fan and now a TV and radio analyst on the Kentucky basketball network. Big Blue Nation is a passionate group to say the least, and its desire to know all about the Cats is legendary. Its basketball IQ is very high, and its deep understanding of the proud history of the UK program is unsurpassed in college hoops.

It never ceases to amaze me where a Cat fan may show up, always wearing the required piece of Kentucky gear. Wherever you are, you hear a chant of "Go Big Blue!" or "Cats! Cats! Cats!" You can feel the warmth of the Big Blue Nation. Hearing those chants in arenas all over the country will put goosebumps on your arms.

So for those of us who are old-school Cat fans or are second-, third-, or fourth-generation fans, this is a book that can remind you of all the things you have enjoyed as a part of Big Blue Nation. It also may introduce you to some knowledge or experiences that you may have missed along the way. If you have a Bucket List for Kentucky basketball in your life, put this book on it and enjoy the ride.

Go Cats!!!

—Mike Pratt
Spring 2012

Acknowledgments

I would be remiss if I did not start by thanking my Lord and Savior, Jesus Christ, in whom all things are possible. Further unending gratitude goes to my lovely wife, Julie, who acted as proofreader, unofficial editor, consoler, motivator, mother of my children, and love of my life. I will try not to be too jealous when her books far outshine my own. Speaking of those children, Natalie and Ryan, thanks for letting me have the time to write this, and I love you both more than you'll know. Thanks to my mom for her love and support—and for taping about ten years worth of games on VHS tapes for me. Thanks to Dad for putting aside his disinterest in sports to give a thorough and efficient proofreading exactly when it was needed. Thanks to my sister, Teresa, for being herself, which has always been entertaining. Appreciation is also due to my in-laws for their thoughtful support.

I have been lucky to have spent my life surrounded by good, decent, kind-hearted people who fostered my love of Kentucky basketball. In naming some of them, I know that I'll accidentally leave out some others, and I beg their forgiveness, but just a few who spring to mind are Carlton Hughes, Jane Mullins and Eugene Kincer, Jay Mujumdar, Garry Bingham, and Earl Costellow. Thanks to all of the other good people of Letcher, Bell, Jefferson, Warren, and Logan Counties who have helped me root for the Cats from almost all corners of Kentucky.

Thanks to Jon Scott for information, and to Ritchie Curtis and Rob Smith, among others, for the research help they provided. Russell Rice should be commended for writing the first—and in many cases the most authoritative—word on most major UK basketball history topics.

I can't leave out the good folks at Western Kentucky University. Professors like Walker Rutledge, John Hagaman, Joseph Glaser, the late Patricia Taylor, Karen Schneider, and Ted Hovet constantly encouraged and guided me throughout my studies with them, and a decade or more on, I hope I've retained most of their lessons. If so, the praise is theirs if not, the fault is mine. While this is hardly a literary book, I still appreciate the "most reverend heads, to whom I owe/All that I am in arts, all that I know," as Ben Jonson put it so well while also admitting, as Jonson did, "How nothing's that?".

Finally, big thanks always go out to my co-author. I was a homesick college freshman with few friends in the fall of 1998 when I met Ryan Clark. I'm grateful for the friendship that we've shared and most of all for his can-do attitude, which made this project a reality. Let's do this again sometime, Ryan.

Thanks to all of the players—once men to me, now just past being boys—who have worn the blue and white, and the staff who coached, taught, and otherwise supported them. While this book is sometimes a bit light in tone, please don't think that I do not appreciate the pressures that these folks have lived with over the years. Without the Wildcats, there are no Wildcats fans.

Lastly, thanks to the game of basketball. To paraphrase what the great Jim Bouton said about his initial vocation, I spent a lot of time, maybe too much, gripping a basketball as a young boy. It's only as a man that I realize that, as often as not, the basketball was gripping me. It's always been a wonderful ride.

—J. Cox

Joe is a wonderful writer, and he did a great job of thanking most of the people I'd also like to thank. Like the guy who gets the microphone second at the Academy Awards, I hear the music playing us off. So without further ado, I'd also like to thank my family: Manda and Carrington, as well as my mom and stepfather, Bart, my sister, Jenna, and my granddad, who started all this craziness back when

I was little. Writing this took time away from them, and I thank them all for letting me have this freedom.

Also, to all of the players, staff, fans, and coaches, this book would not exist without you. To former UK Sports Information Director Scott Stricklin and current UK SID DeWayne Peevy, thank you so much for the access over the past few seasons. It's been a blast.

To Dick Weiss, Billy Reed, Tom Wallace, Gregg Doyel, Gene Wojciechowski, Lonnie Wheeler, Denny Trease, and Russell Rice, your books were invaluable.

To those journalism and writing professors at Western Kentucky University, Northern Kentucky University, and the University of Kentucky, as well as those students on staff at *The College Heights Herald* newspaper who helped me, you know who you are. My eternal gratitude to all.

To Mike Pratt, you were a pleasure while helping us, and you seemed genuinely excited about working with us on this project. Many thanks.

To Joe Cox, you are the perfect writing partner—cheers to the first of many!

And to Noah Amstadter, Karen O'Brien, and everyone at Triumph Books, thank you so much for the opportunity. We love working with you.

—R. Clark

Introduction

Two thousand and ninety wins (and counting), eight NCAA Tournament championships, 45 SEC championships, 27 SEC Tournament championships, 54 All-Americans, 60 1,000-point scorers…and one conversation.

This book began sometime in the fall of 1998 as a conversation between two friends— two friends out of thousands, maybe even millions, who make up the Big Blue Nation of Kentucky Wildcats fans. The conversation was about Kentucky basketball, but it also became about the best of Kentucky basketball—which, as the numbers above illustrate, is simply the best of the best. Which players and teams epitomized the tradition, courage, and excellence that made Kentucky basketball so great? What particular games and plays did we remember, and which had we only heard about from grandfathers and family friends but had analyzed and studied until we knew them by heart? Which wacky Cat fans drew our interest or admiration with their own peculiar zeal and devotion? What were the most fun and entertaining UK-related events or experiences?

In 1998, the conversation was a bit different than it is today. John Calipari was getting fired as the coach of the New Jersey Nets, and Tubby Smith was the head man in Lexington. Tayshaun Prince was a freshman at UK, and Anthony Davis was five years old. On the other hand, Bill Keightley was still on the sideline as the equipment manager, and Cawood Ledford, while no longer the Voice of the Wildcats, was still alive and well, as were Ralph Beard and 1921 UK All-American Basil Hayden.

The conversation shifts, as life always does. But the best part is that it just grows another layer. The success of Anthony Davis in no way makes that of Bill Spivey any less important. John Wall sometimes made us wonder if he was as good, or perhaps even better, than Ralph Beard. Coach Cal's home win streak is impressive, but we wonder if he can hope to match Adolph Rupp's 12-year unbeaten run at home.

In trying to summarize the Kentucky basketball experience, we picked 100 essential touchstones—players, coaches, teams, games, broadcasters, locations, events, and even other fans—and wrote short chapters about each. Some of these items are great, some are heartbreaking, and a few are a little weird. We hope that if you're fairly new to this conversation about Kentucky basketball that we can help you catch on and catch up. If you want to learn the difference between the Fabulous Five and the Fiddlin' Five, then read on. If you know about Michael Kidd-Gilchrist, but have never heard of Vernon Hatton, well, we've got some stories to share.

On the other hand, we hope that even the veterans of this conversation, those who were debating some of these topics before our parents were a gleam in our grandparents' eyes, can relive some of those glorious moments again, and hopefully, pick up a few new wrinkles. If you want to learn which UK legend hailed from Booger Hollow or which has one of the funniest Twitter accounts on the Internet, then read on.

And most of all—enjoy the conversation!

J. Cox and R. Clark
Summer 2012

Adolph Rupp

He was known as the "Man in the Brown Suit." And when it comes to Kentucky basketball, he is the first and most important person to know.

Born in Halstead, Kansas, in 1901, Adolph Rupp grew up in a state that would become known for its basketball history. At 6'2", he starred at the local high school, averaging 19 points per game. Sometimes he also served as the unofficial coach of the team. This led to a playing career at the University of Kansas.

A reserve on the Kansas team, Rupp learned from one of the masters—Kansas coach Phog Allen, who himself learned from James Naismith, the inventor of the game. In fact, Naismith was still serving as an assistant on that Kansas team when Rupp was playing. It was only fitting that Rupp would become a coach himself. After a couple of high school coaching jobs, Rupp landed as the head coach at Freeport High in Freeport, Illinois. Many have undoubtedly heard about Rupp's supposed aversion to recruiting African American players, but it was in Freeport that he coached his first black player. In 1930, after coaching at the high school for four years, Rupp invited Illinois coach Craig Ruby to speak at their postseason banquet. Ruby had heard of a job opening for the head basketball coach at the University of Kentucky.

He recommended Rupp for the job.

It was a position Rupp held for the next 41 years, where he accumulated 876 wins, 27 conference championships, four NCAA championships, and an NIT title. He coached his teams to 27 Southeastern Conference championships and 13 SEC Tournament titles, and 32 of his players were named All-American. By the time he retired in 1972, having reached the state-mandated retirement age of 70 for university workers, he was the all-time winningest coach in college basketball history.

In an age where basketball was still being accepted in many southern states, Rupp was an innovator. He wanted to play fast. He wanted to score points. In order to do so, he emphasized a fast-break style of offense where points could be easily scored in transition.

A superstitious man, Rupp always wore his brown suit to games (it was said he once wore a blue suit to a high school game and lost, so he never wore the blue one again) and he always carried a lucky buckeye in his pocket. He did not mince words when it came to his love of winning—or how important he thought it was to win.

"If it doesn't matter who wins or loses, then what in the hell is that scoreboard doing up there?" he famously asked.

And then there are the stereotypes that have followed Rupp through history.

Pay Your Respects: Visit Adolph Rupp's Grave at Lexington Cemetery

Believe it or not, a Lexington gravesite may be the second-most visited shrine when it comes to UK fans (second to Rupp Arena, of course). There, resting in Lexington Cemetery, is the grave of the Baron of the Bluegrass.

Many fans come to the cemetery to visit Rupp's marker, which is decorated with a basketball as a centerpiece.

In December 2009, just before Kentucky became the first program to reach 2,000 total wins, UK coach John Calipari, former coach Joe B. Hall and Herky Rupp, Adolph Rupp's son, all made the pilgrimage to the cemetery to visit Rupp's gravesite.

"More than half the wins were from your father, and you," Calipari told Herky and Hall.

The trio then placed fresh poinsettias on either side of the marker—just like any other fan.

2

In 1966, "Rupp's Runts," a team nicknamed for its lack of height, was ranked No. 1 in the nation and played Texas Western, also a team ranked in the top 5, for the national championship. What made the game even more interesting was the fact that it was the first time an all-white starting five played an all-black starting five for the title.

Kentucky lost the game 72–65, and the game seemed even more important as it occurred during the time of the Civil Rights movement.

Because many of the schools in the south were slow to integrate, the stereotype became that Kentucky and Rupp did not want black players. It wasn't true. Rupp tried to recruit many black players from across the state, beginning in 1965 with star Butch Beard and he signed Tom Payne in 1969. Kentucky was the fourth school in the SEC to integrate the basketball team.

How did Rupp really feel about black players? No one can know for certain. But we know he hated to lose. And if a player was talented, Rupp wanted him.

"I know there have been a lot of people who thought he was a racist," former UK coach Tubby Smith told the *Chicago Tribune* in 1997. "But I think the times can dictate how people act—where you're brought up, how you're brought up. If he was a racist, he wasn't alone in this country. I'm never going to judge anybody. That's a long time ago, too…. You learn from the past, and you go on."

Rupp was inducted into the Naismith Memorial Hall of Fame and the College Basketball Hall of Fame, and after retiring from UK he actually served as the vice president of the American Basketball Association's Kentucky Colonels.

He was succeeded at UK by his former player, assistant, and Cynthiana, Kentucky, native, Joe B. Hall.

On December 10, 1977, the Kentucky basketball team traveled to Lawrence, Kansas, to play the Jayhawks in a game dubbed

Adolph Rupp Night by Rupp's alma mater. The Wildcats won, but the program suffered its greatest loss.

Rupp died that very night, back home in Lexington, at the age of 76.

He is still the fifth all-time winningest coach in men's college basketball.

In his goodbye speech, Rupp said, "For those of you who have gone down the glory road with me, my eternal thanks."

2 Joe B. Hall

Three men have won NCAA championships as players and coaches. Bob Knight and Dean Smith are two. The third was a bespectacled skinny reserve guard on UK's 1949 title team. The benchwarmer played in three games, missed two free throws, and failed to score a point. He transferred to Sewanee after the season. At that point, Joe B. Hall's total contribution to UK basketball was virtually nil. But where the player left off, the coach would later build a Hall of Fame career.

Hall was the head coach at Central Missouri in 1965 when Adolph Rupp brought Hall back to Lexington as an assistant. Coaching under Rupp and alongside venerable assistant Harry Lancaster, Hall was blessed with an opportunity to learn coaching from a couple of its finest practitioners. Hall himself contributed through his conditioning program, remembered ruefully by the 1965–66 squad, which came to be known as Rupp's Runts paid immediate dividends in Lexington. Hall's first season as an assistant was Rupp's last trip to the Final Four, and the Runts' dream ride ended in a historic title-game loss to Texas Western.

Kentucky basketball coach Joe B. Hall on the sideline.

Hall moved to the main assistant job in 1970, and in 1972 he was placed in a very difficult situation. Adolph Rupp was about to turn 70 years old. Under the laws of the time, Rupp was subject to mandatory retirement. Or was he? Rupp did not intend to retire, and great pressure was exerted on the University to craft some manner of exemption to the retirement rule. Hall was stuck in the middle, torn between being loyal to his current boss and the reality that he was candidate No. 1 on the list to replace that boss. The University eventually held its ground, and Rupp grudgingly retired. Joe B. Hall was immediately hired to replace the icon who had built Kentucky basketball. Hall's first two seasons were solid but unspectacular. UK had a combined record of 33–21. Some within the UK fan base clamored for the return of Rupp, who was doing little to be inconspicuous in his retirement.

However, in 1974–75, Hall took a veteran squad led by Kevin Grevey, Jimmy Dan Conner, Mike Flynn, and Bob Guyette into an NCAA Elite Eight game against undefeated Indiana and Bob Knight—the same Bob Knight who had slapped Hall in the back of the head during IU's 24-point beatdown of UK earlier in the season. Not only was Indiana crowned as the likely champion, but many believed Knight's squad was one of the best ever. However, in the locker room before the game, Hall outlined how UK would beat Indiana, cut down the nets, have a police escort back to Lexington, and celebrate wildly.

And that was exactly what happened. UK shocked IU 92–90. A title-game loss to UCLA kept Hall and UK away from the ultimate prize, but the 1975 season permanently banished the specter of Rupp. Three years later, the freshmen from the 1974–75 squad were now veterans. Jack Givens, Rick Robey, Mike Phillips, and James Lee teamed with Purdue transfer Kyle Macy and led the 1977–78 team to UK's fifth NCAA title. The year was known as the Season Without Joy, but this is hardly representative of Hall's feelings.

Hall continued to coach at UK until 1985. He returned UK to the Final Four in 1984 and won eight SEC titles in his thirteen seasons as UK head coach. Joe B. Hall was 297–100 in his UK coaching career. As the only native Kentuckian to coach the Cats in the last 80 years, he has remained a visible part of the Big Blue Nation in retirement. Hall worked to further the international spread of basketball during and after his career, and he even had a brief career as a color commentator on the UK Television Network. In 2012, he was finally recognized with selection to the National Collegiate Basketball Hall of Fame—quite an auspicious climax to a career that started with three games played and no points.

3 Cawood Ledford

It is a long journey from a place called Booger Hollow to immortality. But it is a journey that radio legend Cawood Ledford knew well. Calling Cawood Ledford a sports broadcaster is like calling Everest a mountain. From 1953 to 1992, from Adolph Rupp to Rick Pitino's Unforgettables, Ledford calling the action remained the one constant in Kentucky basketball. A member of the National Basketball Hall of Fame, Gannett News Service's choice as the best college sportscaster in history, and the first non-player or coach to have his UK "jersey" retired, Cawood Ledford set a standard in his field that is every bit as formidable as Kentucky basketball is on the hardwood.

Ledford was born on April 24, 1926, officially in Harlan, Kentucky, but actually in an area that is known as Booger Hollow. Ledford graduated from Hall High School, and during World War II he served in the U.S. Marines. Ledford graduated from Centre College and was briefly a high school English teacher back at Hall High. In 1951, however, Ledford began announcing high school football and basketball games in Harlan. Only two years later, Ledford began announcing UK hoops. At the time, there were multiple networks, each with its own call of UK games. Ledford went head-to-head with the legendary Claude Sullivan. Sullivan, who was one year older than Ledford and a native of Winchester, Kentucky, was perhaps the feature attraction of UK announcers at that time. Ledford, though, was a viable competitor, and by the time Sullivan's promising career and his life were prematurely ended by throat cancer in 1967, there was no question as to who would then be *the* voice of the Wildcats.

Claude Sullivan

For a time, Cawood Ledford wasn't even the most popular UK radio announcer. Claude Sullivan, who was Ledford's competition-in-chief, called games for WVLK in Lexington, while Ledford came to work with WHAS in Louisville. Indeed, while Ledford is one of the most well-known broadcasters in history, Sullivan is relegated as something of an afterthought. To say that this is undeserved is an understatement.

Claude Sullivan had much of the same professionalism and versatility as Ledford. Like Ledford, Sullivan was also at home at the horse track or at the ballpark. Sullivan was the play-by-play voice of the Cincinnati Reds before cancer took his life in 1967. While Sullivan preceded Ledford as the Voice of UK basketball, he also preceded the venerable Marty Brennaman as the Voice of Reds baseball.

Having the bad luck to die at a young age (42) seems to have been Sullivan's only mistake. While acclaim has been a bit slow to come, in 2006, Claude Sullivan was inducted into the Kentucky Journalism Hall of Fame and the UK Sports Hall of Fame.

Historically speaking, Ledford's career stretched far beyond even Kentucky basketball. Many experts contend that Ledford's best sport was actually horse racing, and he called the Kentucky Derby nationally for many years on behalf of CBS Radio. Ledford also broadcast from events such as baseball's World Series, golf's Masters, and many great boxing matches, including several involving Kentucky native Muhammad Ali. Indeed, Ledford's stature was so great than when President of the United States Bill Clinton made an appearance in Hazard, Kentucky, in 1999, there was no question who the Commander-in-Chief wished to announce him. *The New York Times* reported that the President quipped, "I was thinking that if old Cawood had been a political announcer instead of a basketball announcer, and I could have kept him with me these last 25 years, I'd have never lost an election."

Stylistically, Ledford was exactly perfect. His descriptions were mature and complete but also simple enough for anyone to follow. His own feelings were clear to his listeners, but Ledford never descended into homerism or self-promotion the way that many current announcers do. The extent to which Ledford is and was the gold standard of announcing is hard to overstate. A couple of fascinating artifacts shared by current UK announcer Tom Leach on his website are written critiques that Ledford prepared for Leach, giving him specific instruction on how Leach might improve his calls of UK action. The best is a three-page handwritten letter to Leach after he called UK football's exciting 1997 win over Alabama. Ledford's advice is precise and exact—he offers no suggestion that he himself did not utilize—and the overall tone is kind, supportive, and studious.

For instance, "Tape all of your games, and as you listen, ask yourself how you could have done better." It is somewhat comforting to see the level of dedication and study that Ledford practiced. While Ledford was blessed with supreme talent, it is immediately clear how hard-working and conscientious he was. Like Dan Issel firing in a jump shot or Anthony Davis timing another blocked shot, the results could seem effortless at first notice, but the man who hailed from Booger Hollow took his place in Kentucky basketball lore because of his hard work and relentless desire for perfection. Little wonder that after Ledford's passing in 2001, UK designated the playing floor at Rupp Arena as Cawood's Court—a designation that Tom Leach mentions at each home game to this day. No doubt, it was quite a trip from Booger Hollow.

4 Bill Keightley

The first things you noticed were his hands. Yes, they were aged, spotted, and rough from years and years of hard work. But they were bedazzled—each wore a huge ring sporting jewels and diamonds, and your eyes were automatically drawn to them.

They were his championship rings, and Bill Keightley had three in all, one each from the three years he served as equipment manager when his Kentucky Wildcats won the national basketball championship. In 1978, he earned his first when Coach Joe B. Hall led the Cats to the title. He earned rings two and three with Rick Pitino in 1996 and Tubby Smith in 1998, respectively.

Two hands, but three rings—how to decide which to wear?

"I'm not wearing the '96 one right now," Keightley said hours before a home basketball game in 2007. He smiled. The only thing bigger than those rings was his smile.

He was making a bit of a joke. A few years prior, Pitino—who had served as UK head coach for eight years until he accepted the job to rebuild the NBA's woeful Boston Celtics—left professional basketball and had taken the coaching job with the Wildcats' main rival, the Louisville Cardinals. Keightley detested the Cards.

Normally, the annual Kentucky and Louisville basketball game was played around Christmas or New Year's Eve. Keightley was known to sit on his spot on the bench, counting down the minutes until a win over Louisville would allow him to celebrate the holiday. Three minutes to go? "Three minutes 'til Christmas," he would say. Two minutes? "Two minutes 'til Christmas." And so on.

So when it came time to decide which championship rings to wear, it wasn't a difficult decision to keep the Pitino ring in his pocket.

"You can really only wear two at a time," he would say, laughing.

Keightley laughed a lot—and he made others laugh, too. For 48 years, he served as the equipment manager for the basketball team, gathering up their jerseys and socks and making sure players always had what they needed to wear. But he also served as a listening board for players who needed to vent about their coaches or teammates. He was sometimes a friend to those who just needed someone to talk to.

"You could talk to Mr. Bill, and he could calm people down when they were mad, or he could talk you through some things if

Billy Gillispie (left) shares a laugh with equipment manager Bill Keightley during Big Blue Madness at Rupp Arena in Lexington, Kentucky, on October 12, 2007. (AP Photo/James Crisp, File)

you'd had a bad day or coach had gotten on you," said UK All-American Kevin Grevey. "That's why he was so valuable—he was just a great person."

Also known as "Mr. Wildcat," Keightley was an All-State center at Kavanaugh High in Lawrenceburg. After serving in World War II, he worked as a postal carrier when, in 1962, a co-worker asked him to assist in serving as equipment manager for UK. Ten years later, he took over the job.

In 1997, Keightley was honored when the university retired his jersey, making him just the second non-player or non-coach to receive the honor (radio announcer Cawood Ledford is the other).

Keightley and his wife, Hazel, had one daughter, Helen, who works for the University. And there was only one team Mr. Bill loved like his Wildcats. He loved the Cincinnati Reds.

On March 31, 2008, Keightley was traveling to see Opening Day at the Reds' Great American Ballpark in Cincinnati. He stumbled while exiting a bus and fell, and he was taken to a local hospital. He passed away that day from internal bleeding caused by a previously undiagnosed tumor on his spine.

He was 81 years old.

"Mr. Bill was one of a kind," said UK All-American Kyle Macy. "It's safe to say there won't be another one like him."

John Calipari

On April 1, 2009, John Calipari was hired as the head men's basketball coach at the University of Kentucky.

The program was struggling. The fans were unsatisfied with the performance of the previous coach, Billy Gillispie, who had failed to take the team to the NCAA Tournament for the first time in nearly 20 years. UK needed a coach who would bring top talent to Lexington. Calipari was hired to do just that.

"I am here because I can bring in the very best," Calipari said. And he started quickly, bringing the nation's top point guard, another highly ranked guard, the top power forward, and a pair of other talented wing players to UK. When these players meshed with a few seniors and talented holdover Patrick Patterson, UK was ready to make another run at a national championship.

There was no rebuilding process. The hiring of Calipari was the rebuilding.

But the Calipari story goes back much further than that. Born on February 10, 1959, in Moon Township, Pennsylvania, just outside Pittsburgh, Coach Cal played point guard and earned a scholarship to UNC–Wilmington. In 1980, he transferred to Clarion State where he finished his college career. Immediately, he began coaching at prestigious camps on the East Coast where he crossed paths with another young coach, Rick Pitino. Cal then served as an assistant at Kansas, where he developed a relationship with legendary coach Larry Brown.

In 1985, Calipari became an assistant at Pittsburgh, and in 1988 he was hired as the head coach at Massachusetts—Pitino's alma mater. Pitino has since said that he recommended Calipari for the job, which seems to have irked Calipari. That, coupled with some recruiting friction in the future, caused some tension between the two.

But we're getting ahead of ourselves.

Calipari became a coaching star at UMass, taking a rag-tag bunch of Minutemen and creating a stable, talented program that reached the Final Four in 1996. It was seen as nothing short of a miracle. He recruited Marcus Camby, a 6'10" multi-talented forward who would become Player of the Year in 1996. And UMass' shot at a national title was stopped only by a superbly talented Kentucky team (coached by Pitino) in that year's Final Four.

But that would be just the start of Calipari's problems. After that season Calipari became aware that Camby had taken tens of thousands of dollars in benefits from a professional sports agent, which meant Camby was ineligible for that season. Calipari notified the school and the NCAA himself. As a penalty, UMass was stripped of all its wins that season and its Final Four appearance. Camby declared for the NBA draft, and he became a lottery pick and an instant millionaire.

Calipari did the same, taking the job as head coach and executive vice president of basketball operations for the New Jersey Nets. It did not go well in the NBA. Bad luck, including an injury to Sam Cassell and a lockout in the 1998–99 season, contributed to a bad start for the Nets, who had made the playoffs the previous season. The team started just 3–17, and Coach Cal was fired. He later rejoined Brown as an assistant while Brown was head coach of the Philadelphia 76ers.

In 2000, Calipari took over as head coach of the Memphis Tigers, and immediately he was a rival of Pitino's again, who was then coaching at Louisville. It was there that the two began recruiting the same players, like Dajuan Wagner (Louisville legend Milt Wagner's son) and Darius Washington. This led to more friction between the two coaches, and Pitino called Cal's recruiting tactics "aggressive."

In 2008, Calipari took a team led by national Player of the Year Derrick Rose and played Kansas for the national title. After hitting a three to tie the game, the Jayhawks won in overtime. Calipari was left without his championship. But controversy followed him again. In 2009, Cal was hired to coach Kentucky. He was given the keys to a Cadillac program. And once again, his most fierce rival would be Pitino at Louisville.

"He had proven that he was a coach the best players wanted to play for," said UK All-American and current radio broadcaster Mike Pratt, who helped then-Kentucky president Lee Todd and

John Calipari talks with guard John Wall during the second half of a game against Alabama on Friday, March 12, 2010, at the Southeastern Conference tournament in Nashville, Tennessee. Kentucky won 73–67.
(AP Photo/Mark Humphrey)

athletics director Mitch Barnhart choose the new UK coach. "He became an obvious choice, I thought."

But not long after he was hired, the NCAA ruled that due to improprieties when Rose took his SAT, he would be retroactively ruled ineligible for the 2008 season. To put it another way, a witness claimed that when Rose took his test, it actually wasn't Rose taking it. So even though the NCAA investigated the issue before Rose was admitted to Memphis and originally ruled Rose eligible, the NCAA decided it had made a mistake and punished Memphis by taking away all its wins and its Final Four appearance.

Cal had been to two Final Fours, but both appearances had been vacated by the NCAA for rules violations. Although Calipari was not found to be involved in either situation, it still hung like a black cloud over his head.

"I've been to the Final Four," Calipari would say in a news conference. "I was there. I remember it."

After coming close in his first year at UK, Calipari could officially say he'd been to the Final Four again in 2011, when his Brandon Knight–led squad defeated No. 1 Ohio State and North Carolina to advance to the national semifinals—the school's first appearance in 13 years.

One year later, Calipari put together one of the best teams in Kentucky history. Led by Player of the Year Anthony Davis, Michael Kidd-Gilchrist, Terrence Jones, Doron Lamb, Darius Miller, and Marquis Teague, Kentucky defeated Pitino's Louisville squad in the Final Four, then beat Kansas to win the school's eighth national title.

Calipari came through on his promises.

At last, Kentucky was back on top.

6 Tubby Smith

Within the rarified air of UK basketball coaches, it can be tough for a new member of the group to stand out. All Orlando "Tubby" Smith did in his first season at UK was win the school's seventh NCAA Tournament championship. No other UK coach advanced farther than the Elite Eight of the NCAA Tournament in his first season. Needless to say, Smith raised the bar on UK coaching debuts.

Not so long ago, it would've been unfathomable for Smith to be the UK men's basketball coach at all. Smith's NCAA title came 32 years after an all-white Kentucky team lost to integrated Texas Western in the NCAA finals. Hollywood revisionists aside, Kentucky's segregated status had more to do with the unfortunate politics of the era than with Adolph Rupp or the university being hateful racist monsters. For that matter, if Duke had beaten Kentucky in their semifinal game in that 1966 Tournament, Duke would've been the all-white opponent of Texas Western. It would be interesting to see if Duke would have been vilified as Kentucky has been for the backward climate of the times.

Tom Payne became UK's first African American player in 1970–71. Payne was an All-SEC center in his lone season as a Cat before he entered the NBA Draft. Seven seasons later, Jack "Goose" Givens became UK basketball's first African American All-American. A mere two decades later, when Rick Pitino left town, athletic director C.M. Newton handed the keys to the program to Smith. To be sure, there were critics of that decision—most notably *Lexington Herald-Leader* columnist Merlene Davis, who implored Smith to turn down the job. However, most Kentucky fans were much more focused on Blue and White than black and white.

Kentucky's 1997–98 squad, Smith's first, was a group of veteran players who were solid contributors but not superstars. Smith patiently melded the group into a basketball machine, a tight team that pulled through tough games with experience and chemistry. UK beat Duke in the Elite Eight by two, beat Stanford in the Final Four in overtime by one, and rallied from a 10-point halftime deficit to beat Utah for the NCAA title.

Tubby Smith coached ten total seasons in Lexington. His teams averaged 26 wins per year, and five of his 10 teams won SEC Tournament championships. The Cats won three SEC regular season titles and claimed two more co-championships during Smith's tenure. Smith was 23–9 in NCAA Tournament games at Kentucky, and his teams reached the Elite Eight four times.

While Tubby Smith lacked John Calipari's abilities as a recruiter, his forte was taking solid players and developing them into veteran stars. Among Smith's stable of undervalued UK hoopsters are names like Gerald Fitch, Erik Daniels, Kelenna Azubuike, Chuck Hayes, Cliff Hawkins, and Joe Crawford.

Smith's 2003 team was a superb veteran group led by seniors Keith Bogans and Marquis Estill and juniors Fitch and Daniels. They were the top-ranked team in the nation, and but for an injury to Bogans and meeting a red-hot Dwyane Wade in the Elite Eight, UK might have won an NCAA title.

In 2004, Smith brought in a top-ranked recruiting class. Rajon Rondo, Randolph Morris, Ramel Bradley, and Joe Crawford seemed likely to bring major NCAA hardware back to Lexington. Unfortunately, it never quite worked out that way, and the 2005 team, which fell in the Elite Eight to Michigan State, was as close as it got for that group.

After the 2007 season, Smith, apparently feeling ostracized due to pressure to revamp his assistant coaching staff, moved on to the University of Minnesota. Smith has gone 103–68 in five seasons at Minnesota, and he will begin the 2012–13 season 10 wins short of 500 career wins. Perhaps the only thing Smith did wrong in Lexington was make such a strong debut that he left himself no room to improve.

7 Rick Pitino

"We will win. And we will win right away."

Rick Pitino stood in front of the room of reporters and spoke the words. It was uncertain if he believed them or not. Certainly he believed his team would succeed—the young coach had rebuilt the New York Knicks into a playoff team and taken the Providence Friars to the Final Four.

But right away? Could he really say with a straight face that this 1989–90 Kentucky team, a team with no nationally known players, could win right away?

The year was 1989. The Kentucky basketball program was in the middle of its most trying time. A series of events implied that Kentucky was paying players, and in another instance, a player's test score may have been altered. Because of the scandal, the university president and athletic director left the school, as did most of the so-called "high-profile" recruits and their coach, Eddie Sutton. Kentucky started over and chose a respected son to help in the process.

C.M. Newton was a respected coach in the Southeastern conference, as well as a former UK player under Adolph Rupp. He took the job as athletic director and set out to find the perfect man to rebuild Kentucky's legacy.

He found that man in P.J. Carlisimo. Then the coach at Seton Hall, Carlisimo was respected in the basketball community, and he came within a whisker of winning the 1989 National Championship when his Pirates lost to the Michigan Wolverines in overtime.

There was only one problem: Carlisimo turned Newton down. Duke coach Mike Krzyzewski considered the job and declined, as did Arizona's Lute Olson. Newton thought he may have to coach the team himself for a season while grooming a much less experienced coach as a future replacement. But there was always one person in the back of Newton's mind—someone he thought was perfect for the job.

Rick Pitino.

At first, Pitino also told Newton no. C.M. left the Pitino home in New York, but like any good recruiter, Newton knew his offer to visit Lexington intrigued Pitino. Then the head coach of the New York Knicks, Pitino and his bosses in New York were not seeing eye to eye. It had become such a sore spot that Pitino was thinking of leaving the team.

In a few more days, Newton would have his man. The slick, Armani-wearing Pitino moved to the Bluegrass State where the talent cupboard was bare and his most challenging coaching task lay ahead. Yet he never questioned his winning formula: run, press, shoot threes. Repeat. And when it came time to tell the state and the world what he intended to do, he did not mince words. He was confident. He said UK would win right away. People loved him immediately.

"Coach Pitino has a way of talking that he tells you you're going to do something and you believe it," said UK legend Richie Farmer. "That's one of the reasons he's a great coach."

Pitino was born September 18, 1952, in New York City. After playing point guard for Massachusetts from 1971–74, Pitino served as an assistant at Hawaii and Syracuse before becoming the wunderkind coach at Boston University at age 26 in 1978. His reputation for turning programs around began there when he took a team that had won 17 games in its past two seasons combined and—in five years—led them to their first NCAA Tournament appearance in 24 years. He then left to serve as an assistant for the Knicks under Hubie Brown.

From there, Pitino went to Providence, where the team had just gone 11–20. In two seasons, Pitino had them in the Final Four. He then left to be the head coach of the Knicks, and he had some success, going 52–30 and winning the Atlantic Division in 1989.

Still, with all that success, he was drawn to the challenge of Kentucky. It could be said he would never have as much success anywhere else.

In Pitino's first season with UK, legendary broadcaster Cawood Ledford said it would be a miracle if the team won 10 ballgames. Pitino and the Cats did him four better, going 14–14 (including a 100–95 win over a Shaquille O'Neal–led LSU squad), and winning the hearts of Cats fans everywhere. By the 1990–91 season, the Cats were a better bunch, and with the addition of 6'8" All-Universe power forward Jamal Mashburn, the team went 22–6 and had the best record in the SEC. But because of NCAA probation, Kentucky could not win the tournament or play in the postseason.

The following season, UK began the year ranked fourth in the country. They finished 29–7 and defeated John Calipari's UMass team before pushing the Duke Blue Devils to the brink and losing in the Elite Eight. If anyone was wondering, Kentucky was back. The next season, Mashburn would lead them to the Final Four, and in 1996 Pitino's best squad finished 34–2 and defeated another Calipari squad in the Final Four before claiming the school's sixth national title.

Pitino was king. But there were always rumors that he would return to coach in the NBA. In 1997, his team looked like it could repeat, as it featured two of the country's best players in Ron Mercer and Derek Anderson. Midway through the year, Anderson suffered a shocking knee injury, effectively ending his season and UK career.

The team overachieved, reaching the NCAA finals before falling to Arizona in overtime. It was Pitino's last game at UK.

"We'd heard all the rumors," said UK player Cameron Mills. "But we still really didn't believe it was true."

Pitino told the team he was leaving to coach the Boston Celtics. It did not go well. He was given general manager duties as well as coaching responsibilities, and because Boston had the league's worst record the previous season, the team had the best shot to get Tim Duncan, the consensus No. 1 player in the draft. At worst they could settle for Keith Van Horn, the No. 2 player.

They got neither. Purely by chance, the Celtics missed out on both players, and Pitino's NBA career got worse. His managerial decisions and drafts were not the best; his most successful season was his first, a 36–46 campaign. In his fourth year, Pitino resigned.

In 2001, he returned to college coaching. Instead of taking jobs at UNLV or Michigan, Pitino became the coach of UK's most hated rival, Louisville. It was then that most UK fans severed ties with the former coach. Many had not forgiven him for leaving UK in the first place, and to a lot of them, coaching Louisville was unforgivable.

The coach suffered much embarrassment in 2009 when he was the victim of an extortion attempt. Karen Sypher, the wife of the Cardinals equipment manager, was convicted of blackmailing Pitino. The two had an affair, and Sypher wanted money to keep quiet. Pitino admitted to the affair, and Sypher faces up to 26 years in prison.

Pitino led Louisville to Final Four appearances in 2005 and 2012. He has since admitted that leaving Kentucky was his greatest mistake in coaching.

8 Dan Issel

If there was a UK basketball version of Mount Rushmore, one face that would certainly appear on it would be Dan Issel. A brief check of the UK record book will unearth Issel's name time and time again. In only three seasons (he played before freshmen were eligible for varsity competition), Issel totaled 2,138 points and 1,078 rebounds. Both stats are still UK career records. Issel held the single-game UK scoring record for 38 years. While the record was broken in 2009, to this day Issel ranks second, third, sixth, and ninth in single-game scoring at UK. He broke 40 points in a game nine times and broke the 50-point barrier twice. He managed 29 rebounds in one game against LSU. Issel was a two-time All-American, had his jersey retired at UK, and went on to score more than 27,000 points in the ABA and NBA. Pretty impressive for a guy who wasn't UK's first choice and initially didn't sign with UK.

Issel recounts in Russell Rice's *Big Blue Machine,* "I really wasn't interested in Kentucky.... The big guys UK wanted had

Pistol Pete vs. the Horse

As high scoring as Issel was, he didn't top the SEC in scoring during his career. LSU was fielding a series of mediocre one-man teams centered around Pistol Pete Maravich during Issel's career. Rupp's strategy for playing Maravich was to let the Pistol score his points and shut down the rest of the Tigers. It worked on both accounts. Maravich scored a staggering average of 52 points per game in six career matchups with UK. Issel countered with a merely human average of 30.8 points per game in the six contests, although he did put up 51 on LSU in the last of the six games. Maravich outscored Issel that day by 13 points, but the Wildcats outscored the Tigers by 16. UK won all six games, each by 12 or more points.

signed somewhere else. I changed my mind [Issel had previously signed scholarship papers with Wisconsin] and signed with UK. Later I learned that I really was their third choice at center." The mind boggles at the possibility of two players who were a higher priority than the man who was known as "the Horse."

Assistant Coach Joe B. Hall apparently realized that Issel was special. In Denny Trease's *Tales From the Kentucky Hardwood*,

Dan Issel, shown here with the Kentucky Colonels of the ABA, beats Utah's Austin "Red" Robbins for an easy layup on May 18, 1971, in Salt Lake City. (AP Photo)

Hall's whirlwind recruiting is illustrated. Hall visited the Issel family on an evening when young Dan had a date, and the younger Issel advised Hall that he would only be able to stay for an hour. Issel was true to his word, and left on his date, and apparently Issel's father retired to bed at his usual 10:00 PM hour. When Dan Issel returned home from his date at 11:00 PM, there sat Coach Hall, making his pitch to Issel's mother.

Issel played center at Kentucky but would likely project as a power forward in today's game. At 6'9" and around 225 pounds, Issel was rugged enough to play the post and work the glass, but he was also a deadly mid-range jump shooter. In his sophomore season, 1967–68, Issel contributed 16.4 points and 12.1 rebounds per game. UK was two seasons removed from Rupp's Runts and was ranked No. 5 in the nation when it was upset by Ohio State on a buzzer beater in the Mideast regional final in Lexington.

An inspired Issel upped his contributions in 1968–69, earning All-American honors. Issel averaged 26.6 points and 13.6 rebounds per game. The 1968–69 squad was another talented group, with Issel teaming with Mike Casey and Mike Pratt to lead UK to a No. 7 national ranking. However, Marquette upended UK in their first game of the 1969 NCAA Tournament.

At first glance, 1969–70 was a season that looked like a great opportunity for Adolph Rupp to add a fifth NCAA title to his resume. Before the season began, however, Mike Casey was in an auto accident that knocked him out for the season. Again an All-American, Issel simply picked up the slack, scoring a UK–record 33.9 points per game and adding 13.2 boards per contest. Issel was so consistently great that there was only one game in the 1970 season in which he failed to score 20 points (he had 17 in an easy win at Mississippi State).

A No. 1 national ranking stuck with UK into the NCAA's Mideast regional final where the team ran into a combination of shaky officiating and a semi-unknown Jacksonville center named

Artis Gilmore. UK lost a heartbreaker 106–100 as Issel fouled out on an especially shoddy charging call midway through the second half. Rupp never seriously threatened to win another title, but Issel did enjoy some championship success by winning an ABA title with the Kentucky Colonels in 1975—this time playing with, instead of against, Artis Gilmore.

9 C.M. Newton

He played for Adolph Rupp, he played with Joe B. Hall, and he hired Rick Pitino and Tubby Smith for UK. C.M. Newton's Big Blue blood lineage is basically perfect. Indeed, until 2012, C.M. Newton was intimately connected with every head coach who won a title at UK. It is hard to imagine a career that touched much more glory. That said, his association with UK had its share of challenges and difficulties.

Newton the player's career was much less decorated than Newton the coach or Newton the athletic director. Charles M. "Fig" Newton spent two seasons on the end of Adolph Rupp's bench. He scored just 27 points in the two years, although he was part of the 1951 NCAA championship team. Newton played but did not score in the Championship Game. Newton was more accomplished in baseball, where he excelled at UK, and landed a brief minor league career as a pitcher in the New York Yankees organization. Available records indicate that Newton was 11–9 in 51 appearances in the low minor leagues from 1952–55.

Newton left baseball when the pull of family life directed his energy in a safer direction. He returned to Lexington, and at the ripe old age of 26, Newton became the head basketball coach at

Transylvania University in Lexington. Newton won 169 games at Transy and integrated the university's basketball team.

In 1968, former UK football coach and then Alabama coach/athletic director/grand poobah Bear Bryant brought Newton on board to revitalize Crimson Tide basketball. Newton stayed for twelve seasons, again integrating the squad, compiling 211 wins, and at one point winning three consecutive SEC regular season titles.

Newton left Alabama to become assistant commissioner of the SEC. That move lasted only a year, as Vanderbilt brought him back to coaching circles. Newton won 129 games in eight years at Vandy and landed the Commodores in NCAA tournaments in 1988 and 1989.

In 1989, Kentucky basketball was in a terrible situation. The team was being placed on probation, which would cripple an already historically bad team. *Sports Illustrated* headlined an issue "Kentucky's Shame," and the Bluegrass' proud tradition was horribly fractured. Newton stepped into the void, hired by president David Roselle to restore integrity to the UK athletic department. Newton's first (and perhaps biggest) task was to hire a new coach to replace Eddie Sutton. The search was lengthy and arduous. Newton considered coaching the team himself for the 1989–90 season if the right candidate did not work out. However, Newton ultimately struck on Rick Pitino, and the rest is history.

Eight years later, Newton was left with almost as tough of a decision. Pitino had left for the greener pastures of the NBA's Boston Celtics, and Newton had to replace a coach who was coming off back-to-back NCAA title game appearances. Again, Newton acted boldly and wisely, bringing Georgia coach and former UK assistant Tubby Smith to Lexington. Newton certainly scored a public relations jackpot in countering Kentucky's reputation for being a bit backward on racial integration with the hiring of Smith. When April 1998 rolled around, Newton scored a bigger hit when Smith promptly led a tough and gritty UK squad to the university's seventh NCAA Tournament title.

Newton's reputation for excellence in coaching and administration extended far beyond UK basketball. From 1979–85, Newton was chair of the NCAA rules committee, and his watch brought the shot clock and the three-point shot into the college game. Newton was also President of USA Basketball from 1992–96, meaning that he was associated with the compilation of the 1992 U.S. Basketball Dream Team. Newton retired from UK in 2000, and in the same year he was honored with membership in the Naismith Basketball Hall of Fame.

Bob Wiggins

You'll see him at most games, sitting not far from the UK bench, dressed in a charcoal suit with a blue tie. Everyone seems to know him—and for good reason. If you stop to say hello, he'll shake your hand and ask your name.

Meet Bob Wiggins, Super Fan.

Many seem to think Ashley Judd is Kentucky's No. 1 fan. Those people are incorrect. While she is certainly Kentucky's most famous fan, Wiggins has to be No. 1.

Wiggins, 83, is a retired engineer from Falmouth, Kentucky, who first bought season tickets in 1954. He went to his first game in 1944. In his time as a fan he's seen four Kentucky championships in person, and now he flies to most games on the team plane.

John Calipari created a kind of platinum fan status for him, *Sports Illustrated* reported in 2011. Wiggins has access to practices, tickets, and team meals—something no other fan could ever dream of.

On the Cats' most recent run to the Final Four in 2012, senior forward Darius Miller brought Wiggins to the foot of the ladder the team used to cut down the regional championship nets. Instead of having Wiggins climb the ladder, Miller snipped off a piece of net and handed it to Wiggins himself. The crowd who had stayed to watch the ceremony cheered madly.

Wiggins actually saw every game for 19 consecutive years before missing some at the Great Alaska Shootout in 1997 when he had a mild heart attack. Since then, some games have tested that heart, but he keeps right on ticking, right on seeing his beloved Cats.

"I had to take nitroglycerin [for some games]," Wiggins told the Metro New York website in 2011, "just to prevent anything from happening."

He's developed special relationships with various players, like recent sharpshooter Doron Lamb. Wiggins told the *The Villager* newspaper in 2011 that whenever Lamb hits a three-pointer, Lamb will find Wiggins and hold up three fingers. Wiggins will do the same.

"It's just a way of life," he told the Metro New York website. "There is only one Kentucky basketball. I don't have any passions other than this. Just this team and the University. I love it so."

11 Big Blue Madness

"You people are crazy," UK head coach John Calipari said, laughing. Together, he and members of the 2010 UK basketball squad passed out doughnuts to the crowd of people waiting outside in the cold. The previous night, players handed out pizzas. It was a thank-you gift, a present to all those fans who'd come out to wait.

*Nine-year-old Logan McDonald of Greenville, Kentucky, waits for the
beginning of Big Blue Midnight Madness at Rupp Arena in Lexington,
Kentucky, on Friday, October 12, 2007.* (AP Photo/James Crisp)

That is, to wait for a *practice* to begin.

It was a chilly night in mid-October, one requiring jackets and sleeping bags. Still, hundreds of people came to wait outside Memorial Coliseum on the Kentucky campus to get tickets for Big Blue Madness, the first Kentucky basketball practice of the year, held inside Rupp Arena.

That's right. Like Allen Iverson once said, we're talking about practice. We're talking about hundreds of fans, some who wait outside for weeks, for a chance to see the Kentucky Wildcat basketball team officially kick off the basketball season with a practice that showcases the team's new players with dunk contests and a scrimmage.

It's really just a pep rally—but one with 24,000 fans. It's called Big Blue Madness.

I (Ryan Clark) remember waiting outside myself for a chance to get tickets to Big Blue Madness in 1996. My family and I got as close as being able to see the door of the arena, but we were turned away. The place had already filled up. But in a way we were lucky—we'd only waited outside for an hour or so.

Some fans use their vacation from work and camp out for weeks to be first in line for the practice tickets. And now, most every season, the Wildcats players come out to mingle with their most fanatic of fans. Sometimes they pass out food. In 2011, Anthony Davis and others played basketball with those who dared. Go to YouTube and watch the video. It's hysterical.

But how did the madness get started in the first place?

In 1971, Maryland coach Lefty Driesell began the practice of Midnight Madness when he hosted a 1.5 mile run at 12:03 AM on October 15 of that year—marking the first minutes that the NCAA would allow a program to legally begin practice. About 3,000 students showed up to watch the occasion.

It was, as they say, madness. Other schools recognized a good thing when they saw it.

Kentucky started marketing their own event in 1982 when Joe B. Hall was coach. Now you can find Midnight Madness, or some version of it, at schools all across the country, from Michigan State to Indiana, from Connecticut to Kansas. It has become a major recruiting tool for coaches who try and outdo each other at these events.

In the past, Kentucky coaches have ridden motorcycles onto the court (Pitino), emerged hidden from inside the cheap seats high within the crowd (Tubby Smith), or given political-like, State of the Program Addresses, complete with podium and teleprompters (Calipari).

Each year, the crowd loves it.

Until 2005, Kentucky had held its Madness event in the practice facility on campus, the 8,700-seat Memorial Coliseum. But the event became so popular that the Cats started to host it in Rupp

Wally Clark

No one knows more about Big Blue Madness—or about waiting in line for it—than Wally "Wildcat" Clark.

Clark, a Lexington native, became a legend in 1995 when he was determined to be first in line for Midnight Madness. He arrived 17 days early and camped out to get the first tickets available.

But he bested himself in 1996 when he waited an amazing 39 days for the free tickets.

For 18 straight years Clark camped out—until 2010, when complications from a fall stopped the 59-year-old. That year, he was forced to stay at his Lexington home, where he also suffered from diabetes and gout.

"You have no idea how much I miss it," he told the *Lexington Herald-Leader* in 2010. "I miss it a lot."

He missed the following year's Madness when he reportedly moved with his family to Arizona. To this day, everyone agrees: no one waited like Wally.

Arena. Most of the tickets, which are now released online, are gone within the first 30 minutes.

A few years ago, in response to the growing popularity of Madness, the NCAA allowed schools to officially begin practices at 9:00 PM that night. Hence, Kentucky—which had called the event Midnight Madness—now refers to it as Big Blue Madness, and it starts at 9:00 PM. Other schools still begin at midnight.

But none compare to Kentucky's annual Madness celebration. Think about the 1991 event—one week after Madness, all four of Kentucky's main target recruits, Rodrick Rhodes, Tony Delk, Walter McCarty, and Jared Prickett, committed after attending, according to ukathletics.com.

That class went on to win a national title in 1996.

12 Attend a Senior Night Game

Darius Miller said he wasn't nervous when he got ready to run through the hoop. His only concern?

"I was trying not to cry," he said later.

And who could blame him? After playing four years at the University of Kentucky, after all the wins and losses, the hoop signified one thing: the end of it all. It was Senior Night—the last home game for the seniors on the Kentucky basketball team—and it is a must-see for any UK fan.

Why? About 15 minutes before the start of the game, the hoops are gathered behind the entrances to the court. They are huge—taller than the height of your average basketball player (so he can run through it). On the hoop is a kind of tissue paper with the face and number of the player on it.

Each senior is then introduced and runs through the hoop to the clapping of the adoring faithful. He is normally presented with a framed jersey and picture of himself, and his parents are waiting to hug him at center court.

(Or, in the case of Eloy Vargas, the player is represented by some of the coaches' wives, because Vargas' parents could not make the trip from the Dominican Republic.)

The seniors then all line up in the center-court area and the cheerleaders sway, and the band starts to perform "My Old Kentucky Home," the state song of the Bluegrass State. Most of the time there isn't a dry eye left in the house. Al McGuire, the former Marquette coach who later served as a broadcaster, was moved to tears when he saw the famous Senior Night ceremony.

(Author's note: My own wife, Manda Clark, does not love basketball, though she will cheer for UK. But she never could have predicted how emotional the ceremony can be. We saw Chuck Hayes' Senior Night in person. When he cried, my wife cried, too).

Because Kentucky used to show the senior ceremonies on television, rival schools complained it gave UK an unfair recruiting advantage; Kentucky can no longer broadcast the senior ceremonies on TV.

It's always interesting to see how seniors will react to Senior Night. Will they be nervous? Will they be pumped?

We'll always remember a few highlights:

- Richie Farmer introduced legendary announcer Cawood Ledford in 1992 when Cawood announced his last home game. It was also Farmer's Senior Night, and he ended up getting the first few buckets of the game himself.
- That same game was also Sean Woods' last at home. He responded by getting into a fight in the first half and being ejected. Never let it be said that Sean Woods wasn't entertaining.

- In 1984, former governor and Major League Baseball commissioner Happy Chandler sang "My Old Kentucky Home," which is when Al McGuire became so choked up he had to pause to regain his composure.
- In 1995, Tollesboro High star Chris Harrison got his career-high of 16 points on Senior Night.

(Note: Some stars like Ron Mercer and Patrick Patterson, who have already decided to turn pro before they are seniors, are honored after the game, even though they are not seniors.)

13 Kentucky and Louisville— the Dream Game

It took 29 years, but the 2011–12 Cats made the so-called Dream Game stand up to its name for the Big Blue Nation. This is just the latest, and perhaps greatest, but surely not last chapter in the in-state rivalry that divides the Commonwealth annually. Red or Blue—there are simply no other choices.

Of course, Kentucky has a proud college basketball tradition that extends far beyond UK and UofL. E.A. Diddle made Western Kentucky University a major player in early March Madness tournaments, and the Hilltoppers still make periodic NCAA runs. Murray State is a perennial March upset-maker, and other Kentucky universities and colleges dot the landscape of successful lower-level hoops—Northern Kentucky University (NKU), Kentucky Wesleyan, Georgetown College, and the list goes on.

But in Kentucky, thanks to the Dream Game, the quest for ultimate excellence in Kentucky basketball comes down to Red or Blue. Of course, it wasn't always this way. Adolph Rupp made it a choice of Blue or Blue, and Joe B. Hall would have been quite content to keep it this way. UK and Louisville met nine times between 1913 and 1922, and they bumped into each other three times in the NCAA Tournament from 1948 to 1959. They would not play each other again for 24 years. When Adolph Rupp retired in 1972, UK had won four NCAA titles and the Louisville Cardinals had just made their second ever Final Four appearance. New Louisville coach Denny Crum had matched the school's total for such events in his first season, and it would take Crum only three more seasons to return to the Final Four.

Denny Crum led Louisville to six Final Four appearances in his first fifteen seasons, with NCAA titles in 1980 and 1986. During the same period, UK totaled three Final Four appearances and one NCAA title. It wasn't so much that UK slid as that Louisville exploded. Crum brought a high-flying, high-octane attack to Kentucky, and he recruited many of the state and the nation's top prospects.

For years, Crum and Louisville wanted an annual in-season matchup with Kentucky. So long as UK was the clear top dog, it had no interest in such a game. It ultimately took another NCAA pairing, in the 1983 NCAA Tournament Elite Eight, to show everyone that politics aside, the rivalry was real, and the annual game needed to happen purely for basketball reasons. Louisville knocked off UK 80–68 in overtime in the so-called Dream Game, and the following November the two teams began their annual rivalry.

The annual series has been a thriller for teams of both programs. At present, UK leads the regular season scorecard 19–10 since the Dream Game made the UK/UofL series an annual event. Some of the most dramatic games in the series came after Rick Pitino returned to the Commonwealth on the red side of the rivalry after a failed stint in Boston. Rupp Arena echoed with calls of "Tubby! Tubby!" in December 2001 after the true-blue

Smith defeated his turncoat former mentor 82–62. Louisville fans had their moment, though, as Pitino's Cardinals won the next two meetings. In 2004, Patrick Sparks delivered three pressure free throws in the final seconds to edge UofL 60–58 in a marvelous comeback. In recent years, Pitino was 2–0 against Billy Gillispie, and Coach Cal has returned the favor, winning his first three regular season UK/UofL games.

That said, the Dream Game returned to dream status, albeit this time for UK rather than UofL fans, in another NCAA meeting. On March 31, 2012, the two rivals met in New Orleans in the Final Four. Led by 18 points, 14 boards, and five blocked shots from Anthony Davis, UK held off a second-half Cardinals rally to win 69–61 and advance to the NCAA Tournament title game.

Twenty-nine years after UK/UofL became an annual affair, it's safe to say no one can imagine it not being so. The tickets are scarce, and the pregame and postgame scenes can be raucous, but the Dream Game, in whatever incarnation it can be found, is a must for UK fans.

14 The Greatest Game Ever

Sean Woods' floating one-hander, shot on the run across the lane, arced just over the fingers of Duke's Christian Laettner, kissed off the glass, and fell softly through the net. UK 103, Duke 102. The crowd in Philadelphia's Spectrum exploded at the astonishing end to a great game, maybe, some thought, the greatest game. UK's Unforgettables, college basketball's loveable losers, had forever and unequivocally shed the loser role. They had gone from a 14–14 team to the Final Four in only three years. Hollywood might have rejected such a script because it was too implausible to ever take place. But now it had. Almost. There were still 2.1 seconds on the clock.

All day long, Duke had the answer for whatever Kentucky threw at them. Of course, they would have. The 1991–92 Duke team was the defending NCAA champion, and stood at 31–2 and No. 1 in the nation coming into the NCAA regional final against UK. In Duke's main six-man rotation, future NBA lottery picks Christian Laettner, Bobby Hurley, and Grant Hill were featured. UK, on the other hand, was a plucky 29–6 squad that had just recovered from time spent on NCAA probation. Other than Jamal Mashburn, no other Wildcat in this game logged an NBA minute.

The pundits gave Kentucky little chance. On paper, the game looked to be a rout. But on one magical evening, the greatest game ever played transpired between two gutsy, dogged, and ultimately amazing teams.

Duke jumped to an early lead. At halftime, the Devils led 50–45. Kentucky remained committed to playing the game in their up-tempo run-and-gun style, confident that if they did so, their run at the Blue Devils would come. With 11:08 remaining, Duke stretched its lead to 12 points. And then the run came. Kentucky scored eight unanswered points. The two teams went back and forth, and made clutch shot after clutch shot, neither fading under the pressure.

The two teams were tied at 93 at the end of regulation. Until the bitter end of overtime, the two teams traded baskets. Christian Laettner, strangely not ejected after stomping on UK reserve center Aminu Timberlake in the second half, hit a tough runner. Duke led 100–98. Mashburn answered for UK with a basket and a foul. The free throw put UK up 101–100 with 19.6 seconds remaining. Just 5.5 seconds later, Mashburn committed his fifth foul and went to the bench. Christian Laettner sank two free throws—he hadn't missed a shot all game. Duke led 102–101.

The Greatest Villain Ever

Christian Laettner, by virtue of stomping Aminu Timberlake and remaining in the game to make his buzzer-beater, became the super villain of all UK super villains. Among the many derisive mentions Laettner drew was a horse running at a Lexington racetrack shortly after the game under the name Laettner Be Gone. One suspects that a large number of UK bettors backed that horse.

As for Laettner, he was pretty chippy about his role in the greatest game over the years. However, during the 2011 NBA lockout, Laettner came to Rupp Arena as the coach of a team of Villains, who matched up with some UK All-Stars in an exhibition. Late in the game, Laettner, to the delight of the partisan crowd, went to all fours and wiped the Rupp Arena floor. The exhibition earned $50,000 for the V Foundation, which funds cancer research. As for Laettner, he may have laughed last again, as the Villains won 152–149.

And then Woods, finding the guts to take the biggest shot in the biggest game, threw up his running bank shot in the lane. The Big Blue Nation erupted. Kentucky had done it.

Duke coach Mike Krzyzewski knew better. "We're going to win," he told his team in the huddle, and he drew up a long pass from Grant Hill to Laettner. Pitino, for his part, decided not to guard the in-bounds pass. He would double-team Laettner with Unforgettable seniors John Pelphrey and Deron Feldhaus. He cautioned them not to foul. They certainly did not.

With an uncontested sight line, Hill launched a perfect baseball pass, 75' on the fly. Pelphrey and Feldhaus both froze, with Laettner catching the ball at the foul line, dribbling, firing, swishing his shot at the final buzzer. The UK jubilation turned to disbelief. Winning and losing players alike cried on the court. The greatest game ever had ended, and Duke had made one more play than Kentucky.

For Kentucky's part, the greatest game loss was just another sign that UK basketball was back. Four years later, UK would celebrate its sixth NCAA title. Pelphrey, Farmer, Feldhaus, and

Woods each admit that they still haven't forgotten their brush with glory, or the bitterness that their heartbreaking near miss inspired. As long as UPS and CBS have air space, each March brings numerous replays of the heart-breaking shot. Big Blue Nation awaits a commercial about four hard-nosed seniors and a never-say-die team who overachieved to the brink of college basketball's greatest miracle and lost only to perfection.

Anthony Davis

With the game's final rebound grabbed, Anthony Davis did something uncharacteristic. After he bounced upcourt, Kentucky having secured a 69–61 national semifinal win over Louisville in the biggest UK game in at least a decade and a half, Davis flipped the ball in the air as the horn sounded and gestured emphatically at the court, shouting, "This is my stage!" The emotional display was unusual for the reserved Davis, but the statement was exactly correct. The rebound was Davis' 14th, and he had added 18 points and five blocks, as well. Each total was the game's highest individual output from either squad. In the biggest game of his young UK career, Davis, as he had all season, came up big. Anthony Davis, in his one season as a UK Wildcat, was shining like no one had before.

Two nights later, in the New Orleans Superdome in the NCAA Championship, Davis was up to his old tricks again. Unlike the Louisville game, when Davis shot 7-of-8 from the field en route to his epic game, the big man simply could not buy a basket. Davis shot 1-of-10 against Kansas. However, in a rare off shooting night,

Anthony Davis (23) dunks the ball in front of Florida's Scottie Wilbekin (5) and Kentucky's Michael Kidd-Gilchrist (14) during the first half of a game in Lexington, Kentucky, on Tuesday, February 7, 2012. (AP Photo/James Crisp)

Davis showed how many other things he could do to impact a game. While he only scored six points, Davis grabbed 16 rebounds, blocked six shots, had five assists, and added three steals. His value was never clearer than on one late-game possession. Kansas had trimmed Kentucky's lead—as high as 18 in the first half—to six points. A Kansas player caught the ball and faced up for a three-point attempt. The guy jumped to shoot, saw Davis fly at him, and dropped back to the court with the ball. He then launched the shot, which swished through cleanly. Of course, it didn't count because Davis had forced a travel by the simple fact of his presence. UK was never challenged again. On a night when he couldn't make a shot, Anthony Davis wrapped up the Final Four's Most Outstanding Player award.

Anthony Davis was not always a super prospect. As one local high school coach from his native Chicago told *Chicago Sun-Times* columnist Michael O'Brien, "Most of the coaches on the South Side knew him as the little guy who would shoot threes from the corner in junior high." Davis grew to 6' at the end of his freshman year of high school, then to 6'4" by the end of his sophomore year, and to 6'7" by the start of his junior year. He was 6'10" when he committed to UK as the top college basketball prospect in the nation.

Davis maintained some guard-like skills in his lengthy frame, including a 7'3" wingspan. He was quick, athletic, and had good hands. His jump-shooting form was unusually smooth for a post player. Somewhere during his growth spurt, Davis happened to become a freakishly great shot blocker. Blessed with a gift for rarely jumping at ball fakes and a knack for keeping his blocked shots in bounds, Davis was an eraser on defense. On offense, his shooting touch was developing, and the speed with which he could fly to the rim and dunk a lob pass or missed shot was breathtaking.

Before the season, Calipari indicated that Davis was physically ahead of his former UMass star Marcus Camby at this stage of

Camby's career. What some didn't realize was that he was ahead of the rest of college basketball. Davis scored 14.2 points per game, the most on the 2012 Wildcats. He shot 62 percent from the field and 71 percent from the foul line. Davis added 10.4 rebounds per game and set an NCAA freshman record with 186 blocked shots.

Numbers do not do justice to Davis' skills. He won every reputable national Player of the Year award, led Kentucky to the 2012 NCAA title, locked up being the top pick in the 2012 NBA Draft, and he was named to the 2012 U.S. Olympic Team. He made the unibrow a fashion statement and the blocked shot an art form. In 2012, with apologies to Shakespeare, all the world was Anthony Davis' stage.

Memorial Coliseum

$3,925,000.

That was the total cost of the white elephant that became the home of University of Kentucky basketball in 1950. Its critics scoffed that even basketball crazed Kentucky could not consistently expect to fill 11,500 seats. Of course, the critics were wrong, and Memorial Coliseum would become unforgettably intertwined with UK basketball. It was just the sort of raucous and intimate campus gym necessary to give UK an extra edge until the Cats moved on in 1976.

The facility is named as a memorial to Kentuckians who lost their lives serving the U.S. in World War II and the Korean War. Kentucky broke in the gym properly, winning its first 45 games in Memorial until suffering a shocking 59–58 loss to Georgia Tech on January 8, 1955. It had been 12 years and four days since a UK team had last lost on its home floor.

Alumni Gym

Before there was Memorial Coliseum, there was Alumni Gym. That facility, too, had its critics, as the $100,000 needed to build it and its 2,800 seats was again considered by some to be too risky. It ended up being risky for opponents. UK was 247–24 in Alumni Gym. Even more amazing, they won the last 84 games they played there. Adolph Rupp posted a career home record of 203–8 in Alumni Gym.

If those numbers didn't make your head explode, this just might. Alumni Gym still stands and contains basketball courts—and on certain specified dates and times, UK students can play pick-up games where Ralph Beard, Alex Groza, and Bill Spivey fought for SEC and NCAA titles. Alumni Gym is located on the corner of Limestone and Euclid, next to the student center on UK's campus.

There were not many more losses before the home crowds in Memorial Coliseum. Over the years, UK posted a 307–38 record in the gym. Two NCAA title-winning teams and two other Final Four squads called Memorial home. Seven of UK's 25 teams from this era posted unbeaten records at home.

Aside from more than quadrupling the number of available seats, Memorial provided an aesthetic advantage over UK's previous home, Alumni Gym, as well as Memorial's ultimate successor, the nearly gargantuan Rupp Arena. Tom Wallace wrote in his *University of Kentucky Basketball Encyclopedia*, "Old-timers will tell you that [Rupp Arena] doesn't match the atmosphere of Memorial Coliseum. The character of great tradition permeates the air with near spiritual force, even today."

And what a tradition it is. The list of Wildcats who played in Memorial spans from the Fiddling Five with Vernon Hatton and Johnny Cox, to Rupp's Runts with Pat Riley and Louie Dampier, and even up to Jack Givens and Rick Robey, who won the 1978 NCAA title.

That tradition is still available under certain circumstances. In 2009, Kentucky found itself in an odd position, playing in the

NIT. As such, Rupp Arena was booked for the Kentucky High School Athletic Association boys' high school basketball tournament. For one night, UK set back the clock thirty-three years and again called Memorial Coliseum home. While the crowd was small (8,327 were seated, as the Coliseum was renovated and seating capacity decreased in recent years), it was vocal, and was rewarded with a 70–60 UK win over UNLV. Through 2006, Memorial Coliseum also housed the annual Blue-White men's basketball scrimmage. Some 8,000-plus fans would annually pack the house, to see UK play against UK. Memorial also was the practice home of the Wildcats until the Joe Craft Center opened, which allowed for a move into more state-of-the-art digs immediately behind the old gym.

The UK women's team has been the most recent beneficiary of Memorial magic, as the facility has been the primary home for that squad since the mid-1970s. UK Hoops has an all-time mark of 357–140 in Memorial. Through the last three seasons, Coach Matthew Mitchell's team has gone 47–2 on its primary home court. Home attendance averaged 6,282 in 2011–12, which was a record for the team. The women's team currently boasts a 20-game home winning streak. Even Adolph Rupp would be impressed with those numbers.

17 Tom Leach and Mike Pratt

"Here's how you count to eight! Three, two, one! And for the eighth time, college basketball's national championship trophy is coming home to Kentucky!"

With those words, Tom Leach, broadcasting live on the UK IMG Radio Network on April 2, 2012, fulfilled a lifelong dream—calling an NCAA title for his beloved Kentucky Wildcats. While many Kentucky schoolboys grow up shooting jump shots in driveways or schoolyards, dreaming of following in the footsteps of UK stars like Dan Issel, Kenny Walker, Rex Chapman, or Doron Lamb, Leach grew up hoping to follow in the footsteps of broadcasting stars like Claude Sullivan, Cawood Ledford, or Ralph Hacker. Indeed, Leach's official biography on the University of Kentucky Athletics' website states that as a senior at Bourbon County High School in 1979, Leach listed his ultimate goal as becoming the next voice of the Wildcats.

Tom Leach began his broadcasting career at the ripe age of 16. His official website features a few brief moments of a nervous young Leach reporting the halftime statistics at a 1977 high school football game. It would be wonderful to report that Leach was a brilliantly gifted broadcaster from his first game behind the microphone and that he soared to reach his glory as quickly as John Wall, Brandon Knight, or Anthony Davis did at UK.

Instead, it was not until 1989 that Leach was tabbed to join the UK Radio Network. He had attracted a great deal of notice with his excellent radio work during the Kentucky High School Athletic Association state basketball tournament. Even then, Leach spent eight years working the scoreboard and call-in shows after games.

In 1997, Ralph Hacker stepped down from calling UK football, and Leach assumed play-by-play duties. Tom's dynamic style fit well with rookie coach Hal Mumme and his explosive Air Raid attack. On January 1, 1999, Leach called UK's appearance in the Outback Bowl against Penn State. He has gone on to call six more Wildcat bowl games, amongst many other football highlights.

In 2001, Leach finally made good on his old high school aspirations. Hacker handed over the basketball reins, and the long-ago

Mike Pratt and the Final Four

Long before his announcing days, Mike Pratt was an All-American on UK's superb 1969–70 squad. That team, generally accepted as Adolph Rupp's last real NCAA title contender, ran into Artis Gilmore and Jacksonville in the Elite Eight and lost 106–100. Not only was Pratt denied a title, he never played in a Final Four.

One of the many highlights of UK's improbable 2011 run to the Final Four was that Pratt was awarded a Final Four ring, just like the players and coaches. He wears the ring proudly. While Mike Pratt's Final Four dreams seemed broken with his last college game loss in 1970, they were instead only deferred for 41 years.

Bourbon County schoolboy had made good on his high school goal. It would take ten long years for Leach to get to call a Kentucky Final Four game and an eleventh year for Coach Cal's gang of stars to give Leach the chance to call UK's eighth NCAA title win.

During those eleven years, Leach has been awarded the Kentucky Sportscaster of the Year Award four times. His crisp, professional style conveys some of the majesty that the legendary Cawood Ledford brought to the airwaves. This is balanced with a healthy dose of genuine enthusiasm, as in the wildest moments, the boy from Bourbon County seems to resurface. The two traits combine to make Leach the ideal Kentuckian for the job. Rarely falling into homerism but still leaving the listener in no doubt that his heart pumps Blue and White blood, Leach is the type of announcer who can inspire fans to turn down the TV and fill the silence with his superior broadcast.

Leach is ably assisted by Mike Pratt, who has provided the color commentary on the UK Radio Network for the past ten seasons. Pratt, who starred as a player at UK and was head coach of the University of Charlotte for four seasons, brings an insider's expertise to the broadcast table. His rapport with the players during his postgame chat with the Player of the Game is obvious to any listener. That said, Pratt is also capable of delivering his insights with a surprisingly acerbic wit. Pratt has been unflinchingly honest about what he sees on the floor, whether the Cats are clicking or struggling. He was also credited with helping convince Mitch Barnhart and then UK president Lee Todd to hire John Calipari in 2009.

Between Leach and Pratt, UK fans have been blessed with a decade of quality broadcasting. After the two endured some tough times during the end of the Tubby Smith era and the two-year Billy Gillispie era, the last three years seem to have been the culmination of many basketball dreams—for both the announcers and the listeners.

18 Kenny Walker

"Skywalker." It was an appropriate nickname for a player who could seemingly jump from anywhere on the court and finish off a play with a jam.

One of the most versatile athletes to ever wear a Kentucky uniform, Kenny Walker, a native of Roberta, Georgia, played for the Wildcats from 1983–86, making the Final Four in 1984 and earning consensus All-American.

If there was ever a chance for a player to surpass the amazing accomplishments of all-time scorer Dan Issel, it would have been Kenny Walker, one of the last great talents to stay at Kentucky and play for four years. Walker, a prolific scorer and rebounder at 6'8", finished his career with 2,080 points—still good for second all-time on the UK career list. He holds the UK career record for free throws attempted (773) and made (550), and he was voted All-SEC in each of his four seasons.

While many point to his first season at UK when the Cats made the 1984 Final Four before losing to Georgetown, Walker likes to remember his senior year. In Coach Eddie Sutton's first season, a loaded Kentucky team went 32–4, but in an NCAA Tournament quirk, UK was forced to face two teams in a row that they had already defeated three previous times.

"On our way to the Final Four, we played LSU, a team that we had already beaten three times," Walker told CoachCal.com in 2012. "This was after the game we beat Alabama, the game before, for the fourth time. For some strange reason, the NCAA stacked all these SEC teams together. We lost the game, then LSU lost in the semifinals to Pervis Ellison and Louisville, who we had beaten earlier that year."

It was a painful end to a college career, but more accolades would follow for Skywalker.

His jersey now hangs from the rafters at Rupp Arena. He became the No. 5 pick in the NBA Draft and went to the New York Knicks. And of course, there was the 1989 NBA dunk contest.

Long thought of as one of the premiere dunkers in the league, Walker entered the '89 dunk contest. Could he win? The smart money was on defending champion Clyde "The Glide" Drexler. But Walker was determined to show the world what he could do.

Then tragedy struck. Just days before the contest, Walker's father passed away. With the passing of his father, Walker thought about grounding his high-flying act.

"I wasn't going to compete because of the circumstance," Walker said. "But my mom gave me a lot of encouragement to go out there and do it because that's what my dad would have wanted me to do."

Not only did Walker compete, he won, defeating Drexler and becoming the first and only Wildcat to win the NBA dunk contest.

"If you've gone through something tough, tragic, or hard, if you can get through it, you can learn to deal with life because if it knocks you down, you have to just get back up," Walker said.

RYAN CLARK AND JOE COX

His professional basketball career spanned eight years with the Knicks and the Washington Bullets and took him to play in countries like Japan, Spain, and Italy. In 1997, he retired and began his post-basketball career. Sort of.

Using his communications degree, Walker hosts pre- and postgame UK radio shows on WVLK radio in Lexington. Always outspoken, Walker was an early critic of Billy Gillispie, and the former All-American is not afraid to say what he feels. After all, he knows what being a UK superstar is all about.

19 Visit the Joe Craft Center

Just down the Avenue of Champions, located on the University of Kentucky campus and attached to the famed Memorial Coliseum, lies the Joe Craft Center.

A Kentucky fan should not only know this place—a fan should visit it.

Opened in 2007, the Craft Center is Kentucky's basketball practice facility, and it also houses all of the athletic offices. The 102,000-sq. ft. structure was built for $30 million, and it was named based on a $6 million donation made by Hazard, Kentucky, native Joe Craft. Also located in the facility are the basketball team's championship trophies and various other memorabilia that any fan can see during regular Craft Center operating hours.

In the summer of 2008, the Kentucky Basketball Museum, which housed these trophies and memorabilia for nearly 10 years, closed its doors due to lack of funding. The museum opened in 1999 and was located in the Lexington Civic Center next to Rupp

Arena. Thousands of fans came to listen to radio calls of great Kentucky moments or play virtual one-on-one games against UK greats. But attendance figures were greatly overestimated, and the museum struggled financially from its inception. When it closed its doors, much of the memorabilia went to the Craft Center.

The Craft Center is second to none when it comes to practice facilities, including space for both men's and women's basketball teams, gymnastics, and the volleyball squad. There is a 3,000-sq. ft. weight and training room and two full-sized basketball courts.

"In the lower level, the men's and women's basketball teams each get their own practice court, locker rooms, video room, and lounge," the UK athletics website reports. "There is also a huge weight room and training room utilized by both programs.

"The main level features the men's and women's basketball offices, the K Fund department, and the ticket office. On the upper level, you can find the athletics director's office, compliance, media relations, marketing, publications, and business offices."

On one wall, there is a tribute to all of the current Wildcats alumni playing in the NBA. And lining the walls of the basketball courts are banners marking each of Kentucky's national championships.

Not tournament appearances, as Coach John Calipari likes to say. Or conference titles. Or even Final Fours. No—only national championship banners are good enough to be hung on the walls where UK student-athletes spend most of their time (outside of the classroom, of course). Only championship banners.

Joe Craft's gift was the largest private donation ever made to the UK athletics department. Craft, who graduated from UK with an accounting degree in 1972 (and a law degree in 1976) is the president of Alliance Resource Partners, L.P., a coal production and marketing company.

The Craft Center has earned national acclaim since its opening. And it doesn't hurt to show it to prospective recruits, either.

"The practice facility and offices at Kentucky are amazing," ESPN broadcaster Dick Vitale told ukathletics.com. "I cannot believe what they have available there."

Sports Business Daily may have said it best, calling the center "the biggest, the best, the nicest" facility around.

Learn "My Old Kentucky Home"

It is played at the end of every basketball and football game. Slow, soulful, and symbolic, this song represents a state, a fan base, and a university. Fans need to know its history.

It is "My Old Kentucky Home."

Written by Stephen Foster in the early 1850s, legend has it that Foster wrote it after visiting Federal Hill near Bardstown, Kentucky, where he was so moved by the scenery he penned the famous song. Foster, the preeminent songwriter of the day, was famous for tunes like "Oh Susanna!" and "Camptown Races."

But some say the song was not inspired by Federal Hill. Richard Jackson, in *The Stephen Foster Songbook*, argues the song was inspired by Harriet Beecher Stowe's *Uncle Tom's Cabin*, as Foster felt he could profit from the success of the recently published book. Jackson also said that original drafts of the song made reference to Uncle Tom.

Regardless, the song depicts an everyday scene on a slave plantation. According to Kentucky Educational Television's *American Piece* program on Foster, abolitionist Frederick Douglass praised the song for its sympathy toward slaves, saying that is where "anti-slavery principles take root and flourish."

On March 19, 1928, the song became the official state song of Kentucky. But all the way up until the mid-1980s, the lyrics were deemed a bit too controversial and eventually they had to be changed. Carl Hines, then the only black member of the Kentucky General Assembly, proposed a bill that would change the lyric, "Tis summer, the darkies are gay," to, "Tis summer the people are gay." The bill passed, and the song has been sung that way ever since. Sometimes tradition must give way to change.

Besides being played at UK games, it is also played after University of Louisville contests and was adopted by Churchill Downs as the official song of the Kentucky Derby. In 1982, Churchill Downs created a race in honor of the musician, the Stephen Foster Handicap.

"It was hard for me not to cry when that song was played," said UK great Richie Farmer. He said he nearly teared up after every game. But of course, it was especially difficult on Senior Night when he would hear the song at Rupp Arena for the last time.

And I (Ryan Clark) too, remember where I was when I first heard the song after a ballgame. Coincidentally, it was Farmer's Senior Night, which was a victory over rival Tennessee and its star, Allan Houston. I attended the game with my granddad. As the happy crowd around us gathered its belongings to leave, we stopped, fixated on the scene unfolding on the court below us.

The cheerleaders and basketball players lined the sides of the court and interlocked their arms. At once, every person still left in Rupp Arena began to sing.

It had an effect on me, even then.

Just as I'm sure it has an effect on other little fans when they hear the song for the very first time.

Ashley Judd

That smile. Those eyes. That Kentucky T-shirt.

Yes, some would say Ashley Judd is the perfect woman—beautiful, a successful model and actress, and one of the biggest Kentucky fans in the world. Perfect? Or Purrfect?

Judd was born in 1968 in Granada Hills, California, as Ashley Tyler Ciminella. She attended Ashland Blazer High School and the University of Kentucky where she graduated with a degree in French several years after establishing herself as an actress. Judd is the daughter of country singer Naomi Judd and Michael C. Ciminella, a marketing analyst for the horseracing industry. At the time, her mother was unemployed. (The Judds, the country singing group made up of Ashley's mother and Ashley's half-sister, Wynona, would not become popular until the 1980s.) In the early 1970s, Naomi divorced Ciminella, and she and Ashley traveled back to Kentucky where Naomi was from.

Ashley shuttled back and forth from various schools before enrolling at UK. After dabbling in modeling during some breaks and taking classes abroad in France, Judd decided to head for Hollywood, where she lived on her own and studied her craft in acting school. She landed small roles in television shows like *Star Trek: The Next Generation* and *Sisters*.

She was on her way. The independent film *Ruby in Paradise* broke open every door for Judd. Praised for her performance as a southern girl leaving an abusive relationship, she was able to land bigger roles in films like *Heat* and *A Time to Kill*.

By the time the Pitino-led Kentucky teams of the mid-1990s were having their success, Ashley Judd was a full-fledged leading lady, starring in movies like *Kiss the Girls* and *Double Jeopardy*. She

Ashley Judd cheers on the Wildcats during the first half of an NCAA second-round game against Wake Forest in New Orleans on Saturday, March 20, 2010. (AP Photo/John Bazemore)

frequently traveled with the team to its various playing sites like Chapel Hill, North Carolina, Lawrence, Kansas, New York City, or Nashville. And frequently, she stood with other screaming fans in the student section. She had an open pass to the locker rooms after games, and she quickly became the face of the program.

She also caused a bit of a stir when she posed for the University of Kentucky club hockey team's schedule poster. The annual poster was given away free to fans to help promote the team. That poster could probably be found on many a UK dorm-room ceiling. Ashley wore a hockey jersey—and nothing else.

"One thing I love about going to UK games is that I don't feel like a movie star, I'm just another passionate fan," Judd wrote in *Sports Illustrated* in 2004. "In 2002, I hopped on a plane to Gainesville, Florida, took a cab to the arena, and watched the Cats beat the Gators 70–68, feeling as free as I do when I walk the woods surrounding our farm. Later that year, after my brother-in-law's car went out in the first 30 minutes of the 12 Hours of Sebring race

Team for the Stars

The 2009 season not only saw the debut of John Calipari at Kentucky, it also became the season that Kentucky basketball became must-see viewing for celebrities everywhere. It wasn't odd to see superfans like Ashley Judd or country singer Eddie Montgomery, who have always appeared at UK games.

But several times, musicians, athletes, and other actors made appearances, too, including Judd, Montgomery, Jay-Z, rapper Drake, LeBron James, Magic Johnson, Spike Lee, actor Steve Zahn, actress Laura Bell Bundy, former Cincinnati Red and New York Yankee Paul O'Neill, actor Josh Hopkins, world champion Coach Larry Brown, Steelers quarterback Ben Roethlisberger, and Steelers Coach Mike Tomlin, among others.

Aside from those who come to games, other celebrities who have admitted to following the Cats include George Clooney, Matt Damon (who both told ESPN they loved the Mashburn teams), and bestselling author Tucker Max.

in Florida, my husband, Dario Franchitti, and I left earlier than expected. He went home to Tennessee, and I went to St. Louis, where along with the rest of Big Blue Nation, I gleefully watched Tayshaun Prince score 41 points to beat Tulsa 87–82 in the second round of the NCAAs."

Judd is now an activist as well as an actress. A graduate of Harvard's John F. Kennedy School of Government, she has traveled the world in support of organizations like YouthAIDS, Women for Women International, and Equality Now. And even though she is married to race car champion Dario Franchitti, we UK fans feel we can still love her, too.

"I have had so many wonderful memories over the years," she told *Sports Illustrated* before describing one of the best. "It was March 7 and I was sick with bronchitis, but I made it to Rupp for Senior Day. During the first timeout of the second half, the UK cheerleaders spell out "KENTUCKY," and a person from the crowd is asked to come out to make the Y. That day cheerleader Jason Keogh hoisted me onto his shoulder and carried me—and the blue-painted cast on my left foot—to midcourt. Before I was even introduced, I was given a standing ovation. It was the most extraordinary feeling."

For one extraordinary fan.

22 *The Cats' Pause* and Oscar Combs

It was 1975, and Oscar Combs was a man with an idea. Combs had covered UK sports for years for *The Hazard Herald* and *The Eastern Kentucky Voice*. Combs was attending a road game and spoke with three UK fans. These fans had never seen the team play and, living out of state, had followed UK only through the sporadic out-of-state radio coverage that Cawood Ledford and the UK radio network then received. Combs had doubtlessly heard similar stories from similar people. If only there was a consistent, reliable source for UK news, one that would provide more information than the Lexington or Louisville media and would send it around the nation and maybe even around the globe. Like many geniuses, Combs acted on his idea in the most extreme manner possible—he created it.

In 1976, Combs began publishing *The Cats' Pause*, a newspaper covering the in-and-out grind of UK sports, and most especially, UK basketball. Combs published the paper weekly during the season, and monthly during the period between the end of basketball and the beginning of football season. He recruited a crack staff of mostly young and enterprising journalists and turned them loose. The rest, as they say, is history.

Tom Wallace reported in the *Univeristy of Kentucky Basketball Encyclopedia* that then-coach Joe B. Hall was a fan of Combs' newspaper. Football coach Fran Curci, on the other hand, wanted the right to review each article before printing. Athletic director Cliff Hagan eventually provided at least grudging support for the paper, and *The Cats' Pause* soon boasted readers in every U.S. state and several foreign countries. The paper currently serves more than 15,000 annual print subscribers, and apparently had as many as 22,000 per Wallace's book.

In 1997, Combs sold the paper to Landmark Community Newspapers, although he continued to write a column for a time thereafter. The timing was probably ideal because *The Cats' Pause* transitioned into the Internet era. The print magazine is still produced as before, but additional content is available online more or less instantly, with young Kentucky journalist Jeff Drummond leading the charge of information.

In case Combs' dream hadn't spread far enough with *The Cats' Pause*, he was oddly receptive in 1979 when Joe B. Hall complained to Combs that he didn't even have schedules for the next season to distribute to friends who had requested them. Combs created an eight-page pamphlet that was distributed at the Blue/White Game. Two thousand copies were printed, and the initial budget was $110 per Combs. The following year, Combs tested the idea of expansion. He produced a 36-page yearbook with player profiles, a season preview, and SEC predictions.

In 1981, the second *The Cats' Pause Yearbook* had stretched to 90 pages. Recruiting information began to be included, a rare find indeed in the pre-Internet days. The yearbook then moved to 160 pages, to 192, to 240, and with each jump, more information was included—Kentucky high school basketball; other Kentucky colleges; lengthy recruiting sections covering not only UK recruiting but all NCAA recruiting; thorough profiles of UK players, coaches, and recruits; and a wealth of statistical data.

Ten years in, in 1989, Combs indicated that his budget had increased to more than $200,000. That issue featured new coach Rick Pitino on the cover and reached 272 pages. In 2007, the yearbook went to full-color printing. These days, it logs in at just less than 400 pages and is still the single best source of annual UK and related basketball information.

In light of the two impressive innovations that Oscar Combs contributed, it is no surprise that "The Big O" was inducted into the Kentucky Journalism Hall of Fame in 2000. To this day, he remains a beloved figure, particularly among Eastern Kentuckians, and Combs appears on the UK pregame call-in show. It has been quite a run for Combs, who has gone from the man with an idea to an icon.

Bernie Shively

If Adolph Rupp drove the fancy motorcycle that was Kentucky basketball, Bernie Shively rode in the sidecar. They called him "Shive," and as Tom Wallace said in his *University of Kentucky Basketball Encyclopedia*, Shive "is one of the key figures in UK sports history."

Look at the list of accomplishments. He served as athletic director during much of the Adolph Rupp (and the Bear Bryant) eras, from 1938 until his death in 1967. But before that Shive (born in Illinois in 1902) was a football player at Illinois, where he played alongside the legendary Red Grange. At 6'4" and 208 pounds, Shive was no slouch, playing guard and earning All-American honors in 1926.

Shive came to UK as a football coach in 1927, and he served as an assistant coach until becoming athletic director in 1938. But his coaching days weren't over. While serving as athletic director, he also coached football, basketball, and track.

In 1946, when the Wildcats basketball team won its first NIT title on a free throw by freshman Ralph Beard, the football department needed a head coach. Shive, who was then serving as interim head football coach, hired Paul "Bear" Bryant.

In many cases, that hire alone could have made an athletic director famous, but Shive would go on to succeed in other ways, too. In 1953, he was one of the leading voices in the creation of the University of Kentucky Invitational Tournament, or UKIT. For years Kentucky invited teams from all over the country to Lexington as part of (as Wallace put it) "the premiere holiday tournament" around.

And in another prescient move, Shive was the man who decided to create one singular UK basketball network, which then allowed Cawood Ledford to become the Voice of the Wildcats. Prior to that, as many as five networks covered Kentucky games, all with different announcers. Shive changed all that. When G.H. Johnston Inc. of New York City offered to buy the broadcasting rights to UK sports for $44,000 per year, Shive agreed, and Claude Sullivan became the radio man for Wildcats basketball with Ledford playing the role for football. The Johnston Company had made a similar deal with the SEC, which allowed for exclusive rights to a football game each week. Jim Host won the contract away from Johnston in 1974.

When Sullivan's career was cut short by throat cancer, Ledford took over the top spot for basketball in 1968.

"My fondest memories are of the camaraderie that existed among the media group that traveled with the UK teams in those days," former sports information director Russell Rice told the UK Athletics Blueprint newsletter in March 2005. "Bernie Shively was our social director, and he loved to play cards. Jim Host, who worked some of the radio broadcasts at the time, was a notorious bluffer and the life of those card games."

While serving as chairman of the Division I basketball committee, Shively was able to bring several Final Fours to Freedom Hall, then one of the truly great arenas in the nation.

In 1982, Shively was honored with selection into the College Football Hall of Fame, and UK's track and field stadium is named after him.

24 Jamal Mashburn

Little Jamal Mashburn knew exactly what he wanted to be when he grew up.

Throughout his childhood, Mashburn watched grown men leave for work on the subway, dressed in their fancy suits and carrying their briefcases. From his lower-class upbringing in the Bronx, Mashburn wished that someday he too could go to an important job, one where he could make enough money to afford the fancy suits and briefcases.

Mashburn, now retired from the NBA, works for ESPN as an analyst and owns several businesses, among them dozens of Outback Steakhouses and Papa John's restaurants and a few car dealerships. And yes, he does carry a briefcase to work every now and then.

"I always saw those men going to work and that was my goal," he said. "Not to play basketball. Not to make it to the NBA. All that came later. I just wanted to be professional in some way."

He did it. The one they call "Mash" did it all. And along the way he just may have been the most important recruit in the history of UK basketball.

Rick Pitino knew that if he could get Mashburn, then he could kick-start the Kentucky program back to life much quicker than even he thought was possible.

It was 1990, and the Wildcats were on their way to a glorious 14–14 season—glorious because no one, not even home announcer Cawood Ledford, thought the team would be that good. The players fought hard and were supremely conditioned by strength coach Rock Oliver, according to Gene Wojciechowski in his book, *The Last Great Game*. The only problem?

Jamal Mashburn (24) drives for the basket as Michigan's Juwan Howard (25) defends during the first half of their semifinal game of the Final Four at the Superdome in New Orleans, Louisiana, on Saturday, April 3, 1993.
(AP Photo/Ed Reinke)

There wasn't a lot of talent. There was a lot of heart, yes, and pride—but this team needed some talent.

Mashburn was a top-20 prospect, a 6'8", 220 pound Parade All-American jolt in the arm for a program that was most recently on life support. Mash could come in, start right away, and show the nation that he was as good as anyone in the country.

"That really did it for me," Mashburn said. "Coach Pitino said he could make me work and make me better. When I came to Lexington, I knew it was the place for me."

Originally, Mashburn thought about Syracuse, as most talented New York players tend to do, but when he looked at the talent on their roster, he could not see where he would play. He also considered Wake Forest, but the school didn't feel like home.

Not the way Kentucky did. So, like Pitino had done before him, Mashburn made his way from New York to the Bluegrass. Playing time would not be a problem here. Although Pitino said the star would have to work for everything he got, both coach and player knew the high school phenom would play from Day 1. But Mashburn was a worker, a player who wanted to get better, and despite the fact that Rock Oliver's practices made many players want to transfer, Mashburn stayed.

And he got better.

What made him so good was his versatility. He was able to bang inside with bigger players who could not guard his quickness and take smaller players into the post and score over them. He was a coach's dream. And he made an immediate impact.

Mashburn didn't mind that he would sit out one postseason due to probation. It was only a year, he thought. The goal for that season was simple: win as many games as you can. Win them all if possible. The team did extremely well, going 22–6 and finishing with the best record in the SEC. Jamal Mashburn finished third on the team in scoring, averaging 12.9 points per game as a freshman.

His sophomore season was the year that the Wildcats announced they were truly back. While that season ended with the spectacular loss to Duke in the NCAAs, everyone was sure that the Wildcats could win a national title at any time. Mash led all scorers as a sophomore, averaging 21.3 points per game. He was, officially, a superstar.

And he was a first-team preseason All-American leading into his junior year. After such a close call with Duke, there was really only one thing on Mashburn's mind for that season. "That Duke game was such a fun game to be a part of," he said. "Two great teams just going at one another. I'm proud to have been a part of it. But it made me want to get to the Final Four so badly. I wanted to take that next step."

The 1993 team would do just that, blowing out four opponents to crash into the Final Four. There were no more questions. Kentucky was back on the top of the mountain in college basketball, and Mashburn was a huge part of that.

Matt Jones of Kentucky Sports Radio calls Mashburn the most important recruit in the history of UK basketball for the way Mash helped the program get back on its feet. Pitino said much the same in his book, *Full-Court Pressure*. Even now, when a recruit at Louisville shows amazing promise, Pitino and the Cardinals faithful wonder, "Is he the next Mashburn?"

After his third year at UK, Mash declared for the NBA Draft and was selected fourth overall by the Dallas Mavericks. During an 11-year NBA career he was an All-Star in 2003 and—plagued by knee injuries—was forced to retire after the following season. Reports have surfaced that he was interested in buying an NBA franchise.

Mashburn's jersey now hangs from the rafters of Rupp Arena, retired with the greatest players to ever wear Kentucky Blue.

25 Learn "On, On, U of K"

The words echo off the walls of Rupp Arena during every game:

On, on, U of K, we are right for the fight today.
Hold that ball and hit that line,
Ev'ry Wildcat star will shine.
We'll fight, fight, fight, for the Blue and White
As we roll to that goal, Varsity,
And we'll kick, pass, and run 'til the battle is won,
And we'll bring home the victory.

They are the words every fan must know, the words sung to bring home a win. It is "On, On, U of K," the fight song for the Kentucky Wildcats. As a fan, you must learn this song.

"The music for 'On! On! U of K' was written in 1922 by UK professor Carl A. Lampert, the first chairman of the UK music department," the *Lexington Herald-Leader* wrote in 2011. "The lyrics were written in 1923 by student Troy Perkins, who won a $5 prize in a contest Lampert set up for the best lyrics to the music."

The song was then adopted as the UK fight song and was first published in the 1925 Kentuckian yearbook.

"Federal copyright for the song was secured in 1925," the newspaper wrote. "Lampert's widow renewed the copyright in 1952 on behalf of herself and Perkins. In 1941, before his death, Lampert assigned his copyright interest in the song, including all renewal terms, to Thornton Allen Co."

Although he was not a UK graduate, Lampert formed the University of Kentucky Symphony Orchestra in 1918 and founded the UK music department and the marching band. A German immigrant who came to the U.S. when he was six years old, Lampert studied at Elmhurst College in Illinois and the American Conservatory of Music in Chicago, according to Linda Perry in *Kentucky Alumni Magazine.*

"In 1910 and 1911, he studied in Prague and Berlin and also played in an orchestra conducted by Johannes Brahms," Perry wrote. "He was with the Chicago Symphony for two years and also taught at the University of North Dakota. A friend of University of Kentucky president Frank McVey, Lampert arrived on the UK campus to be a professor of music in 1918 and continued to inspire students through 1944, when he retired."

He was known as "Prof" on campus, and without him, there would be no music at UK.

I (Ryan Clark) remember when I was a little UK fan and my grandpa taught me the UK fight song. It was, as he put it, just "something you had to know." I was four years old.

26 The Untouchables

Take six players who scored more than 1,000 points in college. Add three more players who were NBA first-round draft choices. What kind of team emerges? A team that scored more than 91 points per game during its landmark season, won 11 games by 30 or more points, scored 86 points in a half at LSU, put up 120 points at Vanderbilt, and won Sweet 16 and Elite Eight matchups in the NCAA Tournament by 31 and 20 points, respectively. It was the team that eventually brought home UK's sixth NCAA Tournament championship and the school's first in 18 years. This team did it with a running, scoring, pressuring, in-your-face style of play that earned it the entirely appropriate nickname "the Untouchables."

The 1995–96 squad was Rick Pitino's seventh at UK. Expectations were high the previous season, but a disappointing Elite Eight loss to North Carolina had caused Pitino to shake up his team. Second leading scorer and 1,000-point club member Rod Rhodes was shuttled out the door to Southern California. In his place, super freshman Ron Mercer was plugged in. Mercer joined consensus All-American Tony Delk and fellow seniors Walter McCarty and Mark Pope in the 1995–96 team's rotation. Talented sophomore forward Antoine Walker, newly eligible junior transfer Derek Anderson, steady juniors Anthony Epps and Jeff Sheppard, and tough freshman guard Wayne Turner made up the rest of UK's main rotation. Other component parts like sophomore Allen Edwards, freshman project Nazr Mohammed, and junior varsity shooter Cameron Mills could play if needed. This team was, simply put, a juggernaut.

Kentucky honed its team chemistry in a summer 1995 trip to Italy. The group was as tightly knit as it was talented. Kentucky was everyone's pre-season No. 1. When the season began, Pitino started Tony Delk at point guard, along with Anderson, Mercer, Walker, and Pope. The Cats won a tough opener with Maryland, and then were shocked by UMass 92–82. UMass, with star post player Marcus Camby and young coach John Calipari, retained the No. 1 spot for most of the season. But UK would get a second chance at the Minutemen.

In the meanwhile, after the UMass loss, Pitino re-evaluated his squad. Epps would play the point-guard spot with Delk in his natural shooting guard position. Anderson, Mercer, Walker, McCarty, and Pope would shift in and out of the other three spots. With Epps back to running the team and Delk shooting at will, UK simply exploded.

UK won 27 games in a row, with only two of the wins coming by margins of less than 10 points. On any given night, any of UK's superstars could take control of the game. Delk (17.8 points per game), Walker (15.1 PPG), and McCarty (11.3 PPG) were the most likely suspects, but on a team where the 11th man would become an NBA first-round draft pick, a magical effort could come from anyone or everyone. With their full-court pressure, great ball movement, and plethora of shooters, once the Cats got a lead, they went for the jugular. On five occasions during the season, UK broke 110 points.

With a perfect SEC regular season, Kentucky rode a lengthy win streak into the SEC Tournament finals. There, Mississippi State outworked and outplayed the Cats, delivering a shocking 84–73 defeat. For his part, Pitino benched the talented but streaky Walker, delivering a message about the kind of fortitude needed to win the NCAA Tournament.

He didn't need to worry. UK destroyed San Jose State by 38, beat Virginia Tech by 24, thumped Utah by 31, and knocked out Wake Forest and Tim Duncan by 20. UK was back in the Final Four where it would meet its old foe, UMass. This time, with Delk scoring 20 to lead the way, the Untouchables got their revenge with an 81–74 decision.

Two short days later, on April Fools' Day 1996, Syracuse awaited in the title game. The Orangemen kept the game close, trimming UK's lead to two points with just inside 5:00 to play. But UK responded, pulling away to a 76–67 win. Delk led the way with 24 points, and freshman Mercer added 20. As was the case all season, when it mattered, UK had been simply untouchable.

27 The Won and Dones of 2012

As "One Shining Moment" started to play, confetti fell from the ceiling of the New Orleans Superdome. Finally, John Calipari could watch one of these highlight reels and see his own team winning a championship.

It was his first title and Kentucky's eighth. After 40 games, UK stood 38–2 and were the champions of college basketball. But it could be said the foundation for that title was laid three years before when Calipari arrived and introduced a new brand of basketball in Lexington, one where he and the fans embraced the so-called one-and-done players, who played one season of college basketball before leaving for the NBA.

Critics wondered—could it work? Could Cal take young players and mold them into a national title team? Many hoped he could not—or would not. He'd come close a few years before when his Derrick Rose–led Memphis squad lost to Bill Self and Kansas in overtime.

In Calipari's first season, he brought in John Wall and others, and they finished one game short of the Final Four. In Year 2, Brandon Knight and Josh Harrellson led their team to the Final Four.

It only seemed fitting then that Calipari would take his third team to the championship. And heck, when you've made it that far, you might as well win the thing. For players like Doron Lamb and Terrence Jones, for Darius Miller and Eloy Vargas, they tasted the success of college basketball's biggest stage—and they wanted more.

Calipari brought in another No. 1 recruiting class and combined those four talented freshmen with the elders. The best point guard in high school came to UK, as did the best small forward and the best center.

They were long and athletic. They could shoot. They could rebound. They had experience. Fans knew this team could be good.

"Along the way, there were memorable moments—an early win over Kansas that would prove to be much more important than we thought; Anthony Davis' block that saved a win over North Carolina in Rupp; Michael Kidd-Gilchrist's superhuman effort against Louisville (24 points, 19 rebounds); a last-second loss to Christian Watford and IU in Bloomington," Ryan Clark recalled in *Game of My Life: Kentucky.* "And as the team rambled on through a competitive SEC, we watched the team grow. Marquis Teague, the precocious point guard from Indianapolis, became a steady force through which the offense flowed. Terrence Jones showed that he could be a leader and role player. Doron Lamb was the assassin from the outside, and Kyle Wiltjer was valuable off the bench. And of course, there was the Man—all year it was Davis who would go on to become UK's first National Player of the Year."

Kentucky ran the table in the SEC conference, defeating good Vandy and Florida teams twice apiece. They dropped just their second game of the year in a third matchup with Vanderbilt (a third game in three days) in the SEC Tourney final before earning the NCAA Tournament's overall No. 1 seed as the best team in the land.

But for UK to win the title, they would have to defeat some teams they knew very well. In fact, no team would have to face the kind of rivalry games the Wildcats would in the NCAAs. And no team may ever have to do it again.

First up was Western Kentucky, the team with the worst record in the tourney, in a game played in the Yum! Center—home of the Louisville Cardinals. The Toppers were dispatched by 15 points. Next was Iowa State, blistered by the Wildcats with a 20–0 second-half run.

"We've got nothing to hang our head about," Iowa State coach Fred Hoiberg said after the game. "We got beat by the No. 1 overall seed that played an incredible game. We're going to walk out of Lexington, I'm sorry, where are we? Louisville, with our head held high."

"Then the fun began," Clark reported, "as Indiana also won its first two games, setting up a rematch of their buzzer-beating win in Assembly Hall. It turned out to be a major statement game by UK." Indiana decided to run with the Wildcats. It was not a good decision. Kentucky outscored Indiana 102–90 in what may have been the most entertaining game in the tournament.

Baylor, a top-10 team all season, came next. The game was over by halftime as Kentucky built a 20-point lead and held on to win by 12. At times Kentucky looked like it could never be stopped.

"Then came the biggie," Clark said. "After being left for dead in March, Louisville surprised everyone by winning the Big East Tournament championship and upsetting No. 1 seed Michigan State on the way to the Final Four.… Where they would meet Kentucky."

For a week the entire state was the center of the basketball world. And the game lived up to the hype. With 9:13 to go, Louisville hit a three to tie the game. But like they had done all season, the Wildcats found a way to win. Kidd-Gilchrist had two dunks, and hometown hero Darius Miller drilled a three to put the game away. UK won by nine.

At the end of the game, the two coaches shook hands.

"I just said, 'John, I'll be pulling for you, bring the trophy back home to Kentucky,'" Pitino said. "Louisville will be rooting for Kentucky, which doesn't happen very often.

"I'm really impressed with them, not only as basketball players, the way they carry themselves, their attitude," Pitino continued. "They're a great group of guys doing a tremendous job."

UK had another rematch with Kansas for the title, and Calipari would have another matchup with Bill Self in the Championship

Game. The game was only close in the final moments. UK led by as many as 18 in the first half and by 15 with 5:00 to play. Kansas came back to cut the margin to five, but again, the Cats made the plays to win.

It was party time in Lexington—and in New Orleans, which had been painted Bleux. Nets were cut down. Championship shirts and hats were worn.

Kidd-Gilchrist and Davis embraced. "This is what we came here for—to win a national championship," Davis said.

"This is the happiest I've ever been," Kidd-Gilchrist said.

Calipari explained why the team was so successful. "We're not just a talented team," he told the press. "We're a defensive team and a team that shares the ball. We were the best team."

Afterward, the entire starting five left UK early for the NBA. Few seemed to mind. They had given their fans a title, and that was enough.

It was time for the young men to go chase other dreams. But no matter what, Big Blue fans in Lexington and across the world will love them forever.

The Unforgettables

The four players were at the bottom of the dung heap of one of the biggest messes in college basketball history. Today, when someone says the names Pelphrey, Feldhaus, Woods, and Farmer, visions of three-point barrages and basketball glory spring to mind. But after a 13–19 season in their freshman season in 1988–89, the Unforgettables might well have been the Forgotten Four.

Deron Feldhaus, a 6'7" forward from Maysville, Kentucky, was probably the most notable of the bunch. Feldhaus, whose father Allen had lettered at UK under Adolph Rupp, had been lightly recruited by UK and redshirted during the 1987–88 season in order to grow into a physical specimen worthy of Eddie Sutton's last squad. Feldhaus had scored 3.7 points per game in 1988–89, sixth best on the worst UK team in memory, which made him the best of the group.

Richie Farmer, the 6' shooter from Clay County, was buried even deeper in Eddie Sutton's bench. He scored 3.2 points per game, and shot only 28 percent as a freshman. John Pelphrey, the rail-thin 6'7" forward who hailed from Paintsville, had also redshirted in 1987–88. The results were not terribly impressive, though. Pelphrey played very little in 1988–89, and when he did play, he averaged 1.7 points per game.

Sean Woods had missed the season as a Proposition 48 casualty. He lost the year of eligibility and was buried behind Sean Sutton on the UK depth chart. At this point, it seemed unlikely that any of the four would even be significant contributors at UK. Of course, somebody forgot to tell the Unforgettables—or Rick Pitino.

With an incredibly short roster that was light on talent and height, Pitino simply had no choice but to hitch his first UK teams to the Unforgettables. That said, he set about with the help of strength coach Rock Oliver to make the group the toughest, most in-shape group of basketball rejects ever.

And a funny thing happened on the way to NCAA probation and mediocrity. The Unforgettables forged a team spirit, an unquenchable thirst for basketball glory, and an inability to accept their perceived shortcomings. Because of them, 1989–90 was perhaps the most remarkable 14–14 season ever. Pelphrey and Feldhaus turned into double-figure scorers, Woods led the team and managed almost six assists per game, and Farmer was a dead-eye clutch shooter.

The 1990–91 season was even more amazing. UK went 22–6 and won the SEC regular-season title, although as part of their NCAA punishment, the squad could not claim the championship. Pelphrey was the team's leading scorer, Feldhaus and Farmer also averaged double figures, and Woods nearly did, too. A hot-shot freshman named Jamal Mashburn certainly helped out, as UK finally had a McDonald's All-American caliber player, instead of just guys who looked like they worked at McDonald's.

Finally, in 1991–92, the NCAA restrictions were gone. UK went 29–7 with the Unforgettables continuing to play over their heads. Whether it was Woods driving and creating, Farmer shooting over zone defenses, Feldhaus outworking and outhustling bigger post players, or Pelphrey taking over games, the Unforgettables were everywhere. Add in a more seasoned version of Mashburn as well as Dale Brown, Gimel Martinez, Travis Ford, and others, and UK had gone from the 98-pound weakling to the bully of the SEC.

In the SEC Tournament, UK raced into the finals against Alabama. According to Gene Wojciechowski in *The Last Greatest Game*, Mashburn told the four seniors at halftime of the title game that while he couldn't give them any money, he could give them an SEC championship, and he was going to do just that. Big Mash had 28 points and 13 rebounds, and UK rolled in the second half.

The Cats fought all the way to the Elite Eight of the NCAA Tournament where it took basketball magic from Christian Laettner to eliminate the never-say-die Cats. From insignificant players on a terrible team, the Unforgettables had grabbed the heartstrings of the Big Blue Nation and led them on a wild ride. The four seniors' jerseys hang in the rafters of Rupp Arena. There have been better players but never any who were more unforgettable.

Sam Bowie

Yes, it's true, for all of those unbelievers out there: Sam Bowie was chosen ahead of Michael Jordan in the 1984 NBA Draft.

Who? Yes—Sam Bowie.

You would have most certainly heard of him by now, either as a frequent NBA All-Star or a Hall of Famer. But there were too many injuries that plagued him throughout his career.

Life is sometimes cruel and ironic, and as it was, the Portland Trail Blazers already had an All-Star caliber guard in their stable. His name was Clyde Drexler, and they had drafted him in 1983. So why would they want another similar player in Jordan?

They chose Bowie, a 7'1", 230 pound center from Kentucky who had "star center" written all over him. Long and athletic, every college wanted Bowie when he came out of Lebanon High School in Lebanon, Pennsylvania. He was seen as a game-changer, a player who could help you win a national championship. Averaging 28 points and 18 rebounds per game in high school, he was named a McDonald's All-American, and the star said he knew exactly when he wanted to come to Kentucky.

"Yeah, I got off that plane for my visit, and there were hundreds of fans there at the airport cheering for me," he said. "That's when I knew I was coming to Kentucky."

In his first two seasons at UK, the Wildcats were upset in the first and second rounds of the NCAAs. But Bowie was a star, earning All-America honors as a sophomore and leading the team with a 17.4 points per game average.

Between his sophomore and junior years, Bowie broke his leg. He missed a full season. And, more bad news: the bone didn't heal

Sam Bowie (31) goes against Ralph Dalton of Georgetown during a battle for possession of the ball on Saturday, March 31, 1984, during their NCAA semifinal in Seattle's Kingdome. (AP Photo)

properly and required more surgery, and one more full season had to be missed.

"That was the toughest time, realizing I had to miss another full season," Bowie said in the book, *Game of My Life: Kentucky.*

Finally, in 1984, Bowie came back to help lead Kentucky to the Final Four where the team lost to Patrick Ewing and Georgetown. Bowie was not his former self, a step slower on both offense and defense. But he still had talent. He still had skill.

And he was still 7'1". And that made the Trail Blazers want to take a chance. At the time, it made sense for the team. Their previous center, Bill Walton, had led them to a World Championship but was hampered due to injuries.

So the Blazers took the chance, passing over Jordan to take Bowie. And it's something Bowie has had to live with ever since. Even though he played 10 years in the NBA and averaged more than 10 points per game for his career, he is still considered one of the most disappointing picks of all time due to having five leg surgeries that limited his production. In 2005, ESPN called it the worst pick of any North American sports franchise of all time. That same year, *Sports Illustrated* called it the worst NBA pick ever, explaining that teams should always draft for talent, not for need.

But none of that can be blamed on Bowie. He was amazingly talented when healthy, and eventually he came back from injuries to lead the Wildcats to a Final Four.

And for that, he will always be remembered fondly in Wildcat Land.

30 The Fabulous Five

If it seems amazing that UK's most recent NCAA title team was led by several true freshmen, one-and-done players, then you may question your vision when you see that the first UK NCAA champions, the Fabulous Five, included a 27-year-old junior war veteran who had been a prisoner of war for more than a year, a 24-year-old team captain who had served in the navy, and three upper-class all-time UK legends.

The unique circumstances that surrounded the outbreak of World War II left the 1947–48 UK Wildcats with one of the most veteran, experienced teams in the history of college basketball. They were also one of the most talented, and the Fabulous Five, as they were known, turned college basketball on its ear.

Louisville point guard extraordinaire Ralph Beard led the Cats. Beard, a junior, was everyone's consensus All-American in 1947–48, and he played the part. Beard led the Cats in scoring average, and he ran the team flawlessly. Due to the sparse statistics of the time, there are no statistics for assists or steals for Beard, but it is safe to say he excelled in both categories.

Also a junior, the man in the middle, 6'7" Alex Groza, towered above the competition in 1947–48, figuratively and literally. Groza was neck and neck with Beard for high-scoring honors, and was a tenacious rebounder and defensive presence in the middle. Big Alex was chosen second team All-American by most nominating bodies in 1948.

Harlan superathlete Wallace "Wah Wah" Jones played the power forward spot beside Groza. An All-SEC performer who made a few All-America squads himself, Jones, yet another junior, was a solid third scoring option and another daunting interior presence.

Truly veteran presences, senior Kenny Rollins (the 24 year old) and junior Cliff Barker (the 27-year-old former POW) filled in the lineup well enough that each was honored as an All-SEC selection, with Rollins chosen for the first team. Supporting players like Jim Line and Dale Barnstable would've been stars at many other programs but put aside their egos and stats in the quest to build a champion.

The team was talented, but it took Adolph Rupp some time to figure out exactly the right combination of stars to unleash on his opponents. Jones was recovering from the grind of SEC football and an ankle injury, and he could not play against Temple on December 20, 1947. The Owls upset the Wildcats 60–59. UK struggled through another tough task on January 10, 1948, as Michigan State, with former UK star Bob Brannum scoring 23 points, almost took down the Cats in a 47–45 decision.

In the next game, on January 12, 1948, against Ohio University, Rupp started Beard, Groza, Jones, Rollins, and Barker. The Fabulous Five was born, and the Big Blue Beast was unleashed. UK suffered an early February loss at Notre Dame but otherwise tore through the remainder of its schedule. The 1948 team won a total of 15 games by 30 or more points. For the season, UK averaged 24.6 points per game more than their opponents.

The SEC tournament was played in Louisville and UK rolled, winning by 56, 16, 23, and 11 points. The NCAA Tournament offered little more competition. In the semifinal, Beard matched up with Holy Cross and all-time legend Bob Cousy. *The New York Times* noted that Beard spent the game "running the Crusaders dizzy." He scored 13 points, and meanwhile defensive stopper Rollins held Cousy to a mere five points. That eight-point difference was the exact total of UK's victory margin, as the Cats triumphed 60–52. Groza scored 23, and Jones added a dozen.

In the final, UK tamed Baylor early, jumping to a 13–1 lead. The Cats led by 13 at the half and won easily 58–42. The attack was balanced, as Groza scored 14 points, Beard added 12, and Jones and Rollins each added nine. UK had won its first NCAA tournament championship.

Cawood Ledford notes in *Six Roads to Glory* that Rupp believed that the Fabulous Five was his best UK team. Assistant Harry Lancaster went even further. Ledford quoted him as saying that the Fabulous Five "was the best college basketball team that has ever set foot in a gymnasium." Indeed, the 1948 NCAA Tournament was only the beginning of the glory of the Fabulous Five.

31 Cheerleaders

It could be that somewhere, out in a small Kentucky town, there's a young boy in his driveway pretending he's Darius Miller and draining threes from all angles of the Rupp Arena court. It's also possible that the boy's sister—if she's not dreaming of playing for the UK women's squad—is practicing her cartwheels and back hand springs, hoping to one day be part of the most successful sports team on the Kentucky campus.

The cheerleading squad.

Yes, it's true—the country's best cheerleaders come from UK, and as a fan, you should take a moment at halftime to watch them.

No other cheerleading squad in the nation can claim what UK's squad can—19 Universal Cheerleading Association national championships, including the unbroken stretch from 1995 to 2002. UK has the only squad to win back-to-back titles three separate times, and the only team to win up to eight championships in a row.

"UK's eight-year streak of championships was broken in 2003 when they finished runner-up to Central Florida," UKAthletics.

com reported. "They regained the title in January 2004 and won their third straight in 2006. Central Florida regained the championship in 2007 when UK finished in third place. But the next year, UK came home with their 16th title."

The same fear Kentucky basketball can cause in other teams is felt among other squads when the UK cheerleaders compete in a tournament.

"The squad receives substantial media exposure," UK officials said. "Having finished in the top 10 every year since the existence of the UCA National College Championships, each year the UK squad is seen on the ESPN televised Championships Program, which airs at least eight times nationally. In addition, the UK squad is seen on television as every UK basketball game is televised nationally."

The squad has been featured in highlight stories by television, radio stations, and newspapers, such as the *CBS Evening News*, Connie Chung's *Eye to Eye*, the *CBS Morning Show*, *Southern Living*, *Gentlemen's Quarterly*, *ESPN the Magazine*, and *Seventeen* magazine.

The cheerleaders have performed at many events, including for the Denver Nuggets, the Miami Heat, and for the Denver UK Alumni Club function.

"Each one we win is just as special as the first one," head cheerleading coach Jomo Thompson, who also cheered at UK, told television station WKYT. "It is great to see the kids work so hard and accomplish a goal. We always have adversity; it comes up every year. A couple of kids got the stomach bug down here, but we battled through it and didn't let anything stop us from our goal. We did what we set out to do: win another national title."

Thompson said winning the title was particularly sweet in 2012 because the team took second place by a slim margin in the Universal Cheerleaders Association Division 1A competition in 2011.

"We're just happy to have it back in the Bluegrass State," he said.

Now, he said, the team will come home to yell for the UK men's and women's basketball teams and, "hopefully cheer them on to a national title, as well."

"It never gets old," Thompson said. "I enjoy winning. I want to collect as many rings as we can get, and so does this program. That is something that we strive for every year. If we get second or third, we are not satisfied with that. We want first place."

So the next time you're at a UK game, take a moment at halftime or during a timeout to notice the hardworking student-athletes tumbling and pepping up the crowd. They're the most successful team on campus.

They're the cheerleaders.

32 Read—and Possibly Loathe— the *Lexington Herald-Leader*

If this book were a crossword puzzle, the next clue would probably read, "Well-respected Lexington publication that seems intent on making itself a pariah to Kentucky fans." Indeed, the *Lexington Herald-Leader* has the sort of Jekyll and Hyde existence that often makes it essential reading, both for those who agree with it and those who agree to loathe its very existence.

In 1983, the *Lexington Herald* and the *Lexington Leader* merged. Newspaper readers, aside from the few who preferred the Louisville *Courier-Journal*'s coverage, now had a single source to turn to for daily printed UK news. Rather than glory in this media monopoly, the *Herald-Leader* inaugurated its new name by quickly cranking out a series of columns regarding purported corruption in the Kentucky basketball program.

The *Herald-Leader* was rewarded with a Pulitzer Prize for investigative reporting (two other Pulitzers have since followed) and an irate pro-UK readership. Granted, many of the allegations in the 1985 articles apparently had more than a smattering of truth to them. Regardless, many UK fans perceived that the *Herald-Leader* had sided with the anti-UK camp. Ensuing years have done little to change or invalidate this perception.

In 1989, *Herald-Leader* reporter Jerry Tipton nearly cost Kentucky its only shot with head coaching candidate Rick Pitino. Tipton cornered Pitino, who was in town to meet with athletic director C.M. Newton and other UK dignitaries, at a local restaurant, asking about some possible links between Pitino and NCAA rules violations that had occurred in the 1970s when Pitino was an assistant at University of Hawaii. In the wake of the Eddie Sutton scandal, the line of questioning was probably legitimate, but many of his detractors felt that Tipton's tactics were bush league. Pitino intended to take his name out of consideration for the job but was prevailed upon by Newton and UK President David Roselle to stay the course.

Pitino's reception was positively kind, however, compared to that afforded to Tubby Smith. Merlene Davis, an African American columnist with the *Herald-Leader*, somehow managed to work a bizarre, paranoid rant into print as a column, asking Tubby Smith to turn down the UK job and all but convincing him that white-sheeted Klansmen would run him out of town if he accepted. Fortunately, Smith had the good sense to listen to people who were wiser than Davis, even if the column did little to make Smith's transition more comfortable.

No figure is more polarizing in the love/hate relationship of the *Herald-Leader* and its readership than Jerry Tipton. Tipton has long been a nationally respected reporter. However, in his old age, his critics believe that he seems content to play the contrarian and the curmudgeon. Whether it's asking insensitive questions to Michael Kidd-Gilchrist regarding the death of a family member, mocking Ryan Harrow for having a high voice, attempting to insinuate falsely that Patrick Patterson was suddenly driving an expensive new vehicle, or generally writing as negatively as possible about Coach Calipari and the UK program, his critics say that Tipton is the man for the job—so long as the job is making much of Big Blue Nation's blood boil.

This is not to say that the Big Blue Nation has accepted the *Herald-Leader* quietly. Definitely the funniest response has to go to Kentucky Sports Radio, whose NotJerryTipton contributes a weekly parody notebook to that website, written in exactly the style that Tipton's opponents love to hate. For instance, during the NCAA tournament, NotJerry wrote, "Absolutely nobody cares about a 30–1 regular season because, let's face it, this Kentucky team has accomplished exactly nothing so far." He closed the column by noting, with tongue firmly in cheek, "On this date in 1998, Kentucky edged Duke to advance to the Final Four. There was a great deal of luck involved, though, as Duke guard William Avery somehow missed a wide-open 50-footer that would have given the Blue Devils the victory."

Hilarious parody aside, the Internet in general has provided the only antidote for UK fans who can't tolerate the *Herald-Leader*. While there have been a few *Herald-Leader* basketball writers who have handled the job with unquestioned class and aplomb, John McGill, Mark Story, and John Clay being a few such examples, the *Herald-Leader* remains the only major print media in Lexington and appears destined to remain both a viable news source for some and a written hemorrhoid for others.

33 Wildcat Lodge

Just across from the Craft Center practice facility and Memorial Coliseum sits a smaller building designated by a simple sign that reads, "Wildcat Lodge."

Back in the days before the NCAA got involved, the Lodge was the place made solely for Wildcats basketball players. Just them—no one else. With its posh environment and proximity to classes and practice, the Lodge was a great recruiting tool that UK coaches used to emphasize that the best of everything was in Lexington, Kentucky.

Of course, the NCAA decided that wasn't fair.

Even though the Lodge was built in 1978 entirely with private donations, NCAA officials decided the place was too nice and that other students should be able to enjoy the space, as well. It made sense. The athletes had extra-large beds, places to relax, and private showers and bathrooms, among other amenities. In 1979, the NCAA said the Lodge went against a rule that said athletes may not receive better accommodations than other students.

The funny part? The NCAA created the rule after the Lodge was built.

Still, it was a rule and UK had to comply. Athletes were forced to have roommates, the bigger beds were taken out in favor of more regular-sized ones, and private bathrooms were replaced with communal ones. It was still luxurious but now less so.

Then in 1991, the NCAA attempted to close all athletic dormitories, saying no dorm of the kind could have more than 50 percent athletes on a floor. UK then opened 50 percent of the Lodge to students who were non-athletes. So the Lodge still remains the home of the basketball team to this day.

But that doesn't mean there isn't controversy.

The Lodge was outdated, both in look and size, and a group came forward in 2009 with funding, looking to update the dormitory. Joseph W. Craft III, the CEO of Alliance Coal and a UK graduate, "organized a group of donors to give $7 million for the building; an anonymous donor later gave an additional $1 million," the *Lexington Herald-Leader* reported.

The lodge will be 20,000 sq. ft., house 32 students, and will open in fall 2012. Its name? Wildcat Coal Lodge. Even that has rubbed some people the wrong way. Some think the university has, in essence, jumped into bed with the coal barons, selling out to an industry that some critics think has had such a negative affect on the mountains of Kentucky.

"Coal has not been good for Kentucky," Teri Blanton of Kentuckians for the Commonwealth, an environmental activist group, told the *Herald-Leader*. "I don't think UK is making a good decision."

Still, the athletes love it. And the new Wildcat Coal Lodge will be built.

"The Lodge has been a great place to live the last three years," star Darius Miller told the UK athletics website. "It's where we spend most of our down time together. I think it's great to have a place to get away, and it helps to build team chemistry, plus it's pretty close to our practice facility."

34 Nike and the Changing Uniforms

Long before the University of Oregon held the reputation as trend-setters in the sports uniform fashion world—before each game the Ducks strutted out in camouflage or glow-in-the-dark jerseys—the

University of Kentucky was the school setting the trends, especially in the 1990s.

Throughout much of its basketball history, Kentucky sported Converse shoes and uniforms, making white and blue Cons iconic with the program. Children would buy these shoes and pretend they were Kyle Macy or Tony Delk while shooting jumpers in the backyard.

But times change.

When Michael Jordan became the young legend of the NBA and his shoes became the most popular on the planet, Nike reached out to several schools, including UK, to wear the Jordan shoes. The year was 1985. Joe B. Hall had just retired, and Eddie Sutton had taken over as coach at Kentucky. With a wonderful team including stars like Kenny Walker coming back, and in the future Rex Chapman, UK was known for high-flying dunkers.

It made the Cats an obvious choice for the Nike line.

But in 1989, when Rick Pitino became coach, Kentucky switched back to Converse, and the company began experimenting with all kinds of interesting uniform ideas. Converse focused on the jersey shorts, trying to make them look different. There was the Zubaz-like jungle pattern. And the wave that swooped from one leg to the other. There were the icicles that jutted down like stalactites. And, of course, there were the denim jerseys.

In the middle of the 1996 season, the Cats—who had only lost one game and were on their way to winning a national title—went through a uniform change. It had been planned since the beginning of the season, and fans were used to seeing different uniforms. But these were something altogether different.

Some complained the uniforms looked like Carolina blue. Others just felt they were strange. Many of the players liked them—they were denim in color with special new Converse denim-colored shoes. One thing was sure, no one had ever seen anything like them. And when the Cats won their national title, they were wearing Converse denim.

Whatever anyone ever thought of the uniforms, they were never seen again after the 1996 title-game win over Syracuse.

By 1998, when Kentucky was in the hunt for its seventh championship, they had a new coach in Tubby Smith and new uniforms and shoes. Again UK had gone with Nike. With a simple, throwback style, the Nike uniforms were generally lauded by the fans.

With the growth of summer AAU programs luring more high-profile basketball high schoolers, it seemed necessary for schools to affiliate with one of the two largest shoe companies: Nike or Adidas, which sponsor many of those AAU tournaments. Merging the two powers that are Nike and Kentucky basketball seemed a natural thing to do.

Nike was the biggest shoe company in the world. It's what children, teenagers, and their parents wanted to wear. And anything that could help bring the best players to Lexington was fine with the fan base.

Nike began to outfit the entire school's athletic department, experimenting with the basketball team in particular. Various uniform styles would follow, including platinum, black, and checkerboard versions. LeBron James even sent along his own special style to the team.

Another one-game addition involved a black "K" on the uniform with the name "Keightley" on the back of each (to honor the recently fallen equipment manager Bill Keightley). Yet another involved a re-creation of champion thoroughbred Secretariat's silks. And one more depicted iconic scenes of the UK campus.

But one thing is certain when it comes to Cats fans: no matter what the team wears, as long as they win, no one cares.

35 The Blue-White Scrimmage

Every year, smack in between Big Blue Madness and the beginning of the basketball season, there is a game that finally allows fans to see their beloved Big Blue Kentucky Wildcats play real basketball—kind of.

It's the annual Blue-White Scrimmage, where the team divides up and plays itself in front of a crowd of thousands at Rupp Arena. The team will attempt to actually play, but of course, most of the players will be going at half-speed, defense is normally at a minimum, and dunks are most likely at a premium.

The Blue-White Scrimmage has been known for producing amazing performances but not necessarily being a great indicator of what to expect from the upcoming season. As a fan, it's important to remember that.

Jonathon Davis once had a great scrimmage performance in 1989 with 37 points. It made some think he'd be an amazing scorer. It wasn't really an accurate predictor.

In 2012, the results were mixed. Many fans already thought the team had a chance to win a national title. UKAthletics.com said it best, "With an athletic and long combination of experienced and young talent, the Cats electrified fans with an arsenal of dunks, drives, and alley-oops as the Blue team defeated the White 126–104 behind a scrimmage-record 52 points from Terrence Jones."

That's right. Terrence Jones had 52 points and 16 rebounds in his last Blue White Scrimmage. Jones went on to play a key leadership role in the 2012 team's run to a national title. But he never had a real game with those kinds of stats.

Most years, the game is played like this (from UKAthletics. com), "As fun as the Cats were to watch, John Calipari made sure to point out just how far his team has to go to reach the heights so many are expecting of them.

"'Everybody's excited because you saw a lot of high-flying dunking, blocking, tipping,' Calipari said. 'That doesn't win, though. We have to play basketball. We have to be a great team. We're not right now.'

"Jones converted on 24 of his 31 field-goal attempts on the night, while six other Cats had at least 19 points. The Blue team shot 55.9 percent from the field and repeatedly had easy looks at the basket. Calipari's teams have come to be known for defense, but this edition of the Wildcats just isn't quite there yet.

"'I bet you we'd be really good against the Washington Generals,' Calipari said. 'We've got to be a great defensive team, and we're not.'

"In particular, the White team, which featured three of UK's four freshmen, had trouble containing the opponent. Jones wasn't the only one to take advantage of their inexperience either as Doron Lamb scored 31 points and Michael Kidd-Gilchrist added 21. The teams were split just as they have been throughout UK's two weeks of full practice since Big Blue Madness, which has made it tough at times for the trio of newcomers."

Every year, fans love seeing their team play—even when the team is only playing against itself. Just remember that sometimes the scrimmage will show you things you can't really believe. But that doesn't mean you can't have fun watching.

Pat Riley

Could it be that Pat Riley is the most famous alum the UK basketball program has ever produced? It's possible.

Consider this: Riley, a 6'4" forward from Schenectady, New York, was a multi-sport star in high school and the leading scorer and rebounder for one of Kentucky's most popular teams, Rupp's Runts. Even though he was a bit undersized, Riley still jumped center and displayed unnatural speed and quickness, according to Tom Wallace's *University of Kentucky Basketball Encyclopedia*. He averaged 18.3 points per game for his career, shooting 47 percent from the field and 71.4 percent from the free throw line.

But his best season was his junior campaign, the Runts year, when he averaged 22 points and nearly nine rebounds a game. He scored 36 points against Notre Dame in Freedom Hall and went for 29 four times, including twice in back-to-back wins in the NCAA Tournament over Dayton and Michigan. He also scored 19 in a semifinal win over Duke and in the loss to Texas Western in the Championship Game.

He was named All-American that season, as well as SEC Player of the Year.

Unfortunately for both UK and the player, Riley injured his back in the off-season, limiting his full potential as a senior, though he still earned All-Conference honors and averaged more than 17 points per game.

Riley was drafted in the first round of the 1967 NBA Draft by the San Diego Rockets—and also as a wide receiver in the 11th round of the NFL Draft by the Dallas Cowboys. He decided to play basketball and pinballed from one team to another before settling with the Los Angeles Lakers. There he backed up Jerry West and helped the Lakers win the 1972 World Championship.

Riley's career lasted just nine years, and he served as a role player most seasons, averaging just more than seven points per game. His real popularity came after he retired from playing.

After working as a radio announcer for the Lakers, Riley was asked to be an assistant coach after head coach Jack McKinney was injured in a bicycle accident. Paul Westhead took over the team and hired Riley as an assistant.

Six games into the 1981 season, Magic Johnson threatened to quit the team if Westhead wasn't replaced, so Riley became the head man in L.A. He won four NBA championships there with Johnson. After a stop in New York to coach the Knicks, Riley settled in Miami, where he won another title in 2006.

He became a member of the Basketball Hall of Fame as a coach, and in 2011 he won another major award as he was named Executive of the Year. He still serves in that role with Miami today, and won another championship with them in 2012.

"I think probably what I cherish most is the fact that I went to an institution that really cared about sports and cared about basketball," Riley told UKAthletics.com in 2000. "Kentucky basketball is probably one of the most important things in the state of Kentucky, and we took great pride in that. All the fans throughout the state of Kentucky took great pride in it. I felt very special being part of that kind of program. There was a lot of pressure there, but I think the one thing that I took away from Kentucky was that we were in something that was real, that was important, and also fun. We did the very best we could do at it."

Rupp's Runts

Louie Dampier said it was one particular loss that hurt the most.

"It was just hard because Coach Rupp never made it back to the tournament championship game," said Dampier, one of the most talented guards to ever play for the Big Blue. "We just really wanted to get him another championship."

But it wouldn't happen in 1966, even though it was one of the more magical seasons the Big Blue faithful had ever seen. Coming into the 1965–66 year, expectations were low. And that made sense. No starter stood more than 6'5". There was no true center. Who would rebound the ball? Luckily, the team had great scorers, including Pat Riley and "Deadeye" Louie Dampier. And although the team had very little size on the front line, the backcourt of Dampier and Tommy Kron stood at 6'0" and 6'5", respectively. Both could be a matchup nightmare for opponents. And 6'3" forward Larry Conley could pass as well as any point, giving another added dimension to the group.

Sophomore Thad Jaracz would be the center. At 6'5" he was best suited for the role. Because of the lack of height, the team became known as Rupp's Runts. But the team would really become known for Riley and Dampier, who would both average more than 20 points per game that season.

Many of these matchup problems weren't obvious to fans and the media at the beginning of the season, which meant expectations remained uncharacteristically low. The team began the year unranked, then won its first 23 games. The team cracked the top 25 at No. 10 on December 22. By February 12 the Wildcats were No. 1 in the land.

The two forwards were doing their best to rebound. Riley averaged more than nine per game. And the passing is what set the team apart.

"Why was this team, thought to be average at best, able to become a great team?" Tom Wallace asked in his *University of Kentucky Basketball Encyclopedia*. "There were many reasons why, among them: It was a superbly conditioned team. The reserves were better than expected. Shooting, passing, and defense. Dampier and Riley [both became All-Americans that season]. Team chemistry. And Conley and Kron."

Thad Jaracz (55) of Kentucky and David Lattin (42) of Texas Western vie for a rebound in the first period of the NCAA championship game in College Park, Maryland, on March 19, 1966. Kentucky players at rear are Tommy Kron (30) and Larry Conley (40). (AP Photo)

Conley and Kron in particular were singled out in later years as being the true MVPs of the team, sacrificing their statistics to get the ball to the other three teammates.

After dropping a game at Tennessee 69–62, the Cats entered the NCAAs at 24–1, still No. 1 in the land. They dispatched unranked Dayton and ninth-ranked Michigan, both by seven points. Riley led the way, scoring 29 in both contests.

Then came No. 2 Duke in the Final Four, which many thought would be the true Championship Game. Dampier scored 23 and Riley scored 19 as the Cats edged the Blue Devils 83–79 to advance to the title game against third-ranked Texas Western.

Later, many people called this the Brown vs. Board of Education game, because it was symbolic as five white players from Kentucky faced the all-black starting five from Texas Western. *Brown vs. Board of Education* was the court case that made it illegal for states to utilize separate public schools for black and white children. Though most of the players seemed only concerned about winning a championship that day, the symbolism could not be overlooked.

Still, a game had to be played. And when UK took the court, they were overmatched.

"Their quickness stunned the Cats," Wallace wrote. "Lightning-fast Bobby Joe Hill proved to be the biggest thorn in UK's side. His two early steals resulted in layups that gave the Miners a lead they would never relinquish."

UK would cut the lead to one in the second half, but the Miners responded with a run. The Cats never got close again, losing the game 72–65.

"The title game was a very, very big disappointment," Riley said years later when being honored by having his jersey retired in Rupp Arena. "It's one of the black holes in my life, basically. When you think about it, having the opportunity to win the NCAA title and you get there and you don't, you'll never forget it. At that particular time, it was a great game. Texas Western was a great team."

Still, the Runts gave fans one of the most enjoyable and surprising runs in UK basketball history.

"We had grown together," Riley said. "Most of us had come in together. We were in our third year together. We caught everyone by surprise and caught the attention of the basketball public. We had a great year because we had great togetherness. We had great leaders in Larry Conley and Tom Kron. We had a young center in

Thad Jaracz. We had two shooters in myself and Louie Dampier and a great bench that was playing in a great system. So we got on a roll, and we believed in ourselves. It all culminated [in] being the No. 1 team in the country in 1966."

UK vs. Duke, Part II 1998

Revenge is allegedly a dish best served cold, but six days short of six years after Christian Laettner broke Kentucky fan's hearts in the 1992 NCAA Tournament, UK was ready to serve a scalding helping of the dish to Duke. The two schools had not met since Christian Laettner's shot broke the hearts of the Unforgettables, but the two schools were seeded No. 1 and No. 2 in the South region of the 1998 Tournament. To the delight of UK fans, the bracket held form, and the second-seeded Wildcats met the Blue Devils in St. Petersburg, Florida, with a Final Four berth on the line.

Tubby Smith's squad, his first at UK, later to be dubbed "the Comeback Cats," had been a slow-starting bunch, losing three home games by mid-February. However, by March, the team had come into its own, winning its first three NCAA Tournament games by 15, 27, and 26 points. Duke, one suspected, might not go quite so easily.

Duke sported a fine roster with future first-round NBA Draft picks Elton Brand and William Avery leading a superb supporting cast that included shooter supreme Trajon Langdon and Shane Battier. Kentucky countered with an experienced veteran cast, the sum of the team being much greater than its individual components, although such components included Jeff Sheppard, Nazr Mohammed, Wayne Turner, and Scott Padgett.

Duke began the South regional final looking like a team that could well waltz past UK and through the Final Four. Duke shot better than 54 percent in the first half, including one 17–0 run, and led UK 49–39 at the break.

The second half did not start much better for the Cats. While Duke was cooling, Kentucky had yet to mount a substantial offensive rally. And then with Duke ahead 59–45 and just less than 15:00 to go, Duke seemed to add injury to insult.

After a loose ball, UK back-up center Jamaal Magloire became tangled with Duke point guard Steve Wojciechowski. For some reason, Wojo decided to turn the occasion into his Academy Award campaign, contorting his body as if Magloire was undertaking some medieval torture move on him rather than merely trying to stand up. Coach K continued the boorish Duke behavior by spending a timeout smirking and sarcastically berating an official after a Duke

Scott Padgett

Scott Padgett's "Three-Pointer Heard Around the World" was amazing in more ways than one. Padgett, the 6'9" forward from Louisville's St. Xavier High, seemed likely to disappear entirely off the Kentucky radar screen after he essentially flunked out of UK after his freshman season in 1995. Padgett, who played only 57 minutes that season, indicated that he didn't think professors would fail a UK basketball player. Learning the error of his ways, Padgett missed the 1995–96 season and the first eight games of the 1996–97 season while he earned his way back onto the squad.

The results justified the patience of Rick Pitino and Tubby Smith. Padgett scored 1,252 points at UK and made two All-NCAA Regional Teams and two All-NCAA Final Four teams. He also was a two-time academic All-SEC selection, proving that his turnaround on the court was no less remarkable than his turnaround in the classroom. Padgett became a 1999 first-round draft choice of the NBA's Utah Jazz, and married former UK volleyball player Cynthia Dozier. It has been a storybook ending to an unlikely story of riches to rags and back for Padgett.

charging foul. Six years had certainly done nothing to make Duke one iota more likeable.

Everything was moving Duke's way, and its lead extended to 71–54 on an offensive rebound basket with 9:37 remaining. When hopes were fading, along came Kentucky's run.

Heshimu Evans nailed a three-point shot, followed by another from Padgett, and an old-fashioned three-point play by Turner, who blew by Wojciechowski. Edwards drained a trey, Jeff Sheppard made three free throws, and Turner again blazed by Wojo in the lane, scoring to cut Duke's lead to one. During this run, UK scored on seven consecutive possessions and held Duke to a lone free throw. It was 72–71 with 6:00 to play.

Duke fought back gamely, trying in vain to hold its dwindling lead. With 2:15 to go, Cameron Mills got an open look from behind the three-point arc and tossed in his first basket of the tournament, giving UK its first lead at 80–79. Suddenly, an NCAA title was so much gravy. UK fans wanted blood, and they wanted Duke's blood. Meanwhile, the Blue Devils had burned all of their timeouts and were looking noticeably fatigued.

With the score knotted at 81, Kentucky had possession inside the final minute. Who would drive the stake through Duke's heart? Turner curled off a high pick from Padgett. Duke raced to cut off Turner and left Padgett alone at the top of the key. Turner swung the ball, and Padgett's three-pointer ripped through the net with 39 seconds to play, putting UK ahead 84–81.

Duke would not go away, fighting to within 86–84 with 4.5 seconds and one last possession to go. Tubby Smith called a 20-second timeout and set his defense (this time, thank-you-very-much Rick Pitino, with a man guarding the inbounds pass). With Wildcats fans holding their breath, Will Avery's 30' heave smacked harmlessly off the backboard. UK had won, and revenge, albeit red-hot, was served.

John Wall

After compiling a stellar freshman season during which he averaged nearly 17 points and seven assists per game, John Wall went on to set a couple of firsts as a Kentucky player.

Wall, a 6'4" point guard from North Carolina, went on to become the first UK player to win a National Player of the Year Award (the Rupp Award). Then he would go on to become the first player chosen in the 2010 NBA Draft—another first for the Kentucky program.

Simply put, Wall was one of the most important recruits in the history of the UK program. Why? At the time, Kentucky basketball was on life support. The situation wasn't as dire as the one Rick Pitino faced in 1989, but the program wasn't far from that. After two disappointing seasons under Coach Billy Gillispie, he was dismissed and John Calipari was hired, as he said, to bring in the best.

Wall was the No. 1 recruit in the land, a McDonald's All-American. Freakishly athletic, Wall combined a lightning-fast first step to get to the basket with superb passing ability. He was, as many experts would say, a reliable jump shot away from being unstoppable.

Calipari had already secured a commitment from the best power forward in the country, DeMarcus Cousins, and one of the best guards in Eric Bledsoe. But Wall was the player who could lead the team to a national title.

And after watching what Calipari had done with his previous two point guards at Memphis (Derrick Rose won an NBA MVP award while Tyreke Evans won Rookie of the Year) Wall said the choice was simple. He would be a Wildcat.

Immediately, Kentucky soared into the preseason national rankings. Some services had the Cats ranked as high as No. 2. With the addition of Calipari's first recruits, Kentucky was back. Now they just had to get it done on the court.

Wall became a legend in his first game. After sitting out a game due to an NCAA violation, Wall's first contest as a Wildcat was actually the Cats' second game of the season, this one against Miami of Ohio. The undermanned Miami squad was thought to not have a chance against fourth-ranked UK.

But that's why they play the game, right?

With new point guard John Wall at the helm, the Wildcats found themselves down 18 points in the first half. But UK fought back and took a three-point lead with less than 1:00 to play. Miami's Kenny Hayes then drilled a three of his own to tie the game with six seconds to play.

Coach Calipari wondered if he should call a timeout to set up a play for his young Cats. Normally, he would let his teams run and let them decide how to make a play to catch the other team off guard. But this team was so young. Maybe he should call a timeout...

While Calipari was deciding what he should do, Wall took the inbounded ball, glanced at the clock and raced up court. He stopped about 15' out, pulled up, and drained the game-winning jump shot 72–70.

It was a remarkable start to a college career.

Many thought the Wall-led team was either the best or second-best in the land and was thought to be a lock for the Final Four. But the only piece the team lacked was a reliable outside shooter. It came back to haunt the team when they faced West Virginia in the Elite Eight round of the tourney. Combined, UK shot 4-of-32 from three-point range in a 73–66 loss to the Mountaineers.

While the end of the season proved to be disappointing, Wall and his team set a new standard at UK.

Suddenly, everyone thought Kentucky was the cool place to be again. All the top recruits—especially point guards—wanted to go there.

The stage was set for a run to a national title. John Wall was one reason why.

Paul "Bear" Bryant

There was a time in Lexington, Kentucky, when the sun shone every day. The birds sang sweetly in the sky, all the women were beautiful, all the men were handsome, and everyone was kind and charming. The Wildcats basketball team was coached by Adolph Rupp, and the Wildcats football team was coached by Paul "Bear" Bryant. Okay, so not all of that is quite true. But it had to seem that way because Rupp and Bryant were indeed patrolling their respective Wildcats sidelines. Alas for UK gridiron fans, this era of paradise ended abruptly after the 1953 season when Bryant headed west to Texas A&M. From there, he ended up at the University of Alabama, where his Crimson Tide rewrote the SEC and NCAA record books and generally whipped the Wildcats like so many red-headed stepchildren.

Wildcats lore has indicated that the last straw in Bryant's decision to leave was that after he and Rupp each won an SEC championship in 1950, at a postseason banquet, the University presented Rupp with a new Cadillac and Bryant with a cigarette lighter. Bryant's SEC title was the team's first, and in the ensuing 60-plus years, one more shared championship is the total sum of UK football's SEC hardware. Rupp's dominance, meanwhile, was simply another brick in the wall of SEC ownership by the basketball Cats. Such a story certainly explains the different standards of the two programs, a difference that many football fans bitterly complain of to this day. It explains why Rupp stayed and won and won, and why Bryant took his act to greener pastures.

There is only one problem. The story isn't true. The source of the story is impeccable—Bryant himself. He told the story to *Sports Illustrated*, and the magazine printed the account in its August 22, 1966, issue. The facts simply do not support Bryant's account. UK hoops historian Jon Scott has researched the issue thoroughly and has been unable to find any banquet for both the football and basketball teams or any gift of a car to Rupp in this era. Bryant did tell an audience in Oklahoma this basic story in December 1950, but the newspaper reports that Jon Scott has found indicate that the story was essentially a joke by Bryant.

The University did give Rupp a car in 1956, two years after Bryant moved on to College Station, Texas, in celebration of Rupp's 25 years at the school. Incidentally, Russell Rice, in his UK football history, *The Wildcats*, relates that on December 28, 1952, a group of 25 Kentuckians presented a UK coach with a new automobile in Frankfort—and that the coach in question was Bear Bryant. Rice reported that Kentucky's governor, in presenting the gift, proclaimed Bryant a lifetime Kentuckian. So much for underappreciation.

Rice, without ever acknowledging the legend noted above, does take the time to point out two giant reasons why Bryant left UK. First was the point-shaving scandal that had enveloped UK basketball and led to the cancelation of the 1952–53 basketball season. Football was secondarily involved in the scandal, and both the University and the NCAA were going to great lengths to taper back the athletic program in Lexington. The second reason was a new University policy that the football program would not recruit out of state at all and that no more than five scholarships in a given year would be awarded to non-Kentuckians. Kentucky, in the 1950s as well as today, was not a high school football powerhouse like Georgia or Florida, and Bryant may well have realized that the deck was stacked against further success.

And so in February 1954, Bryant left for College Station, Texas. He was 60–23–5 as UK's head coach, a record that has not been approached, much less equaled. Unfortunately, his memory does not seem to have been as sharp as his coaching abilities.

41 The Season Without Joy

It had been 20 years since UK had won an NCAA title. There was no precedent for such a drought. Four titles in the first eighteen years of the tournament had spoiled UK fans. But then John Wooden made UCLA a dynasty, and Adolph Rupp struggled with old age and bad luck. Joe B. Hall took the reins as UK coach in 1972 and nearly broke the drought in 1975 before Wooden stole UK's thunder by announcing his retirement and picking up an emotionally charged title victory in his last game.

That 1974–75 Kentucky team featured a superb freshman class, including Jack Givens, Rick Robey, Mike Phillips, and James Lee. All four were three years stronger and more experienced in 1977–78. Kyle Macy had transferred from Purdue to UK and would provide point-guard play and shooting precision. Givens was a rock-solid scorer and rebounder at forward. Phillips and Robey were both talented big men, and Lee was a difference maker off the bench. Guards Truman Claytor and Jay Shidler added depth.

Expectations were sky high for UK in 1978. With such a talented roster and a lengthy title drought, nothing short of NCAA title number five would satisfy either the Cats or their fan base. The media called it, "a season without joy."

UK was ranked No. 1 in the nation by their second game against Indiana on December 5, 1977. The Cats beat Bobby Knight and his Hoosiers by 14 points and won their next 12 games, starting the season 14–0. Midseason losses at Alabama and at LSU in overtime gave Coach Hall enough ammunition to ensure that complacency would not overtake the Cats. UK was back to No. 1 by the time the regular season ended.

The NCAA Tournament began with a tense matchup against Florida State University in Knoxville, Tennessee. FSU led by seven at the half, and Hall bravely elected to bench three of his starters for several minutes, grabbing his heralded players' attention in the nick of time. A re-energized group of starters pulled away from FSU 85–76.

After an easy win over Miami of Ohio, UK was matched up with Michigan State in the Mideast Regional Final in Dayton, Ohio. Michigan State was led by superstar freshman point guard Earvin "Magic" Johnson. Johnson was frustrated by UK, which held him to six points and five assists against six turnovers. Kyle Macy scored 18 points and drained six critical free throws in the final three minutes to give UK a 52–49 win and a return trip to the Final Four.

In the national semifinal, UK met a talented Arkansas team coached by Eddie Sutton and led by All-American Sidney Moncrief. Arkansas played close, but UK outlasted the Razorbacks 64–59. Coach Hall eschewed any postgame celebration, admitting at the postgame press conference, "We want to win the championship. We're going to celebrate after it's over."

On the Sunday preceding the next night's title game, Joe B. Hall wanted to give his team a break. Cawood Ledford in *Six Roads to Glory* recounted Hall telling Rick Robey to select a movie for the team to go out and watch. Hall was thinking of relaxing and decompressing. Robey asked if the coaches had taped Duke's win over Notre Dame in the other semifinal. When Hall admitted they had, Robey said that the players would prefer to stay in their rooms and watch the game film. If it wasn't a season without joy, it certainly was a season of great focus and intensity.

The following night, Duke simply could not weather the UK attack. Jack Givens put up 41 points, and UK cruised to a 45–38 halftime lead. UK led throughout the second half, and the only anxious moment came when Coach Hall cleared his bench a bit too early and Duke closed the Cats' margin to four. Hall rushed the regulars back into the game in time for James Lee to throw down a dunk and clinch the victory 94–88.

The drought was over. Kentucky had delivered on expectations and fought off all opponents. While the press called it the season without joy, in fact, the joy was merely delayed until the ultimate goal was achieved.

Rex Chapman

Before there was John Wall, there was Rex Chapman.

Chapman, also known as King Rex, was a 6'4", 185-pound wunderkind from Owensboro, Kentucky, who could shoot, pass, and dunk like few players anyone in Kentucky had ever seen. In fact, he was so good, he was so cool, it was deemed a necessity that Kentucky sign him—even though Chapman was really a fan of the high-flying, dunking Louisville Cardinals.

"Oh, no," UK fans thought. "No—our homegrown Kentucky boy will not be taking his talents to Louisville."

Guard Rex Chapman goes up for a shot against University of Cincinnati defender Levertis Robinson during the first half of their game on December 1, 1987, in Lexington. (AP Photo/Tim Sharp)

Luckily for UK fans, he didn't.

"An exceptional leaper who could dunk over taller opponents or step outside and bury the trey," is how Tom Wallace described Chapman in his *University of Kentucky Basketball Encyclopedia.*

His arrival was one of the more anticipated in the history of UK basketball. One sportswriter dubbed the college town "Rexington." The star did not disappoint.

He scored 18 points in his college debut, but it's his performance against the University of Louisville that still has people searching for the highlights on YouTube. On national television, Chapman dropped 26 points on the Cards, nailing 5-of-8 three-pointers in the process. And of course, there was the hellacious dunk he threw down. It was nasty. Go online and check it out.

Unfortunately, Chapman only stayed two seasons in Rexington. As a sophomore he led his team to an SEC Tournament championship and won MVP honors. But neither of his teams reached the Final Four.

Chapman declared for the NBA Draft and was chosen with the eighth pick by the Charlotte Hornets. Over the course of his 12-year career, Chapman played with several teams but never quite reached the superstar status many thought he would. He averaged just less than 15 points per game in his NBA career.

After his career, Chapman worked in the front office of several NBA teams and as an analyst for TNT. His son, Zeke Chapman, also a basketball player, committed to play at Ball State.

Chapman now has three daughters and a son and lives in Scottsdale, Arizona, with his wife of 20 years.

"Watching your kids do something is so much more nerve-wracking and emotionally draining than it ever was to play," Chapman told CoachCal.com. "Playing was easy; you could have some sort of control of what was going on out there."

In the summer of 2011, Chapman was elected into the Kentucky Athletic Hall of Fame. But his most fun was had back

Rex on Twitter: @rexchapman

Want to be one of the 26,000 or so people who follow Rex Chapman on Twitter? You should. He's hilarious, and he knows his basketball. You can find sports insights like this:

*Archie Goodwin's strides look like Memphis'
#RodneyCarney from a few years back. #Athletic #Speed*

Or you can find life lessons like this:

*A guy having a joint in his pocket doesn't
mean he's gonna smoke it. Oh wait . . . #Nvrmnd*

Or you can find fun comments like this:

Pulled my groin just watching this game.

Rex Chapman. He'll always be Blue, and he'll always be cool.

when he played, when he was able to watch seniors go through Senior Day.

"It was just special," Chapman said on the website. "Everyone in Rupp was alive and singing 'My Old Kentucky Home.' That's just Kentucky basketball. Getting to enjoy the crowd from the bench and seeing my teammates I love so much having their special night was probably my greatest memory."

And it was no coincidence that Chapman got involved in the program when Calipari was hired. "Man, those few years right before John got there were tough, not only for the fans but for players past and present," Chapman told the CoachCal site. "When he got there, I can't even explain it. What a welcome sight he was. I do feel like he was the absolute perfect guy for the job."

Now a new generation of fans is following Chapman on Twitter—about 23,000 of them to be exact. After his friend, Jim Rome, urged him to, Rex became a Tweeter.

But he was already cool on the Internet before that.

While looking through some old things, Chapman stumbled on some home videos. It was a trip to Disney World, and the trip included a chance to make your own music video. After a little encouragement and a few dares from his family, Chapman decided to do his own hilarious rendition of the popular 1980s Prince song, "When Doves Cry."

It was a huge hit.

All these years later, Chapman is still a rock star, still the coolest kid in school.

Bob Knight

"We've gotten into this situation where integrity is really lacking, and that's why I'm glad I'm not coaching. You see, we've got a coach at Kentucky who put two schools on probation and he's still coaching. I really don't understand that."

—Bob Knight, December 17, 2009,
at the Indiana Basketball Hall of Fame

Like most of the time when he talks about Kentucky, Bob Knight got his facts wrong. For a guy employed by ESPN who is supposed to be a college basketball expert, he messed it all up on this one. In a speech to the Indiana Basketball Hall of Fame, he incorrectly said the coach at Kentucky (John Calipari) had left two programs on probation. Wrong. Calipari turned in his own program at UMass because star Marcus Camby took money and gifts from an agent, which resulted in forfeited victories, while Memphis had victories taken away after the NCAA reversed its own decision that allowed Derrick Rose to play.

Calipari was never implicated in either situation. Neither school was placed on probation.

Knight has been a longtime outspoken critic of all things Kentucky, and the UK/IU rivalry became highly contentious because of it. Many like to trace it all back to one moment: when Knight hit UK Coach Joe B. Hall (and Knight's supposed friend) in the head in the middle of a game.

In *Bob Knight: The Unauthorized Biography*, the situation was described as a bit of a misunderstanding, when in December 1974 Indiana was on its way to beating UK 98–74. With less than a minute to go, Knight was still on the referees and ran down to the UK side of the court to chastise them after a call.

"And as he turned to go back to the bench, I said, 'Way to go, Bob, give 'em hell,' good-naturedly, because this was a friend of mine," Hall said in the book.

Then Knight turned back to Hall and shouted at him to coach his own team and slapped him on the back of the neck. Afterward, Knight claimed it was a friendly pat. The Kentucky coaches felt differently. "All I want is another chance to play them," Hall said. "Knight personally humiliated me, and I'll never forget it."

Later in the year, an underdog Kentucky team beat the same Indiana squad 92–90 to get to the Final Four. As they say, it was on.

Knight was open about disliking how the Kentucky program was run under Hall and Eddie Sutton, yet he seemed to cool when C.M. Newton, also a Knight friend, was hired as athletic director. Knight respected Rick Pitino and his coaching abilities, and complimented the Newton/Pitino pairing publicly. Tubby Smith also earned Knight's respect.

But John Calipari would become a target of Knight's criticism.

After the 2010–11 season, Knight spoke to a group in Wabash, Indiana. The subject of Calipari came up in a question-and-answer session, and Knight responded with this gem: "Kentucky, year before last, started five players in the NCAA Tournament games that had not been to class that semester. And that's that one-and-done philosophy that we have now."

Hoosiers Roasting

Back in the heyday of the Kentucky/Indiana rivalry, when Bob Knight roamed the Hoosier sideline, my Granddad put pen to paper to describe the love/hate relationship between Wildcats and Hoosiers fans.

Because the game is normally played around the holidays, the tune is to "The Christmas Song (Chestnuts Roasting on an Open Fire)." And because Knight gained a considerable amount of weight as he got older, he is referred to as Blobby instead of Bobby. The coach for UK has changed over the years, but it always seems to work, no matter what his name is.

Now, without further ado:

"Hoosiers Roasting on an Open Fire"
By Hubert "Goose" Tatum

Hoosiers roasting on an open fire,
Hoosiers picking on their nose.
Hoosier carols, being sung by a choir
And boogers falling on their toes.

Every Hoosier knows,
The patsies on their easy list
Help to make the season bright.
Hoosier tots, with their eyes all aglow
Think Santa Claus is Blobby Knight.

They know that Blobby's on his way.
He's loaded lots of patsies for his team to play.
And every Hoosier child is gonna spy
To see if chairs really know how to fly.

And so, I'm offering this simple phrase
For Hoosiers one to ninety-two:
Although it's been said, many times, many ways,
Calipari's got a present for you.

Have a Big Blue Christmas everybody!

Again, for someone who is supposed to be an expert Knight is completely out of touch with what is really going on. Because UK could be punished by the NCAA for players not attending class, Kentucky makes sure to strongly encourage its athletes to remain in class until the end of the semester, even if that player has decided to go to the NBA. In fact, only one player has not done so—Daniel Orton—and he was strongly criticized by Calipari and the fan base for his actions.

Players like Patrick Patterson, who went to class his last semester and graduated, took offense to the claim and said so via Twitter. Athletic Director Mitch Barnhart issued a release refuting the claims. John Wall earned a 3.5 grade-point average that semester, and all the other starters remained in good academic standing.

ESPN issued a statement that was termed an "apology" by Knight, but it came off half-hearted. "My overall point is that 'one and dones' are not healthy for college basketball," the statement said. "I should not have made it personal to Kentucky and its players, and I apologize."

As Knight continued to take cheap shots at Kentucky through its 2011–12 championship season (frequently Knight would not discuss UK in his analysis of the best teams and players in the country) the UK and Indiana rivalry raged on. In December 2011, No. 1 UK came into Indiana with an undefeated record and wins over powerhouses like Kansas and North Carolina. But the Hoosiers would not be denied. Christian Watford's three-pointer at the buzzer won it for IU, signaling the team's return from several years of mediocrity.

After the game Calipari told current IU coach Tom Crean (the two happen to be great friends) that he was certain the NCAA would match up the two teams again in March. Cal was correct.

In the 2012 NCAA Sweet 16, Indiana and Kentucky faced off again, and the two teams played one of the most entertaining games of the tournament. Neither could seemingly stop the other, and just like in the 1975 season, UK gained revenge, winning 102–90.

"It was a war," Calipari said afterward. "I love coaching this type of game."

And Kentucky and Indiana fans love watching them. Unfortunately, the teams ended their rivalry that year. Fans hope they play again someday.

44 Ralph Beard

The two-sport star had a rough freshman season. He started for the football team as a freshman but separated both shoulders early in the season and was out for the year. With time to sit and stew, he wondered if UK was his best college choice. He eventually decided that no, it wasn't, and that he should transfer to Louisville. He met with the UK basketball coach to explain his decision. The coach heard the freshman out and according to the player, as recounted in Russell Rice's *Big Blue Machine*, looked him in the eye and told him, "I can't keep you from going to UL, but I will tell you one thing. We here at the University will not cancel our schedule." The star's high school coach took a slightly more gentle tone, telling his former star that he thought he was making a major mistake. And so Ralph Beard, one of UK's best players ever, did not transfer to Louisville but stayed in Lexington to lead the Cats and Coach Rupp to their first two NCAA Tournament championships.

Ralph Beard had been all-everything at Louisville Male High School. He spurned the hometown Cardinals to play for Coach Rupp. Beard, not unlike John Wall six and a half decades later, was an explosive athlete. He could break down defenses, swipe errant dribbles, and drill the outside jump shot when necessary.

Beard and *Sports Illustrated*

How big of a star was Ralph Beard? In February 1949, a new magazine called *Sports Illustrated* was planning its initial issue. Its cover boy? Ralph Beard, the "fiery guard" who was "helping Kentucky defend its title." This magazine was not the same as today's *Sports Illustrated.* That magazine would not begin publication until 1954, picking up the title from its extinct predecessor. Still, a college basketball player was an unlikely cover boy for a late 1940s national sports magazine.

Had Beard's NBA career not been prematurely curtailed, he might have had the same type of following in the NBA. Beard and Bob Cousy had bumped heads occasionally throughout their college and NBA careers. Of course, today one is an NBA legend, and the other is nearly forgotten. Still, *SI* wasn't leading off its first issue with an article on the Couz. A December 1948 article in *The All-Sports News* speculates that James Naismith might have named his game Basketbeard had he seen Ralph play. We'll never know.

Beard benefitted from some unusual NCAA rules—for a brief period following World War II, freshmen had NCAA eligibility. In his freshman season, Beard scored almost 10 points per game and was a dazzling point guard, earning All-SEC selection. He scored 13 points and made the winning free throw in UK's 1946 NIT Championship over Rhode Island. It may not sound like much, but hoops aficionados regard that as UK's first national title. In *Game of my Life*, Beard recalled, "The NCAA [tournament] was more like YMCA…. Everyone wanted to be a part of the NIT at the time." Not only had Beard and Kentucky been part of it, but they won it.

Beard had an All-American sophomore campaign, which was diminished only slightly when UK lost to Utah in the NIT finals. Beard was held to one point, and the loss motivated him to fine-tune his outside jump shot. College basketball would spend the next two seasons paying for the adjustment.

Beard led UK to the 1948 and 1949 NCAA Tournament titles. He added two more All-American campaigns to his resume as well as an Olympic gold medal in 1948. In four seasons at UK, Beard and the Cats were 130–10 and finished 55–0 against SEC opponents. As for Beard himself, he scored 1,517 points, which at the time was second most in UK history and still ranks 15th. There is no telling how many assists or steals Beard would have registered had such statistics been officially tracked. It is certainly safe to say that Beard would have been one of the all-time UK leaders in both categories.

No less of an authority than Adolph Rupp called Beard the finest basketball player he ever saw. After his stellar career at UK, Beard seemed to have a lock on a long and productive career in the relatively new NBA. Beard played for the Indianapolis Olympians and seemed well on his way to such a career. In his second season, 1950–51, Beard was chosen as an NBA All-Star and a first team All-NBA selection. He was seventh in the league in scoring average and fifth in assists (Bob Cousy was fourth).

But then Beard was implicated in the NCAA point-shaving scandal. Beard confessed to taking money but denied fixing games or shaving points. Nonetheless, he was banned from the NBA and was sadly forgotten by many casual fans. He was honored by the Louisville *Courier-Journal* in 1999, sharing a cover photo with Louisville's Darrell Griffith after being named to the paper's all-time basketball team for the state of Kentucky. Astute UK fans will be forever grateful that Beard, who passed away in 2007 at the age of 79, stayed with the Big Blue rather than switching to Cardinal Red, and thus began the UK parade of championships.

45 The Comeback Cats

In 1958, Adolph Rupp coached a group of overachievers, whom he had derisively referred to as "barnyard fiddlers," to a surprising national championship. Forty years later, history, in an odd sense, repeated itself. First-year coach Orlando "Tubby" Smith took a cobbled-together group of leftover players and wildly exceeded the expectations of even the most optimistic Kentucky fans, taking home NCAA title number seven in the process.

Tubby Smith's 1997–98 squad, like Rupp's forty years before, had some barnyard fiddlers but few concert maestros. Jeff Sheppard was a redshirt senior and scored just 5.5 points per game in his last action back in 1996. Allen Edwards, who scored 8.6 points per game in 1996–97, and Cameron Mills, who was a season removed from scoring six points total in 1996, were Smith's other seniors. His lineup was rounded out by junior forward Scott Padgett (the top returning scorer at 9.6 PPG in 1996–97), junior point guard Wayne Turner (6.6 PPG), and junior center Nazr Mohammed (7.9 PPG). Transfer Heshimu Evans would add depth, along with sophomore Jamaal Magloire, four unheralded freshmen, and one walk-on.

Kentucky came into its season opener ranked No. 9 in the country. Sheppard became the leading scorer on this squad, but he had layers of rust on his game. Mohammed continued to improve at an amazing pace, but the team was inconsistent. After two wins, UK met defending champion No. 1 Arizona in Maui and lost by 15 points in a game that wasn't really close. UK rallied to top No. 13 Clemson, No. 6 Purdue, and Indiana in consecutive games. A few games later, though, UK lost to a putrid Louisville squad in Rupp Arena.

This appeared to be the pattern for this team. They were capable on a good day of almost anything, beating six top-25 squads in the regular season. But on a bad day, UK could lose at home to unranked Florida or to Ole Miss.

Kentucky entered the SEC tournament ranked No. 7 in the nation—a good but not great team. UK blazed through the SEC tournament, winning by 11, 25, and 30 points en route to the title despite losing Sheppard to a sprained ankle in the first half of the semifinal.

UK was seeded No. 2 in the South region. UK continued to play like a well-oiled machine as Sheppard showed few ill effects of injury. Kentucky won by 15, 27, and 26 points to earn an Elite Eight matchup with Duke. UK looked to be peaking at just the right time.

It looked that way until No. 3 Duke raced to a 10-point lead, which Duke extended to 71–54 with 9:38 remaining before the late-breaking Cats took over and rallied to an 86–84 victory. Five Cats scored in double figures with Sheppard (18) and Turner (16) leading the way. In the national semifinal, Stanford raced out ahead of the Cats, leading by five at the half and holding a 46–36 advantage early in the second half. UK would again rally late, with Sheppard scoring 27, Mohammed adding 18, and Kentucky winning an 86–85 overtime nailbiter.

Could UK have anything left in the tank for the title game? Utah led 41–31 at the half and rested secure in the knowledge that no team had rallied from such a halftime deficit to win the NCAA title game. No team, that is, until the Comeback Cats.

UK gave its greatest performance on the largest stage. UK trailed 50–40 early in the second half when the mojo kicked in. Utah managed only four baskets in the last 16 minutes, and Sheppard, Padgett, Evans, Mohammed, Turner, Edwards, Mills, and Magloire powered over, around, and through the Utes. When the horn sounded, UK was a 78–69 winner, and the NCAA title was headed back to the Bluegrass. With three amazing comebacks in its last three games, like Rupp's 1957–58 squad, the 1997–98 team had fiddled and fiddled with the end result being sweet music to Cats fans.

Tony Delk

Tony Delk caught the ball near the left corner. He squared his shoulders, rose up, and fired up a three-point try. As it had 282 previous times for Delk in his official UK career, the ball glided toward the hoop and softly swished through. Syracuse's Todd Burgan, rushing over too late to contest Delk's seventh three-point basket in the 1996 NCAA title game, crashed into Delk, fouling him, and sending Delk sliding into the UK bench. The triumphant Wildcats bench happily roughed up Delk excitedly before pulling him to his feet. In the biggest game of his career, Tony Delk continued to do what he did best.

Delk's career was not always so smooth. In 1992–93, Delk was perhaps the least heralded of UK's three freshmen. Rodrick Rhodes was named freshman All-SEC, and Jared Prickett had a big NCAA Tournament. Delk's contribution was much quieter. He drained a few threes, played steady defense, and mostly fit in on a veteran squad that lost in the Final Four to Michigan. Delk scored 4.5 points per game, good for eighth on the team.

The 1993–94 squad was a disappointing one, ending its season in a second-round NCAA Tournament loss to Marquette. Delk, however, was hardly disappointing. He led the team with 16.6 points per game, draining 95 three-point baskets, still the fourth most in UK single-season history. Delk was chosen All-SEC by both the coaches and media.

In 1994–95, Delk continued his consistent roll up the UK scoring list. He entered the 1,000-point club late in the year and again led the team in scoring, this time with 16.7 points per game. Delk was a first team All-SEC selection, but UK fell short of its championship goals, losing to North Carolina in the Elite Eight despite 19 points from Delk.

Delk's senior squad, the Untouchables, did not fall short. Pitino briefly flirted with playing Delk at point guard, looking to improve Tony's NBA prospects before realizing that his team ran smoothest with Anthony Epps at that position and Delk manning his usual shooting guard spot. Delk provided consistent leadership, scoring 17.8 points per game and making everyone's All-American team. Delk canned 93 three-point shots, one less than the combined total of the players who had the second-, third-, and fourth-most threes on the team. He also led the team in steals and knocked down 80 percent of his free throws.

A few particular moments stand out in Delk's 1995–96 campaign. He set a school individual record with nine three-point baskets against TCU in January. In Kentucky's tense last three games of their title run, an Elite Eight win over Wake Forest, the semifinal win over UMass, and the title victory over Syracuse, Delk scored 25, 20, and 24 points, respectively. He was the high scorer in each game and was 12-of-22 on three-point shooting in that span.

Delk finished his career with 1,890 total points, fourth in school history at that time. His 201 career steals set a school record, although his Untouchables teammate Wayne Turner would break the mark three years later. Delk's 283 three-pointers remain the school's standard. On the strength of his UK career, Delk was a first-round draft choice of the Charlotte Hornets.

Delk played for ten seasons in the NBA, making the rounds of eight different teams. His scoring skills never deserted him, though.

On January 2, 2001, Delk, playing for the Phoenix Suns, dropped 53 points on the Sacramento Kings. For Kentucky fans who saw the game, or Delk's lengthy highlight reel, it was, to steal a line from the great Yogi Berra, déjà vu all over again.

47 The 1948 Olympic Gold Medal Winners

How fabulous were the Fabulous Five, UK's 1947–48 NCAA title team? Fabulous enough that after winning that NCAA title, the school's first, they took aim at being not only the greatest team in college basketball but the greatest team in the world.

The Olympics were held in 1948. Due to World War II and the mass political chaos that it brought about, there had been no 1940 or 1944 Olympic Games. Basketball had debuted in the 1936 Olympics in Berlin, the games made famous for Jesse Owens' thumping of Hitler's Aryan sprinters on their home turf. In those games, basketball was a demonstration sport and was played outdoors. The U.S. had won the gold medal game 19–8. Much changed in the next twelve years.

Fresh off their NCAA title victory, the Wildcats were entered into a qualifying tournament against the other top amateur teams in the nation for the right to represent the U.S. in London in the Olympic Games. Kentucky's first qualifying foe was none other than the Louisville Cardinals. UK had not played Louisville in 26 years, and they made Louisville wish it had been many more by winning 91–57. UK point guard Ralph Beard was superb with 22 points, and forward Wah Wah Jones added 19 more. Next, UK drew the same Baylor team it had beaten six days earlier for the

NCAA title. UK proved that 16-point win was no fluke by beating Baylor again, this time by 18 points, 77–59. Alex Groza personally torched the Bears for 33 points.

This brought UK to the finals of the qualifying tournament. They would meet AAU giants, the Phillips 66ers. Phillips Petroleum sponsored the world-class squad, who worked for the company and then played with its basketball team. Seven-footer Bob Kurland was the biggest and best of the 66ers. The game was highly anticipated, and 44 years before Duke and UK played a game which was given the moniker, it was termed the greatest game of all time.

UK jumped to a 20–13 lead in the first half before Phillips answered with an 11–0 run. The game was tied at 26 at the half. In the second half, however, Cliff Barker was unavailable with a broken nose, and Wah Wah Jones fouled out. Despite a 23-point effort by Beard, Phillips had too much firepower. Kurland had 20 points and held Groza to a mere four. Phillips won 53–49.

Despite the outcome, the five UK starters were named to the Olympic team. Along with Phillips' first five and four other players, this was the 1948 U.S. Olympic Team. Because of the results of the tournament, Phillips coach Bud Browning was the team's head coach, with Coach Rupp serving as associate coach.

The two coaches quickly realized that the team played best when the respective five starters were allowed to play as a unit, a strategy that they employed as often as possible. The team, naturally, was a juggernaut. They faced only one real test, struggling in an early game with Argentina, winning by just a 59–57 count.

From there, the U.S. romped. The team won the gold medal game against France by a score of 65–21. Groza was the leading scorer on the team, totaling 11.1 points per game. Cawood Ledford notes in *Six Roads to Glory* that Rupp called the awards ceremony "my biggest thrill in sports."

The Fabulous Five were pretty thrilling. They weren't just the best team in the NCAA, they were also—with a little help from their friends—the class of the entire world in basketball.

48 C-J and Larry Boeck

While the *Lexington Herald-Leader* has its history of probing and investigating the UK basketball program, down the road is another Pulitzer Prize–winning newspaper in Louisville, the *Courier-Journal*, which has its own sordid history associated with the Wildcats.

In fact, it's possible that a *C-J* reporter may have ruined the chance for Kentucky to have a perfect championship season.

In 1954, the team finished 25–0. Led by the powerhouse trio of Frank Ramsey, Cliff Hagan, and Lou Tsioropoulos, the Cats won the SEC and were set to represent the league in the NCAA Tournament. Adolph Rupp was on the verge of his first undefeated national title squad.

But an interesting series of events were already underway.

The three stars (Tsioropoulos, Ramsey, and Hagan) had technically graduated the year before. When Kentucky was banned from playing for a year because of a prior point-shaving scandal, a year was used up. All good students, the players got their degrees and then focused on their last season of basketball.

What no one knew was that an obscure NCAA rule existed that disallowed graduated players from participating in the NCAA Tournament. The three were deemed ineligible to play.

It was Larry Boeck, a reporter for the *Courier-Journal*, who pointed out the rule. Boeck had already become a bit of a legend in the sportswriting business, having given the 1948 national champs their famous moniker, the Fabulous Five. Boeck had written for both of the two Louisville newspapers, then he left to serve in WWII before coming back in 1946.

For Kentucky, there was a decision to make. It was perfectly acceptable for the rest of the team to play in the tournament—just not those three players. Legend has it that when the team found out, Rupp left it up to the team to vote to see if they still wanted to play in the NCAAs.

The vote was supposed to have been 9–3, with the three stars voting to keep the perfect record. Then, also supposedly, Rupp overruled the majority, and decided to keep the record and turn down the invitation.

Did it really happen that way? In the book, *Game of My Life: Kentucky*, Ramsey said he never heard about a vote. He confirmed that the trio of talented stars did not want to go to the NCAAs but that Rupp made the choice on his own.

"He told us we would not be going," Ramsey said.

And it all happened because a reporter knew the rulebook.

Throughout the years, reporters have done their best to act as watchdogs of the university teams, and while newspapers have been challenged by Internet sites, the number of overall journalists has increased. Sites like Rivals.com, Scout.com, Yahoo! Sports, and others like ESPN and Fox Sports have journalists writing about college sports on a daily basis, as well as a stable of bloggers.

That doesn't even begin to count the number of amateur bloggers and professional blogging sites like KentuckySportsRadio.com or ASeaofBlue.com.

And in most cases, the journalists don't always get along with the subjects they cover. Larry Vaught, multi-year winner of the best sportswriter in Kentucky award as a writer for the Danville *Advocate-Messenger*, seems to be the exception. Everyone from fans, celebrities, and coaches love him.

What price did Boeck and *The Courier-Journal* pay for ruining a championship? According to Tom Wallace's *University of Kentucky Basketball Encyclopedia*, Wallace describes a near-fight occurring between Boeck and UK assistant coach Harry Lancaster.

Boeck went on to cover many memorable UK games. He then went to work for the University of Louisville and died in 1972 at the age of 52.

The Fiddlin' Five

UK's first three NCAA championship teams were basically juggernauts. The 1947–48 and 1948–49 seasons were dominated by the Fabulous Five, a world-class group of players who ran roughshod over everyone who stumbled into their path. The 1950–51 season wasn't much different, as a fine team was led by Bill Spivey, who was the most dominant player of his era. However, after the point-shaving scandal, the lost season of 1952–53, and the undefeated season of 1953–54 that ended without the NCAA tournament, UK had fallen back a bit.

In the fall of 1957, Adolph Rupp was asked about his team for the upcoming year. According to Russell Rice's *Big Blue Machine*, Rupp answered, "They might be pretty good barnyard fiddlers, but we have a Carnegie Hall schedule, and it will take violinists to play that competition." Before the 1957–58 season finished, Rupp's squad was known as the Fiddlin' Five, and they played some sweet string music for the ears of the Big Blue Nation.

Senior Vernon Hatton was perhaps the foremost fiddler on the team. In 1958, he averaged more than 17 points per game, was named All-American, and often came through with clutch plays for a UK team that excelled in close games. Hazard junior Johnny Cox was Hatton's main wingman. Cox was a deadly outside shooter and a tough 6'4" forward who grabbed more than 1,000 rebounds in three seasons at UK.

John Crigler, a hustle machine and defensive stopper, played the other forward. Ed Beck was an undersized 6'7" center who scratched and clawed to get the most from his talent. The fifth starter was a junior college transfer named Adrian "Odie" Smith.

The Fiddlin' Five hit many sour notes early in the 1957–58 campaign. After a December 20 loss to West Virginia in the UK Invitational Tournament, UK stood at 4–3. One of the four wins was a triple-overtime home win against Temple that couldn't have happened had Hatton not sent the game to a second overtime with a 47' buzzer-beater.

While Kentucky did improve enough to win the SEC regular season title, the team was 19–6 entering the NCAA Tournament. No team had ever won the NCAA Tournament after losing as many as six games in the regular season.

UK's NCAA run began in Lexington. UK had lost only one home game all season, so this was a pivotal boost to their fortunes. UK began with an easy 94–70 win over Miami of Ohio. The next opponent was No. 8 Notre Dame. Rupp essentially double-teamed Notre Dame's star, Tom Hawkins, and UK held the All-American to 15 points, stunning the Irish 89–56.

From there it was on to Louisville where Freedom Hall was hosting the 1958 Final Four. In the semifinals, Temple awaited a rematch. It had been ages since UK's triple-overtime win in December, highlighted by Vernon Hatton's miracle shot. Temple had lost only once during the rest of its season—to Oscar Robertson and Cincinnati. Russell Rice recalls in *Big Blue Machine* that Temple star Guy Rodgers told Rupp, "We're going to beat you this time." The Baron of the Bluegrass replied, "There's a possibility of that."

The possibility went unfulfilled. Temple led 60–59 with 24 seconds to play. UK had the ball, and Rupp called timeout. According to Cawood Ledford in *Six Roads to Glory*, Rupp called for Hatton to take an outside shot, but Ed Beck interrupted, saying that if Hatton would drive off his screen, Vernon could get to the basket. Rupp agreed, Beck screened, and Hatton sunk a reverse layup, giving UK a 61–60 lead with 16 seconds left. Temple fumbled away their last possession, and the score held up.

UK advanced to face Seattle and superstar Elgin Baylor in the title game. Rupp and assistant Harry Lancaster struggled with how to stop Baylor. They settled for allowing Crigler to drive at him on defense, luring Baylor into foul trouble and giving UK a huge advantage. Hatton scored 30 points and Cox added 24, with UK turning in an 84–72 win. The Fiddlin' Five's unlikely tune had ended in championship glory and eternal recognition.

50 Pitino's Bombinos

Start with a 13–19 team, the school's worst record in 62 seasons. Let three starters, more specifically the top two scorers and the starting point guard, transfer away. Add in one lightly regarded high school swingman and four walk-ons, replace the coach, ban the team from live TV and postseason play, and what would a reasonable fan expect? Cawood Ledford predicted an eight-win season and said that if the team could win 10 games, its new head coach should be NCAA Coach of the Year.

What Kentucky fans got, even more important than the surprising 14–14 record from the 1989–90 squad, was a new era in Kentucky basketball. *Lexington Herald-Leader* columnist John

McGill nicknamed the bunch "Pitino's Bombinos," and the nickname stuck. New head coach Rick Pitino displayed a love of the three-point shot, a harassing mother-in-law defense, and a refusal to allow small things like a lack of talent or depth to slow his team.

The Bombinos consisted of eight scholarship players, none taller than 6'7", and only two of whom, Derrick Miller and Reggie Hanson, had substantial playing experience. The core of the team was a group of four inexperienced sophomores, Sean Woods, Richie Farmer, Deron Feldhaus, and John Pelphrey, who would come to be known as the Unforgettables. Farmer, Feldhaus, and Pelphrey were Kentucky natives, and Woods hailed from Indiana but had spent much of his youth in Kentucky. This Kentucky team looked more like an intramural squad than a major college basketball team. But what the group lacked in size, speed, or talent, they made up for with heart.

The Bombinos did not lack scoring punch, averaging 88.8 points per game. They did, however, lack defensive talent and depth, giving up 87.9 points per game. Early on, the going was difficult. On December 9, 1989, UK went to Kansas and was blown out 150–95. Still, even in the rough games, a tone was set. Kansas coach Roy Williams, according to Gene Wojciechowski in *The Last Great Game*, approached Pitino late in the game, asking if Pitino would like Williams to call a timeout, as Williams insinuated that he could not otherwise control the thumping. Pitino, in no uncertain terms, told Williams what he could do with his timeout. No quarter would be asked and none taken by this group. Pitino's style was here to stay.

After losing its first two SEC games, UK was at 5–7 on January 6, 1990. However, Pitino's charges were catching on and catching fire. UK won eight of its next 11 games in SEC play. The high point of this streak was a February 15 showdown with LSU. The Tigers featured dominant center Shaquille O'Neal, star shooting guard Chris Jackson, and a host of other talented players, including

Three-Pointers and UK

When the first Kentucky three-point basket of a game goes in, bear in mind that one of the more impressive records of NCAA marksmanship has continued. Through the 2011–12 season, UK had connected on a three-point shot in 827 consecutive games. Only two teams have longer consecutive-game three-point streaks than UK—UNLV and Vanderbilt. The last game when UK did not knock down a three? November 26, 1988, in the Great Alaska Shootout against Seton Hall. The Cats lost 63–60 to Coach P.J. Carlisimo, who was offered the UK head coaching job after the season. UK was 0-for-2 from three-point range.

UK's first official three-pointer was made by Rex Chapman on November 29, 1986, against Austin Peay. Kentucky's all-time top three-point bomber is Tony Delk with 283 treys. Jodie Meeks holds the single-game mark with 10 three-pointers against Tennessee in a 54-point effort on January 13, 2009. Recent favorite Doron Lamb is the most accurate three-point Cat, with a career shooting percentage of 47.5 percent from downtown.

future NBA first-round pick Stanley Roberts. LSU had won in its gym over the Wildcats by 13, and Pitino and LSU coach Dale Brown had gone face-to-face in a shouting match. In Lexington, the largest crowd in UK basketball history was ready to usher UK basketball back to glory.

The Wildcats did their part. Deron Feldhaus held his own against O'Neal, and Derrick Miller was ready to trade three-pointers with Chris Jackson all evening. Reggie Hanson battled his way to a double-double against two big men who were each half a foot taller. John Pelphrey tallied seven steals, and Sean Woods ran the offense at a blur. UK jumped to a 40–18 lead late in the first half.

LSU figured to make a run and certainly lived up to that expectation. Chris Jackson scored 41 points, including seven three-pointers. LSU trimmed the lead to three in the closing seconds. But Richie Farmer canned eight free throws down the stretch and UK's basketball Davids had stunned LSU's Goliaths 100–95.

UK finished 14–14, including a 10–8 mark in the SEC. UK drilled 281 three-point shots, nearly triple as many as the previous season, setting a new SEC record. Never before had a .500 season brought smiles to so many, but then, a UK program that had looked headed for disaster was instead headed for rebirth.

51 Wah Wah Jones

One of the great unheralded names in UK athletics history is Edna Ball. Ball was basically responsible for UK retaining a pivotal part of two NCAA champion basketball teams, a football bowl team, its baseball squads and, according to some, even its track teams. You see, in 1945, Harlan High School's Wallace "Wah Wah" Jones, star multi-sport athlete, agreed in principle to play his college sports at the University of Tennessee. Tennessee boosters loaned Jones and his friend, Humzey Yessin, a car to return to Harlan and gather their belongings. Jones suggested that the two stop in Middlesboro, Kentucky, to see Ms. Ball, who was his girlfriend. Ball and her family convinced Jones that his future lay in Lexington and not Knoxville. Ball would later become Mrs. Wallace Jones, and Jones would become a Wildcats legend.

Jones played basketball for Coach Rupp, played end (the modern equivalent would be wide receiver) for Coach Bryant, and also pitched and played first base for the UK baseball team. Decades before Bo Jackson was even thought of, Jones was a one-man multi-sport wrecking crew.

While his uniform number was retired by the football program, it was on the basketball court where Jones made his ultimate mark. He was a four-time All-SEC selection, a rarity due to the NCAA rule change that allowed freshman eligibility in the immediate aftermath of World War II. He was three times chosen as an All-American by many of the major basketball publications of the day. All of this came despite the fact that Jones never averaged double-figure scoring in any of his four seasons as a Wildcat.

Jones was never called on to be the main cog in the Wildcats' attack. Teammates Alex Groza and Ralph Beard filled those roles. Jones was a rugged 6'4" forward capable of holding his own on the glass, of defending vigorously, and also of scoring when needed. Jones was a pivotal component in the Fabulous Five—the group that posted a 130–10 career record and did not lose an SEC game in four seasons. UK took home an NIT title in 1946, which might be the school's first actual national title, as well as NCAA Tournament honors in 1948 and 1949. The group also represented the United States in the 1948 Olympic Games in London, claiming a gold medal in basketball.

After his stellar college career, Jones was a first-round draft pick by the NBA's Washington Capitols, who traded him to the Indianapolis Olympians. Jones played only three seasons in the pros, but it is telling that in each of his first two seasons, he did average double figure scoring totals, suggesting that Jones' career numbers might have been even more amazing had he not played in the shadow of a couple of other Kentucky legends.

Jones ultimately left pro basketball for a political career. In 1953, only four years removed from starting for the Wildcats, Jones was elected sheriff of Fayette County. Three years later, in 1956, a thirty-year-old Jones ran for a seat in the U.S. House of Representatives. Jones' election bid was unsuccessful, but 54 years later, Jones told the *Lexington Herald-Leader's* Mark Story that he still recalled getting to go to Washington and meet President Dwight Eisenhower.

While his political career never returned to its initial burst of glory, Jones remains a prominent face in and around Lexington. At last note, he was a business owner and is still fondly remembered by those who saw him hit, pitch, catch passes, block, shoot, or rebound. Maybe it's not too late to simply see if Edna Ball could get *her* jersey retired.

# Bill Spivey

The talented big man was bewildered and disappointed. He was highly regarded and considered one of the most talented players in college basketball. His next season, which everyone knew was just a prelude to his NBA career, was much anticipated not only by Kentucky fans but by all followers of college basketball. But before the season started, it was finished. The NCAA stepped in, drawing the ire of the Big Blue Nation, ruling that improper business dealings amongst others would sideline the big man and deprive fans of a spectacular season.

Enes Kanter in 2011? Nope. Bill Spivey in 1952, and the story is much sadder than Kanter's.

Bill Spivey was a rail-thin giant from Warner Robins, Georgia, who came to UK in 1948. In the era before freshman eligibility, Spivey's time was mostly spent lifting his frame from around 175 pounds to about 230 pounds. Spivey used all of his 7' length to go from gangly teenager to dominant college center. In 1949–50, sophomore Spivey scored 19.3 points per game and was named All-SEC and third team All-American in his first taste of college basketball.

The following year, Spivey was even better. He scored 19.2 points per game, totaling more than 1,200 points in two seasons at UK. Spivey grabbed 17.2 rebounds per game, including 34 in a single game against Xavier. He was the Helms Player of the Year and a first team All-American. In a December 1950 matchup with Kansas All-American Clyde Lovellette, Spivey outclassed the KU big man, outscoring him 22–10 and leading UK to a 29-point win over Coach Rupp's alma mater. Lovellette would go on to be a basketball Hall of Famer, but Spivey was far superior at this point.

Spivey led the 1950–51 team to the NCAA title, going for 22 points and 21 rebounds in the title game victory over Kansas State. At this point, UK had won three NCAA championships in four seasons, and with Spivey ready to return for his senior season, UK seemed well on its way to dynasty status.

And then it all turned ugly. Spivey sustained a knee injury and was likely to miss part of the 1951–52 season anyway. But then the UK point-shaving scandal broke, and Spivey was alleged to have been

Point-Shaving Scandal

The point-shaving scandal that sidelined Spivey sidelined the NBA dreams of a great deal of other Wildcats legends. In the late 1940s and early 1950s, gamblers apparently routinely approached college basketball players with the intention of getting them to play over or under the given point spread. A former UK football player and Brooklyn gambler named Nick Englisis soon established a link with the 1948 Kentucky basketball squad.

From 1948 to 1951, Kentucky may or may not have shaved points or thrown games on multiple occasions. As with any other sports-related scandal, in looking at a game after the fact, every missed shot or turnover can be cause for suspicion—or it could be part of the game. UK legend Ralph Beard said on many occasions that his only crime was taking gamblers' money, and he denied shaving points or throwing games. Bill Spivey probably did even less than that. Still, when the smoke cleared, UK was banned from playing the 1952–53 season, making it the recipient of one of the NCAA's first major probation sentences. Ralph Beard, Alex Groza, and Bill Spivey were out of professional basketball, and a string of three championships in four seasons would give way to exactly one over the next 26 seasons.

involved in the scandal. The NCAA would not allow him to play, and Spivey found himself unwelcome at UK and forced to take out a loan to obtain legal representation to attempt to clear his name.

As the legal wrangling over the point-shaving scandal dragged on, Spivey was eventually indicted—not for point shaving but for perjury for proclaiming his innocence. The evidence against Spivey was flimsy, and a New York jury voted 9–3 for his acquittal. A mistrial was declared, and the district attorney declined to try the case a second time. Spivey was readmitted to UK and managed to obtain his degree. NBA Commissioner Maurice Podoloff, however, was uninterested in Spivey's redemption and refused to allow the big Georgian an opportunity to ply his trade in the NBA.

For his part, Spivey promptly sued the NBA for violating antitrust law. Apparently realizing the shaky ground on which it stood, the NBA eventually settled the case in 1959 out of court for a small payment to Spivey. However, Spivey's name was besmirched and he was several years older by the time the legal wrangling was completed. He would never play a second in the NBA.

Spivey instead played in the Eastern League, the American Basketball League, and even against the Harlem Globetrotters. The end of Spivey's pro basketball story was especially tragic. In February 1968, Spivey played in an Old-Timers game of former NBA players. He was 38 years old and was the high scorer in the game. *The New York Times* quoted another player in the game, Bob Davies, as saying, "I always wanted to play with a good big man.... Too bad it was 20 years too late." Davies presumably meant too late for himself, but it was too late for Spivey, too. He retired from basketball after the game.

Spivey eventually became the deputy commissioner of insurance in the state of Kentucky and died while living in Costa Rica in 1995. He will always make those who remember him wonder what might have been.

53 The Mardi Gras Miracle

Rick Pitino was absolutely beside himself. He stomped off the court into the visitor's locker room in Baton Rouge, not staying to watch Walter McCarty shoot his second free throw to end the half. McCarty's shot was good, but this merely trimmed LSU's halftime advantage to 48–32. At many homes around the Commonwealth (including the Cox residence), due to the late night telecast and the poor first half, televisions clicked off. Losing to Arkansas and Syracuse in the last two games had been bad enough. But this was even worse. Kentucky had not lost three games in a row in the decade. This was not Kentucky basketball.

Pitino undoubtedly made the same point at halftime in much stronger language. UK had walked into an LSU firestorm on Mardi Gras, February 15, 1994. It had been more than six years since UK had won at LSU, and this night did not look like a good bet to end that streak. A talented but inconsistent LSU squad featuring star shooter Ronnie Henderson and tough forward Clarence Ceasar seemed to hit every shot they took. UK faltered, fumbled, and fell well behind.

It would be exciting to report that Pitino's halftime words of wisdom or his benching of Rod Rhodes and Jared Prickett changed the game. They did not. UK scored to pull within 50–37 and then allowed an 18–0 LSU run in which Henderson and Ceasar, who had scored 36 and 32 points respectively, seemed to be playing "HORSE" with each other. LSU led 68–37 with just less than 16 minutes remaining in the game.

And suddenly, in the blink of an eye, the roles were reversed. LSU went into a deep freeze, and UK caught fire. UK made its run, or at least its first run, making a 24–4 streak to trim the LSU advantage to 72–61 with 9:52 remaining. The maligned Rhodes scored seven during the run, as did Walter McCarty, and reserve guard Chris Harrison came from deep into the UK bench to add eight more.

LSU did not intend to fold, and Ronnie Henderson scored the next five points to give the Tigers a 16-point cushion again. But UK simply would not go away. Jeff Brassow hit two treys, Rhodes nailed a triple, and Travis Ford added another. LSU still held a 91–82 lead inside 3:30 to play.

The Tigers would not make another basket, but Kentucky was only getting started. Andre Riddick scored on an offensive rebound to cut the lead to 91–84 with 2:44 remaining. Seconds later, Riddick made a steal and hit Brassow for a three that further trimmed LSU's once-insurmountable lead to 91–87 with 2:30 to play. Ceasar made two free throws for the Tigers, but Brassow then hit an NBA-range three-pointer to make it 93–90 with 2:05 left.

Ceasar tried to quiet the storm, knocking down two free throws, but Tony Delk followed with a three from the left wing that drew UK within 95–93. The two teams swapped possessions, LSU was absolutely drained, and Kentucky smelled blood in the water.

With the clock at less than 30 seconds, Tony Delk began to drive to his left, perhaps toward a tying basket. With the shot clock winding down, another LSU player moved to cut off Delk, leaving McCarty open on the left wing. Delk immediately made the pass, and Walter's three-point shot hit nothing but nylon. Kentucky held a 96–95 lead with 19 seconds to play. Jamie Brandon drove for LSU but missed with five seconds left. The rest was merely academic.

UK had pulled the Mardi Gras Miracle, stunning LSU 99–95! UK ended the game on a 62–27 run in the last 15:30. Five Cats finished the game with double-figure scoring totals led by McCarty's 23 points. And on February 16, 1994, untold numbers of Kentucky fans would double check the calendar, making sure it wasn't April 1 when a friend, coworker, or stranger assured them that yes, indeed, UK had won the previous night.

54 Emery Air and Its Unusual Package

Chris Mills is the only UK basketball player ever to record a triple double. However, Mills' on-court production is not what his name is (in)famous for in UK circles. On March 30, 1988, UK assistant coach Dwayne Casey allegedly mailed $1,000 in $20 bills to the father of Mills, then a UK recruit. The package was sent via Emery Worldwide Air Freight. According to Emery, the package "popped open" in transit, and a diligent employee discovered the money and someone apparently alerted the *Los Angeles Daily News*, which began investigating the matter and eventually published a story about the package. Casey denied putting $1,000 in the package, and Chris' father Claude Mills denied receiving the $1,000.

Chris Mills subsequently played one season at UK where he recorded his triple double against Austin Peay. The NCAA had already been investigating UK's basketball program and found many additional rules violations, but the Mills incident may have been the last nail in the coffin that slammed shut on UK's hope of avoiding major penalties. In May 1989, the NCAA dropped the boom on UK, imposing three years of probation, two years without postseason play, and one year without live television coverage. Investigators indicated that there was consideration of leveling the so-called "Death Penalty" of shutting down the men's basketball program at UK.

Of course, Kentucky hired Rick Pitino, who righted the Wildcats' ship in amazing time. In the grand scheme of things, the

Kentucky's Shame

In the aftermath of the NCAA hammer coming down on UK, *Sports Illustrated* famously published an issue with a cover bearing an anonymous UK player and the headline, "Kentucky's Shame." One of the many poignant storylines of the epic 1992 UK/Duke Elite Eight game was that Pitino, after the loss, produced the "Kentucky's Shame" issue of the magazine and told his tearful team, "You've taken Kentucky all the way back from this." And of course, he was right, as the magazine has since featured three UK NCAA champions. UK fans are still awaiting the "Indiana's Shame" or "Tennessee's Shame" issues.

whole incident is more of a bump than a serious roadblock. However, decades later, major questions remain about the whole episode.

It definitely strains credulity to think that a national freight carrier would routinely just happen to have a package "pop open," particularly a package that was purportedly full of gift cash that the NCAA would deem illegal. It is certainly convenient that the employees who "discovered" the cash carefully logged the information about the package, resealed it, delivered it, and forgot about it. Except that someone, somewhere along the line decided that the *Los Angeles Daily News* should be contacted.

This is probably the point when it should be mentioned that Mills, a Los Angeles product, was the subject of an intense recruiting battle between UNLV, Kentucky, and UCLA. One wonders whether the zealous informant who carried the story to the papers would've been as concerned had he or she realized that once the manure hit the NCAA fan, Mills would still attend Kentucky, and then eventually end up at Arizona, not UCLA.

Dwane Casey certainly found the matter suspicious. Casey filed a $6.9 million suit against Emery Worldwide Air Freight. The suit eventually settled out of court for a sum rumored to be in the millions of dollars. Certainly, if Emery and its employees' actions were entirely above board, one wonders why they would have paid money to resolve Casey's suit instead of fighting the battle to its end in open court.

For that matter, it certainly also seems peculiar that if Casey were attempting to buy Mills, as the NCAA would subsequently suggest, that he would utilize such a relatively small sum of money. No less of an authority than sports columnist and UK hater John Feinstein has sarcastically suggested on his blog, "If you're trying to buy a player, *buy* him for crying out loud." No word from Feinstein as to how he and his beloved Duke Blue Devils feel about Corey Magette's business dealings.

Again, at the end of the day, much of the conversation is academic. Casey, while effectively blacklisted out of NCAA coaching, climbed the NBA coaching ladder and has served as head coach of the Minnesota Timberwolves and Toronto Raptors. Mills transferred to Arizona and was drafted in the first round of the 1993 NBA Draft by the Cleveland Cavaliers. He played ten years in the NBA. Eddie Sutton resigned, and Rick Pitino took over. He returned UK to national prominence in two seasons and to the Final Four in four.

Emery, on the other hand, ceased operations in 2001. Today, the name is utilized by UPS, which ran ads featuring Christian Laettner's 1992 heartbreaking shot during the 2012 NCAA Tournament. Apparently, that was yet another amazing coincidence.

The Undefeated Season

During the 1952–53 season, Adolph Rupp was stewing. His Wildcats were banned from fielding a team that season due to the recent point-shaving scandal that had rocked college basketball.

Rupp had won NCAA titles in three of the last five seasons before the ban, so he used the non-season, in the words of Tom Wallace in the *University of Kentucky Basketball Encyclopedia*, "To sharpen his team's skills to a razor-like finish." Rupp used that razor to slash through college basketball in 1953–54.

That team would be led by the Big Three, a trio of seniors who were among the best to play at UK. Cliff Hagan was perhaps the biggest name of the group. The 6'4" Hagan was often undersized but rarely outworked. Hagan was particularly deadly with his smooth hook shot. His foremost partner in crime was Frank Ramsey. Rupp famously said of the Madisonville native that if UK won by 30, Ramsey would score three, but if they won by three, Ramsey would score 30. There were many more 30-point wins than close games in 1953–54, but Ramsey was still a stand-out. Lou Tsioropoulous was the third member of the trio. He had come to UK on a football scholarship and was most known for his rugged defense and rebounding, but Tsioropoulous could also score quite effectively. Billy Evans and Gayle Rose often completed the first five players.

An angry UK team began the year firing on all cylinders. The group averaged more than 87 points per game and racked up an average margin of victory better than 27 points. Only two opponents would play UK to a single-digit margin. In the season's opening game, Cliff Hagan put up 51 points and nearly beat Temple single-handedly in an 86–59 romp. Early in the season, UK took on a tough LaSalle team in the UK Invitational Tournament. The Cats held All-American Tom Gola to 16 points and won 73–60. Three months later, LaSalle won the 1954 NCAA Tournament.

After a tough six-point win over Xavier on January 4, UK worked its way into and through SEC play. Ramsey put up 37 points in a 97–71 thumping of Tennessee. Hagan topped that with

38 points in an 88–62 win against Ole Miss. For the season, Hagan averaged 24 points per game and was everyone's All-American. Ramsey was almost equally respected, totaling 19.6 points a contest, and Tsioropoulous reminded opponents that it wasn't the Big Two, as he added a respectable 14.5 points per game. Combined, the Big Three averaged 58 points per game, while UK's opponents totaled an average of 60 per game. Accordingly, it didn't take much from the supporting cast for UK to steamroll the competition.

Throughout the SEC schedule, UK won every game by at least 22 points. Vanderbilt managed to get that close in an 85–63 drubbing in Nashville. LSU somehow also went unbeaten but did not play UK. Accordingly, on March 9, a one-game playoff was held in Nashville for the SEC title. With All-American Bob Pettit, the Tigers were determined to ruin UK's perfect season. They did hold a 40–36 lead early in the second half, marking the only time all season that UK trailed after halftime.

Ramsey had the answer. He scored 30 in the 63–56 victory. UK had a perfect regular season. Unfortunately, that was the end of the season. The NCAA ruled that fifth-year seniors Hagan, Ramsey, and Tsioropoulous were ineligible for the Tournament. The remaining players voted 9–3 to play without the Big Three, but an angry Rupp vetoed the vote. Rupp, according to Russell Rice's *Big Blue Machine*, thundered, "If we can't play with our full team, we won't allow a bunch of turds to mar the record established in large measure by our three seniors."

As noted earlier, LaSalle, a team that UK had previously beaten by 13 points, went on to win the title. The 1953–54 squad was undefeated and unfortunately didn't win an NCAA title—it was the last team to hold such a distinction.

56 Mitch Barnhart

UK athletics director Mitch Barnhart is important for a number of reasons. Let's list the major one—he hired John Calipari, a decision that brought an eighth national title to Big Blue Nation.

Granted, he also hired Billy Gillispie, a decision that kept UK fans in misery for two seasons. But hey, you can't blame a guy for getting it right on the second try, can you? Nah. Sometimes you have to go through Hell before you get to Heaven.

Barnhart has done some great work since being hired in 2002. He hired Rich Brooks, who rebuilt a UK football team that was on life support and took them to four consecutive bowl games. Barnhart hired Matthew Mitchell, who won an SEC championship with the women's basketball squad for the first time since the early 1980s. He's overseen outstanding growth in sports such as softball, baseball, tennis, and gymnastics. He created the UK Hall of Fame and oversaw construction of the Craft Center practice facility.

In February 2011, Barnhart signed a contact extension that will keep him at UK until 2019. And Barnhart hasn't had the easiest road since being at UK. He watched as a respected college coach (Tubby Smith) became virtually ineffective and chose to leave. He worked with a hiring firm to identify the next great UK coach and instead got an abrasive Texan with an alcohol problem. With the help of Mike Pratt and others, Barnhart convinced university president Lee Todd to take a look at Calipari.

Then things got really fun.

Barnhart, a Kansas City, Kansas, native, served as the athletics director at Oregon State for four seasons before taking the Kentucky job. He earned his undergraduate degree at Ottawa University (Kansas) and his Master's in sports administration from

Ohio University. Previous stops for Barnhart included Tennessee, Southern Methodist, Oregon, and San Diego State.

When Barnhart was hired, many people questioned whether he could (not being a Kentuckian and all) actually understand what it means to be in charge of the UK athletic department and, by extension, the basketball program. Sure, he could say all he wanted about other sports, but fans wondered, "Why does he care? Just get us a coach to win a basketball championship!"

If there was ever a doubt, it was erased in April 2012 when the newly minted men's NCAA champions brought home the eighth such trophy to Lexington. The team pulled inside Rupp Arena in a huge bus and celebrated the championship in front of thousands of raucous fans. And then Barnhart took the microphone.

Larry Ivy

You know how they say you never want to replace a legend?

You want to be the guy who replaces the guy who replaces the legend.

Larry Ivy can attest to that. After replacing the wildly popular C.M. Newton as athletics director at UK in 2000, Ivy's tenure ended in 2002 when he resigned after an independent review panel investigated the athletic department's management practices when the football team was serving probation for rules violations.

The panel said Ivy should be replaced.

"Ivy, a 33-year employee of the school, had overseen Kentucky's athletic budget for 23 years, during which time it has grown from $3 million to $41 million," the *Herald-Leader* reported. "A graduate of the University of Alabama, he came to Kentucky in 1969 at age 26 as director of housing."

"I have decided to retire for a number of reasons, but most importantly it is just time for me to take a different direction with my life and career," Ivy said in a statement. "All things must end. While most of my career has been focused on the university, there are other things and business ventures I would like to pursue. I believe now is the best time to follow those interests."

He tried to hold back his tears as he thanked Calipari and the team, and UK unfurled its championship banner in the rafters.

"That's the beautiful part of my job, that I get to spend time with kids who get to achieve dreams and have fun," Barnhart told the *Herald-Leader* newspaper. "That's what we get in this business for. There's a lot of other stuff that happens along the way, but this is what you get in the business for."

They say it takes winning a championship before Yankees fans finally recognize a player as a true Yankee (think A-Rod). Maybe it took a basketball title for UK fans to truly appreciate Barnhart. Either way, they're appreciating him now.

They're hugging him with open arms.

57 The Attendance Record

Rupp Arena holds 23,000 fans although most of the highest-attended games in Rupp history somehow go way past that mark. In fact, the game with the highest attendance heading into the 2011–12 championship year was the game when Rick Pitino brought his Cardinals to Lexington and 24,479 squeezed into Rupp on January 2, 2010, to watch.

Kentucky beat the Cards that day 71–62, but back to the point.

Because Kentucky has a venue that is so big, it is natural to say that the Cats have an edge on every other team when it comes to winning the attendance record every season. Of course, just because you have a big venue doesn't mean people have to come watch the games (we're looking at you, Tennessee).

The combination of a huge venue and a crazy passion for sports makes for a deadly combination in Lexington. Rupp opened in

1976, and since then, Kentucky has won the overall attendance title (meaning greatest average attendance for the entire season) 24 times. That's 24 times out of 36.

And the Cats are 478–60 (.888) all-time at Rupp Arena through the 2011–12 season.

Coach John Calipari has yet to lose in Rupp Arena, as his first three Kentucky teams have compiled undefeated records at home.

"In 2010–11, for the 15th time in 16 years, UK's average crowd of 23,603 led all of Division I men's basketball," the *Herald-Leader* reported. "A total of 354,046 fans passed through the turnstiles in downtown Lexington for 15 Wildcat games during the 2010–11 season. Syracuse, with an average crowd of 22,312, was second, followed by Louisville (21,832), North Carolina (19,144), and Tennessee (18,952).

"Nationally, 25.1 million attended Division I men's games last season, an average of 5,025 per game. The Southeastern Conference was third among all conferences in average attendance, drawing 11,187 fans, behind only the Big Ten's 12,826 average and the Big East's 11,323 average."

Biggest Crowds In Rupp History

Attendance	Date	Opponent	Score
24,432	December 17, 2005	Louisville	Won 73-61
24,411	February 28, 2009	LSU	Lost 73-70
24,402	February 13, 2010	Tennessee	Won 73-62
24,398	December 3, 2011	North Carolina	Won 73-72
24,394	February 21, 2009	Tennessee	Won 77-68
24,389	February 7, 2012	Florida	Won 78-58
24,388	February 25, 2012	Vanderbilt	Won 83-74
24,387	December 31, 2011	Louisville	Won 69-62
24,386	January 5, 2008	Louisville	Lost 89-75
24,382	March 1, 2012	Georgia	Won 79-49
24,371	February 23, 2008	Arkansas	Won 63-58

Source: Kentucky Basketball Media Guide, 2011–2012.

58 Travel with the Team—to Maui, Alaska, or New York

For UK fans everywhere, there is no greater fun than following your Cats to one of their many travel destinations over the course of the season.

Whether it's jaunting off to the Loveliest Village on the Plain, partying at The Grove or taking in the nightlife in Nashville, there are plenty of towns in the SEC for UK fans to investigate.

Of course, some are more fun than others.

"We used to kind of laugh and call Starkville 'Stark-Vegas,'" UK legend Mike Pratt said. "There wasn't a lot to do."

Then there's the seemingly annual trips to New York City and the various locations for the SEC Tournament, like Atlanta, Tampa, and New Orleans. Each place has been known for great UK moments in the past.

John Wall had his coming out party in a 25-point performance against Connecticut in Madison Square Garden in 2009. A victory against Kansas in 2012 in NYC was a precursor to the national title-game rematch of that year.

Atlanta has become known as Cat-lanta for the number of times the Cats have won the SEC Tournament there. Most recently, Darius Miller was named MVP of the SEC Tourney in Atlanta after a championship win.

And New Orleans has been the site of so many big moments, from Jamal Mashburn facing off against Michigan's Fab Five in 1993 to the most recent UK championship in 2012 when Anthony Davis showed the world he was the best player in college basketball.

For those more adventurous, UK fans need to pay attention to the ever-changing schedule. The Big Blue has been a regular participant in tournaments in Alaska and Hawaii—and both have featured big moments in UK history.

In the early 1990s, Rick Pitino was developing a dynasty of fun in Lexington. Before he won a national title, his teams were still feared for being able to compete with any in the country. In the 1993–94 season, the Cats were coming off a Final Four appearance and had lost their main man Jamal Mashburn.

Yet they returned a load of talent. With sophomores Rodrick Rhodes, Tony Delk, and Walter McCarty, along with senior guard Travis Ford leading the way, the team was again in the top 10. They played in the Maui Invitational Classic and made it to the finals against another talented squad, the Arizona Wildcats. Led by guards Damon Stoudamire and Khalid Reeves, the Wildcats were formidable, and they took UK down to the wire.

With seconds remaining, Arizona took a 92–91 lead. They didn't count on Jeff Brassow.

The UK offense did not look great on the last play. Rhodes put up an awkward, too-far-out three-pointer, which missed badly. Fortunately, Brassow, who was originally part of Pitino's first recruiting class before suffering a slew of injuries, blocked out the world on the left side of the basket and tipped the ball back in the hoop as time expired.

UK won the championship 93–92. Rarely did anyone see the kind of emotion from the UK bench after a regular season win that erupted here. Pitino ran into Brassow's arms as the rest of the team surrounded them. Obviously, for UK fans, it was a fun trip.

In the 1996–97 season, the Cats were coming off a national title season, and things looked good for a chance to repeat. With swingmen Derek Anderson and Ron Mercer both playing like All-Americans, UK was annihilating some opponents—that's what happened when the team traveled north for the Great Alaska Shootout.

Eighth-ranked Kentucky showed just how good it could be when it won the tourney title. Along the way the Cats dismantled

12th-ranked Syracuse 87–53. Supposedly, when the team was enjoying snowmoblie rides between games, guard Wayne Turner got lost. Eventually, he found his way back. Good thing—in his Kentucky tenure, he went on to play in two more Final Fours.

Obviously though, fans have to beware. They have to realize their team may not win. In the 1991–92 season, fans (and coaches) were all prepared to go to New York for the semifinals of the pre-season NIT tourney.

Then reality happened, and UK was upset by Pittsburgh 85–67. Instead, the Panthers made the trip to New York.

That's why, all things considered, Hawaii or New Orleans sound like the best destination. Even if your team loses, it's still a party!

59 UK vs. Tennessee

Against which opponent have the greatest number of UK's 2,090 wins been amassed? The Tennessee Volunteers have been the team that UK has loved to beat again and again—148 times entering the 2012–13 season. Of course, in all fairness, UT has come out on the winning side 66 times in the matchup, which is also the most losses UK has amassed to any opponent. Over the course of 214 meetings, there have been enough twists and turns for a first look to suggest a great college basketball rivalry.

The two schools first met in 1910, with UK beating the Vols 20–5. The *Lexington Leader* described the game as "slow and exceedingly rough." Apparently, little has changed in Knoxville in the ensuing 102 years.

The series was back and forth in the early years. After World War II, when Rupp took Kentucky from a perennially solid team to a frequent visitor to the NCAA winner's circle, UT took a large amount of abuse in its matchups with the Cats. Following World War II, UK reeled off ten straight victories in the series. Tennessee won a home game in the series in January 1950, then UK embarked on a 10-year winning streak in the series. Twenty consecutive UK wins did nothing to improve the spirits of the rocked-topped Tennesseans. Half of those wins were by margins of 25 or more points.

The series was back and forth throughout the rest of Adolph Rupp's tenure. Tennessee actually won four in a row over UK from 1966 to 1968. UK retaliated in January 1969 by winning its 1,000[th] game ever against UT, making the Cats the first NCAA team to reach the mark.

It was during the Joe B. Hall era in the late 1970s that the rivalry reached a boiling point. Ernie Grunfeld played at UT from 1973–77, and Bernard King was a Vol for the last three of those seasons. In the six meetings of the schools when Ernie and Bernie were part of the UT program, UT was 5–1, winning the last five in a row. After the 1977–78 NCAA title team thumped UT twice, Kentucky lost four more to the Vols, including the 1979 SEC Tournament Championship.

The series has tilted to Kentucky in recent years despite Tennessee frequently boasting squads that were full of talent if not entirely positive character. Rick Pitino won his last nine matchups with UT while in Lexington, starting with a memorable 101–40 whipping in the 1993 SEC Tournament. Last man off the bench Todd Svoboda outscored UT All-American Allan Houston in that game. Tubby Smith reeled off eight straight wins over UT at one point, and even Billy Gillispie was 3–1 against UT and the eternally greasy Bruce Pearl. Players like Ron Slay, Tony Greene, Wayne

Chism, and Scotty Hopson have always brought plenty of brawn to the UT sideline, if not much brains.

As of summer 2012, UK has won the last five games in the series. Cuonzo Martin is the newest candidate to right the UT ship after Bruce Pearl was run out of Knoxville by the NCAA. Martin, unlike predecessors Jerry Green and Wade Houston, seems bent on actually coaching his teams. Tennessee is probably destined to be an occasional bump in the road on UK's path to further SEC and NCAA titles.

At the present, UT's 1979 SEC Tournament title is the team's most recent, meaning every SEC school except the league's two brand-new entries and South Carolina has won the Tournament since the Volunteers. Of course, Tennessee's next trip to the Final Four, if it ever occurs, will be its first. To steal a line from the rapper Jay-Z, Kentucky basketball may have 99 problems, but the University of Tennessee ain't one. If in doubt, remember the 148 reasons why this is true.

60 First UK All-American: Basil Hayden

Before there was Anthony Davis, Jamal Mashburn, Kyle Macy, Dan Issel, or Ralph Beard, there was...Basil? Despite standing only 5'11" and being saddled with a name out of a detective novel, Basil Hayden was UK basketball's first All-American. While the era in which he played denied Basil the chance to move on to the NBA after his historic 1920–21 season, he did earn some measure of satisfaction—he lived to be 103 years old, providing lots of time to remind all of those succeeding generations of Wildcats of his heroics. As to the nature of those heroics, and the era in which they took place, consider that while Hayden is one of 36 Wildcats players who have had their jerseys retired, he is the only one who did not have an actual jersey number to retire.

Hayden was born in 1899, making him doubtlessly the only Cat to live in three different centuries. He began his collegiate career at Transylvania but transferred across town in time to lead the Cats to perhaps their first taste of basketball glory. Not content to star in basketball, Hayden was also featured on UK's tennis and track squads. On the basketball court, Hayden's All-American season was 1920–21. He scored 9.7 points per game. While this may not sound like much, UK averaged 36 points per game in that season. Scoring more than a quarter of Kentucky's points would be roughly equivalent to about 20 points per game in the current era. Hayden's accomplishments, however, tended more toward team-focused goals—such as bringing the first major championship trophy back to Lexington.

As a junior swingman noted for excellent passing as well as scoring, he led a 9–1 UK squad into the postseason SIAA Tournament in Atlanta. The SIAA was a forerunner to the modern Southeastern Conference. UK competed in the SIAA from 1895 to 1903 and again from 1911 to 1922. SIAA Tournaments were irregular events, and the 1920–21 Tournament was UK's first.

Hayden led the Cats to wins over Tulane, Mercer, and Mississippi A&M, thus earning a spot in the title game against Georgia. The Georgia defense keyed on Basil, and UGA held a 19–17 lead late in the game as the Bulldogs held Hayden scoreless. However, Basil broke free for a game-tying basket inside the final minute. With momentum now shifted, a UGA foul gave UK a free throw with no time on the clock. William King drained the shot for a 20–19 win, and a multitude of traditions began. Hayden was an All-American, UK won a major conference title, and Atlanta's transformation into Catlanta was underway.

Unfortunately, alongside all of the positive records and benchmarks that Basil Hayden earned, he does hold one Kentucky record no one would want to break. Statistically speaking, Basil Hayden was the least successful head coach in UK basketball history. In 1926–27, mercifully his only season as head coach, Hayden was saddled with a 3–13 record at UK. In Russell Rice's *Big Blue Machine*, Hayden lamented, "I couldn't get a very good effort out of them all season." At least Hayden left some room for improvement for his successor, John Mauer, and then three seasons later for a 29-year-old hot-shot coach from Kansas who just turned out to be Adolph Rupp.

 **Freedom Hall**

While every team needs a home, the Kentucky Wildcats have had a home away from home since 1958—the first year that UK played a game in Louisville's Freedom Hall. The new arena, constructed in 1956, served as the home court for University of Louisville basketball through 2010. The 1958 NCAA Final Four was held in Freedom Hall, and Kentucky laid claim to the gym immediately, sneaking past Temple in the national semifinals and beating Seattle the next day to claim the school's fourth NCAA Tournament title.

In the following season, UK played a pair of neutral-site games at Freedom Hall against Illinois and Temple, and in December 1960, began an annual series in the arena with Notre Dame. The two schools played annually at Freedom Hall until December 1981. UK won 18 of the 22 matchups, and the game featured yearly crowds at or above the arena's seating capacity.

In 1971, UK began playing the home half of its series with Indiana in Freedom Hall, as well. That pattern lasted only three games, with IU winning all three, but from 1991–2005 the two schools switched game sites between Freedom Hall and Indianapolis' RCA Dome. This time, Kentucky won all seven of the games played in Freedom Hall, two of which were battles between IU and UK squads each ranked in the top 10. In December 2002, UK won 70–64 when Indiana coach Mike Davis bolted onto the floor of Freedom Hall in the closing seconds, earning two technical fouls and an ejection.

Of course, once Kentucky and Louisville began an annual regular season series in 1983, UK played as a road team in Freedom Hall once every two years. UK was 7–6 in those games before Louisville moved on to the Yum! Center in 2010. Perhaps the most memorable of those games for UK fans was a December 2004 tilt in which Patrick Sparks of Kentucky was fouled by Ellis Myles just ahead of the final buzzer and drained three free throws, giving UK a 60–58 win over Rick Pitino's Cardinals. UK had trailed by 16 at the half, so the win was especially sweet.

In addition to visiting Freedom Hall as the neutral site for rivalry games with Indiana and Notre Dame and the biannual visit to the Louisville Cardinals, UK began scheduling a non-conference match-up each season for Freedom Hall. The game, as well as a pregame practice, usually gave Wildcats fans in and around Louisville an annual chance to check out their Cats up close and personal. In 2008, UK backers watched Jodie Meeks put up 46 points in a win over Appalachian State.

While attendance had started to lag in these annual tune-ups since UofL deserted the old arena in 2010, Freedom Hall has drawn more than 17,000 fans in each of UK's two subsequent visits. In 2012, fans enjoyed a 73–51 victory over Arkansas–Little Rock. Anthony Davis had 22 points and 16 boards, and Darius Miller joined UK's 1,000-point club in Freedom Hall.

Kentucky has posted a total record of 60–18 in Freedom Hall. Additionally, UK was 61–11 in games played at the Jefferson County Armory, also known as the Louisville Gardens, from 1937 to 1956. The SEC Tournament was held there from 1941 to 1952. Of course, with two 2012 NCAA wins, UK adds a 3–0 record in the Yum Center to its Louisville totals.

To the Big Blue Nation, Freedom Hall is an especially sacred ground. From the Fiddlin' Five's first visit in 1958 to John Calipari's most recent visit in 2012, each Kentucky team has played at least once in Freedom Hall. Five NCAA titles have been won by UK during that stretch, and a portion of each season was played out in Freedom Hall—once the home of the archenemy but today a home away from home.

62 Matt Jones and Kentucky Sports Radio

In November 2005, Matt Jones, an attorney who was originally from Middlesboro, Kentucky, and a group of his friends founded a small Internet blog dedicated to providing UK basketball, football, and recruiting news "in the most ridiculous manner possible." Six and a half years later, Salon.com proclaimed Jones "the chief media villain of the Final Four." As Brian Weinberg went on to make clear in his column, Jones is not a villain to his readers, with as many as 150,000 unique viewers to the once-small blog, which Weinberg notes, "looks like it was made on an Atari." Instead, Jones has rocked the media power structure in part because of his popularity and in part due to what Weinberg terms "his relentless criticism of nationally esteemed basketball writers like Pat Forde of

Yahoo.com and Pete Thamel of *The New York Times*." Make no mistake, Jones' views, stated in his hilarious but articulate manner, tend to align heavily with the rest of Big Blue Nation. It might be ridiculous, but it is must-read stuff day in and day out.

Jones' site, KentuckySportsRadio.com, has literally changed the tenor of modern media. Jones is not constrained by the usual principles of journalistic etiquette—he is an unabashed Kentucky fan, although he is certainly not above criticizing the program when he deems it to be warranted. At the same time, many of Jones' readers appreciate that he pulls no punches. When Jones doesn't feel that Jerry Tipton or Pat Forde or Pete Thamel are honest or objective about Kentucky sports—and here's the rub, in varying degrees, they often aren't—he calls them on it. Jones doesn't need to hide his contempt for Louisville coach Rick Pitino or NCAA president Mark Emmert. He can wear his views on his sleeve, and often does.

None of this is intended to make KSR, as it is known, a one-trick pony. It doesn't exist merely to criticize. It was KSR that published the infamous photo of Josh Harrellson in Lexington on his official visit wearing his soon-to-be-trademark jorts (jean shorts). Absent KSR, who knows what Josh's nickname would have been? KSR delights in exposing some of the more backward elements of Kentucky society—Jones has been known to have a rustic Eastern Kentucky character named Oh Napier featured on the site since its early days. Russellville's erstwhile YouTube correspondent Kige Ramsey and his deadpan takes on potato chips or the proper form of foul shooting often pop up. Greasy eastern Kentucky attorney Eric C. Conn's ridiculous commercials give viewers the chance to laugh with Jones and his friends. A couple of rhythmically challenged UK students found infamy with perhaps the worst rap ever, which happens to be about Kentucky basketball, "Lazy Tuesday."

Kentucky Sports Radio has also attempted to broaden its horizons. "Ms. Tyler Thompson," so nicknamed to make clear that she is indeed female, is one of the more popular KSR contributors. "Radio" Ron Chilton is a senior citizen with gusto who sometimes outshines Jones despite the fact that Chilton could be his grandfather. Additionally, the dunce of the team, the much-maligned Bryan the Intern, seemed to serve as a human lightning rod, throwing up half-baked opinions that often left the site's commenters calling for his departure.

It is tempting to call it all good fun. And there is plenty of good fun. But self-awarely "ridiculous" or not, KSR is a symbol of the new media. The site's success seems to say that anyone with a computer and some ideas can alter the course of modern media. As for Jones, at 33 years old, it is interesting to see where his career and KentuckySportsRadio.com can end up. To paraphrase the most famous of Kentuckians, a website by, of, and for the people of the Big Blue Nation will not perish from the earth—or from cyberspace.

63 Vernon Hatton is Mr. Clutch

Throughout the history of Kentucky basketball, there have been more than a few memorable big baskets in big games—Ralph Beard's free throw to win the 1946 NIT, Shelby Linville's late basket to push UK into the 1951 NCAA title game, Scott Padgett's trey to push past Duke into the 1998 Final Four, and Brandon Knight's jumper to lift UK over No. 1 Ohio State and into the 2011 Elite Eight are just a few. But probably the biggest such shot came courtesy of UK's very own "Mr. Clutch."

Vernon Hatton was a 6'3" guard from Lexington's Lafayette High School. In only his fourth game with UK's varsity, Hatton scored Kentucky's last five points to gain a comeback victory at Maryland 62–61. Hatton was the third scorer on that 1955–56 squad behind All-American Bob Burrow and Jerry Bird. UK finished 20–6 and lost to Iowa in the Elite Eight of the NCAA Tournament.

Hatton's junior season, 1956–57, was a difficult one. He missed a month of the season due to an emergency appendectomy. However, Hatton scored 14.8 points per game when he did play and finished strong, averaging 20 points per game in UK's last four contests. Ultimately, the season again ended in the Elite Eight, this time with a loss to Michigan State.

The 1957–58 season would be different. Kentucky was not very highly regarded but sought to prove itself in an early season matchup with Temple. The Owls brought All-American guard Guy Rodgers and a tough squad to Lexington to meet the 2–0 Wildcats. The game that followed was simply a classic.

Temple led by one at halftime and held a two-point advantage late in the game. Hatton canned two free throws to send the game to overtime with a 65–65 tie. The *Philadelphia Inquirer* noted the next day that William Baughn, the former city commissioner of Lexington, fell dead of a heart attack during the end of regulation. With apologies to the late Mr. Baughn, he hadn't seen anything yet.

Temple made two baskets early in overtime. The Cats rallied to tie the game again at 69. Rodgers of Temple drained a short jump shot with three seconds to go, and Temple appeared to have the game wrapped up. Kentucky called timeout, and with one second left John Crigler inbounded the ball to Hatton near the sideline and a step across midcourt. His 47' heave dropped through the hoop, sending the game to a second overtime.

It would take a third overtime to settle matters, and Hatton scored six of UK's 10 points in that frame, setting UK's 85–83 win.

Hatton and UK rode that momentum to a No. 9 ranking at the end of the regular season and an SEC Championship. Mr. Clutch scored 17.1 points per game to lead the squad.

After two NCAA Tournament wins, in the national semifinal, Hatton again ran into the Temple Owls. Rodgers was superb again, scoring 22 points and staking the Owls to a four-point lead with 2:30 left. It became a 60–59 lead with :23 remaining. After a timeout, acting on a play-calling suggestion from center Ed Beck, Rupp called Hatton's number in the huddle. Hatton was only 4-for-15 in the game with a total of 11 points. But with the chips down, Hatton followed a pick from Beck, drove to the goal, and scored to give UK a 61–60 advantage. When Temple turned over the ball, Mr. Clutch had yet again buried the Owls.

On the following night, UK did not need any late-game heroics to knock off Seattle and Elgin Baylor. The Fiddlin' Five played sweet music in their 84–72 championship win. Vernon Hatton, the master conductor of the Fiddlers, was a first-team All-American. He went on to play four seasons in the NBA. Interestingly, the Temple Owls have never returned to the Final Four. Mr. Clutch apparently did them in.

64 Terry Mobley and the Shot vs. Duke

Before Christian Laettner had The Shot against UK, there was already a world-famous shot in a UK/Duke game—a shot that gave Kentucky a huge win.

What many don't realize is that UK and Duke had a history of big games and a rivalry way before Laettner was ever born.

There were many NCAA Tournament games between the two, including wins by Kentucky in the 1978 NCAA title game, the 1998 regional finals, and the 1966 Final Four. There were other wins in the 1954 and 1970 UKITs. There was a one-point loss to Duke in the 1980 NCAAs in Lexington and, of course, The Shot by Laettner in 1992.

These programs know each other well.

So when the pair met up in the Sugar Bowl Classic in 1964, it was more than just a game. UK had been struggling a bit, held together by duct tape and an All-American named Cotton Nash. But Nash and a supporting cast of Larry Conley, Tommy Kron, and Terry Mobley fared considerably better in the 1963–64 season. Kentucky opened undefeated and rose in the rankings to No. 2 in the land. The only problem was UK had not played a ranked opponent.

That changed when Kentucky met the No. 8 Blue Devils in New Orleans on New Year's Eve 1963. In order for Kentucky to be back on top of the basketball world, the team would have to beat Duke. Of course, the situation was even more tense because Duke featured All-American scorer Jeff Mullins, a 6'4" former Mr. Basketball from Lexington Lafayette High School.

Down 10 at the half, Kentucky was close enough to make a run. The Cats used 6'5" center Nash to continually beat his man for the majority of his 30 overall points in the game. UK finally tied it when Mobley, a native of Harrodsburg, hit a shot from the corner with 27 seconds to go to knot it up at 79.

UK's Ted Deeken then batted the ball out of a Duke player's hand and right to Kron, who caught it and called timeout. In the huddle, Nash said the play was supposed to go to him. Deeken, who had 18 points that night, would have been a nice second option.

Unfortunately, when the team inbounded the ball, Nash was double-teamed, and guard Randy Embry dribbled out most of the clock before finding Mobley open just left of the free throw line. Mobley let it fly, and the shot banked in for a UK win.

"Coach Rupp never came out on to the court to congratulate us after a win," Mobley told Lexington broadcaster Denny Trease. "But this time I noticed him hurrying straight toward me. He said, 'Remember, Harrodsburg, we knew Duke was expecting Nash to get the ball, so we outsmarted them and instructed you to take the last shot.'"

Kentucky then made it back to No. 1 in the polls.

Overall, the Kentucky/Duke rivalry has seen its share of great games. And if the NCAA has its way, there will be more to come.

Kyle Macy

It went like this. Before every free throw shot, he would dry his hands on his socks. It wasn't so much about the actual drying. It was, instead, a mental cue, something he could do to take his mind off the shot and focus purely on the routine.

It worked. Kyle Macy was one of the best free throw shooters in Kentucky history. And he was one of the best point guards to ever wear the Blue and White.

From Peru, Indiana, Macy was one of a long line of great Indiana natives to play for UK. Walter McCarty was from Evansville. Mike Flynn was from Jeffersonville. Marquis Teague was from Indianapolis. And so on.

Originally, Macy, who earned Indiana Mr. Basketball honors, enrolled at Purdue and had an outstanding freshman season. But he wanted to go to a place where he could win a national title, and after looking around he thought he could be the point guard Kentucky needed. The only problem was that UK didn't accept transfers.

Macy said he had to sell himself hard to Joe B. Hall. But it only took Hall seeing the guard play—then the coach realized Macy was too good to pass up. After sitting out the 1976–77 season, Macy was ready to replace guard Larry Johnson. With the height of Rick Robey and Mike Phillips, the scoring of Jack Givens and James Lee, and the guard play of Macy and Truman Claytor, the 1977–78 squad was so good it was quickly favored to win the national title.

With Macy at point guard, the Wildcats won their first 14 games. It was going to be a special year—the fans could feel it. The team went on to win the SEC championship and the school's fifth NCAA title. Along the way the team defeated Florida State and Miami of Ohio, to move on to the regional finals. Then they faced Michigan State and another spectacular young point guard named Magic Johnson.

It was a Final Four battle for the ages, one that Macy had a huge hand in winning. Macy always believed in his free throw numbers (he was about a 90 percent shooter). So if he missed one early on in a game, he figured the pressure was off. By the numbers, he knew he would hit all the rest of them.

Against Michigan State, he missed one early.

"I missed my first free throw of the game," Macy said in the book, *Game of My Life: Kentucky.* "When I missed that first one I thought, 'Good.' I'd gotten the miss out of the way, so I figured I'd make all the rest."

He did. Macy ended up hitting 10-of-11 from the line and finished with 18 points. Kentucky beat fourth-ranked Michigan State 52–49 to advance to the title game.

Magic Johnson said that his Michigan State team learned how to win from that Kentucky team. "They were so professional,"

Johnson said more than 20 years later. "They taught us how to win."

Kentucky dispatched Duke in the title game 94–88, and Macy became a championship point guard. But he did miss one thing—he never got a piece of the net. When his team was cutting the nets down, he was rushed off the court to talk to broadcaster Bryant Gumbel.

Still, fewer players were more beloved than the Hoosier who brought Lexington a title.

While his junior season was a rebuilding year, Macy's senior season was another ride to No. 1. The Cats reloaded with talent, adding Sam Bowie, and they went 29–6, winning the SEC and the Great Alaska Shootout along the way. But a 55–54 upset loss at the hands of Duke in the regional ended the season for UK and the career of the one who came to be known as "Cool Kyle."

Macy played for Chicago, Phoenix, and Indiana in the NBA, averaging 9.5 points and four assists per game. He also shared the backcourt with Michael Jordan in Chicago. After retiring, Macy went into broadcasting and coaching, and in 2003 he guided Morehead State to a 20-win season and a share of the Ohio Valley Conference championship.

Now he works in broadcasting for radio and television in Lexington. He says he still wears his championship ring and that everyone still asks him about his career.

"I couldn't have written a better script," Macy said in *Game of My Life: Kentucky*. "The way it all turned out was the best thing that could've happened."

The Draft Cats

UK coach John Calipari called June 24, 2010, "the greatest night" in the history of Kentucky basketball.

Did the Wildcats win a national title? No.

Did they sign another No. 1 recruiting class? Nope.

Calipari's comment had nothing to do with wins and losses—and in fact, many fans criticized him for saying the words. What happened that was so special?

The Wildcats placed five players in the first round of the 2010 NBA Draft.

It was Calipari's first season at Kentucky, and he brought in a whale of a recruiting class. Included in the class was the No. 1 overall player, point guard John Wall, and the No. 1 power forward, DeMarcus Cousins. Eric Bledsoe, a highly touted guard from Alabama, came into the fold, as did center Daniel Orton, who was originally recruited by former UK coach Billy Gillispie. Rounding out the class was local standout Jon Hood.

The class was the best in the land, and it gave Kentucky exactly the talent it needed to return to the elite group of college basketball. Led by Wall, Cousins, and junior forward Patrick Patterson, the team went 35–3, 14–2 in the SEC. They won the conference and SEC Tournament titles before falling to West Virginia a game short of the Final Four.

Wall led the balanced team in scoring with 16.7 points per game followed by Cousins at 15.1, Patterson at 14.3, and Bledsoe at 11.3. Sophomore Darius Miller averaged 6.5 per game.

It seemed that every night a different hero would emerge, leading the team to victory. Players like Cousins and Bledsoe fared

2,000 Wins

On December 21, 2009, the Draft Cats helped Kentucky become the first program in college basketball history to reach 2,000 wins. The Cats beat Drexel 88–44 live on ESPN, and both Cousins and Patterson led the way with 18 points apiece. UK improved to 2,000–635–1 in 107 seasons. North Carolina was second on the list with 1,992 wins, and Kansas was third with 1,980. "This is a special moment for this program and this state," Coach Calipari said afterward.

better than anyone could have ever dreamed, and they were able to show their athleticism on a national stage.

Prior to the season, most thought John Wall would be a so-called "one-and-done" player; that is, Wall would be a player who only stayed in college for the NBA-mandated one season. The other players, while talented, were not expected to go—save for Patrick Patterson, who would graduate in three years. No one would be surprised if he joined Wall and headed for the draft.

But as the season wore on and the players improved, UK fans began to hear the whispers. Cousins was becoming a first-team All-American. Bledsoe already possessed NBA athleticism. It was all adding up to a mass exodus from Lexington.

No team had ever placed five players in the first round of the NBA Draft. The first round meant a guaranteed three-year contract. It meant a player would become an instant millionaire. No Wildcat had ever been selected No. 1 in the NBA Draft. That ended on June 24, 2010, when the Washington Wizards chose John Wall with the No. 1 pick.

No one was shocked.

Cousins then went fifth to the Sacramento Kings, and again—no one was surprised.

People wondered, could three more Kentuckians be picked? The smart money was on two—Patterson and Bledsoe were sure to be chosen in the first round. The other early entrant—little-used 6'10" big man Daniel Orton—was supposed to go in the second round.

The Houston Rockets chose Patterson with the 14th pick, and everything was going to plan. Four picks later Bledsoe was taken 18th to the Oklahoma City Thunder. That was four—a very successful night for the Wildcats. But everyone's mind was blown when the Orlando Magic took Orton with pick No. 29. That was five players picked in the first round.

No one—aside from one UK official—saw it coming. That was Mike Pratt, who had heard that Orton going to the Magic was a possibility.

"It only takes one team to like you," Pratt said.

They would forever be known as the Draft Cats.

Two years later, UK again made draft history, becoming the only squad ever to have the No. 1 and No. 2 picks drafted from the same team—Anthony Davis and Michael Kidd-Gilchrist.

67 Jack "Goose" Givens

While Kentucky has recruited players from all around the Commonwealth, the nation, and even the world, one of its best finds didn't require leaving town. Jack "Goose" Givens was a Parade All-American at Bryan Station High School in Lexington. Familiarity certainly did not breed contempt in the case of Givens, who committed to UK in 1974.

Givens scored just less than 10 points per game as a freshman on the talented 1974–75 NCAA runner-up squad. He tallied 24 points in UK's semifinal win over Syracuse but had only eight points on 3-of-10 shooting in UK's title loss to UCLA in legendary Coach John Wooden's final game. It would take three seasons for Givens to get another title shot, but that game would prove much more memorable for UK backers.

Meanwhile, Givens wasted little time in going from a supporting player to a superstar. As a sophomore in 1975–76, Givens scored more than 20 points per game. He pulled down seven boards per game and shot better than 82 percent at the foul line. The SEC coaches voted Givens first-team All-Conference, and as a Helms All-American, he was UK basketball's first African American All-American.

The 1976–77 season was simply more of the same. Givens scored 18.9 points per game and improved on his shooting percentages both from the foul line (83 percent) and the field (51 percent). Givens was again a Helms All-American. But the 1976 season had ended in the NIT, and the 1977 team bowed out in an NCAA regional final against North Carolina.

In 1977–78, Givens' scoring stats again decreased slightly to a mere 18.1 points per game. That said, Givens was the top scorer on a highly regarded UK squad, and he shot better than 55 percent from the field. Givens was first-team or second-team All-American on virtually everyone's postseason award list. He was Mr. Consistency, failing to score in double figures only three times all season in 1978.

In the 1978 NCAA Tournament, Givens showed scoring improvement in every game. He went from scoring 11 points in an opening-round win over Florida State to scoring 12 in an easy win over Miami of Ohio. This was followed by a 14-point effort in a narrow regional final win over Michigan State. Givens began his Final Four experience with 23 points against Arkansas. Could the pattern continue?

It could, and it did. Givens began the title game against Duke three points shy of becoming the second Wildcat in school history to score 2,000 points. It took him very little time to crack that barrier. Duke played a 2-3 zone defense, and Givens began the game by exploiting the hole in the middle of the zone. At halftime he had 23 points, and UK led by seven.

Jack Givens leaps for a shot at the basket over the head of Lew Massey of the University of North Carolina at Charlotte during the championship game of the National Invitation Tournament at New York on Sunday, March 22, 1976. The basket didn't count as Givens was charged with a travel. Cedric Maxwell of UNC Charlotte watches the play. Kentucky won the game and title by a score of 71–67. (AP Photo/Ray Stubblebine)

Givens' career game continued in the second half. He finished with 41 points, one of the most remarkable performances ever seen in the Final Four. One particular second-half play summed up Givens' golden day. Givens caught a pass about 15' out near the left baseline. He fired another jumper and watched the ball bank off the glass at a seemingly impossible angle and drop through the net. Small things like the laws of physics were no match for Jack "Goose" Givens on the biggest day of his career. Led by Givens, UK knocked off Duke 94–88 and won its fifth NCAA Tournament championship.

Givens' place in UK history remains secure. Thirty-four years after his last game, Givens is third on UK's career scoring list and 12th on UK's rebounding list. Givens was chosen in the first round of the 1978 NBA Draft by the Atlanta Hawks where he played two seasons. Givens went on to work as a color analyst for TBS and for the Orlando Magic for several seasons. At last notice, Givens was involved in coaching and running an AAU basketball program in Orlando.

68 Coach Cal's No. 1 Recruiting Classes

Even before John Calipari's 2012 Cats made their historical mark by being No. 1 on the floor, their coach had solidly established his championship credentials. No, Calipari didn't win any NCAA titles until 2012, but he has now bagged four consecutive mythical recruiting titles, annually pulling down the best class of college basketball recruits.

Calipari's reputation as a big-time recruiter preceded him to UK, but it's not as if the Wildcats had never made any big recruiting hauls. In recent years, 1992's class of Tony Delk, Rod Rhodes, Walter McCarty, and Jared Prickett was judged as one of the nation's best, and it delivered the 1996 NCAA title. Tubby Smith's highly regarded 2004 class of Rajon Rondo, Randolph Morris, Joe Crawford, and Ramel Bradley didn't quite pan out, but it wasn't for lack of star power.

Still, in 2009, Cal's first class dazzled everyone. ESPN, rivals.com, and scout.com tabbed it as the nation's best. John Wall and DeMarcus Cousins were two of the consensus top half-dozen players in the nation, with Wall being most pundits' choice for best player in the class. Daniel Orton and Eric Bledsoe were only slightly less well-regarded, and Darnell Dodson and Jon Hood rounded out the class.

In 2010, Cal didn't rebuild, he simply reloaded. Again, all three major services placed the Cats on top. Enes Kanter, Brandon Knight, and Terrence Jones were solidly among the nation's top 15 players according to all three major recruiting services. Doron Lamb was very close behind, and Stacey Poole and Eloy Vargas filled in the class.

Even by the standards of the first two classes, UK's 2011 recruiting class was breathtaking. While the one-and-done rule makes it difficult to judge, this class may have been the best class of all time. All three services judged Anthony Davis, Michael Kidd-Gilchrist, and Marquis Teague as the best players in the country at their respective positions. Davis and Kidd-Gilchrist, along with Duke's Austin Rivers, were the major contenders for top player in the class status. Kyle Wiltjer was a solid addition to the class, as well.

The 2012 class was slow to come together, but it again placed Kentucky on top of the national rankings from rivals.com and scout.com (ESPN placed UK second). Alex Poythress of Clarksville, Tennessee, and Archie Goodwin of Little Rock, Arkansas, gave UK two solid top 20 players to kick off its class.

Center Willie Cauley-Stein wasn't quite as highly regarded, but he is still considered an impressive prospect.

On April 11, Shabazz Muhammad committed to UCLA on live television. UK was something of a long shot for Muhammad due to his west coast residence and thorough connections with Adidas, who happens to be UCLA's designated athletic shoe company. Still, the move gave UCLA two elite recruits and appeared to knock UK out of contention for the top class. Nerlens Noel, Muhammad's main competition for top player of the class honors, was announcing later in the evening. Many signs were pointing to Georgetown as Noel's ultimate destination.

Fuel was added to the fire when Calipari appeared via telephone on the ESPNU recruiting show where Muhammad and Noel's decisions were being made. Cal didn't directly tip his hand, but he made comments on how players needed to be "all in" to make it at UK, and indicated that if they weren't, perhaps they should go elsewhere. This sounded like Noel wasn't in the works, either.

Later in the evening, Noel, complete with his boxy, tall, flat-top hair cut, appeared on television to make his announcement. He had three caps in front of him—Georgetown, UK, and Syracuse. The UK hat looked like it wouldn't have fit on a five-year-old version of Noel, while the Georgetown hat was a large, flat billed model. Noel began to announce his choice and flipped his back to the camera, showing "UK" shaved into the back of his head. Who fit Calipari's definition of "all in" more than the player who had shaved "UK" into his head? In a hilariously over-the-top moment, Noel had jumped UK back into the leader's seat and cleared the way for a fourth consecutive recruiting title.

69 Visit Madisonville, Home of Frank Ramsey and Travis Ford

If you travel west on the Pennyrile Parkway, there's a stop near US 41 where a town of about 20,000 is famous for producing two legendary Kentucky basketball players.

Welcome to Madisonville, about 125 miles southwest of Louisville. Here you can attend the state's largest Veteran's Day parade, and on the second Friday in the summer months you can dance the night away at Friday Night Live, a downtown party.

But to really get a sense of what it's like to live in small-town Kentucky, you've got to attend a basketball game at Madisonville-North Hopkins High. The high school was opened in 1968 and replaced old Madisonville High and North Hopkins High.

A public advanced-placement high school with an enrollment of about 1,100, Madisonville-North Hopkins is known for its famous alumni. First there is Sonny Collins, possibly the greatest running back in University of Kentucky football history. But the town's two basketball stars played nearly 40 years apart. They are basketball Hall of Famer Frank Ramsey and current Oklahoma State head coach Travis Ford. Both Ramsey and Ford starred for UK—Ramsey in the 1950s and Ford in the 1990s.

Ramsey

Back when it was known as Madisonville High, Frank Ramsey was a talented baseball and basketball player. He recruited himself to UK, winning over Coach Adolph Rupp by showing off his dribbling skills in a game.

Looking like a young Jon Cryer from *Two and a Half Men*, Ramsey served as a great role player on the 1951 team, averaging 10 points per game and winning a national championship. Of course, by the time he was a senior, punishments from a previous team's indiscretions were being given out. When they resumed playing, that team went 25–0, and because the big three of Ramsey, Cliff Hagan, and Lou Tsioropoulos were ineligible to play, Rupp decided not to take the team to the NCAAs, preserving the team's perfect record.

Of course, that meant Ramsey's college career had come to an end. But in a way his basketball life was just beginning. In the NBA, Ramsey became a true star, developing into what would become known as the sixth man for the Boston Celtics. He played nine seasons, averaged more than 13 points per game, and won seven world championships. He was lucky to play for two amazing coaches in Rupp and the Celtics' Red Auerbach.

After deciding his playing days were over, Ramsey retired, returned to Madisonville, and became president of the Dixon Bank. In 1982, he was inducted into the Basketball Hall of Fame. "What an honor," he said.

Ford

Travis Ford grew up hearing all about Frank Ramsey.

As a senior at North Hopkins High School, Ford averaged 31.7 points per game and became a Parade All-American. But in order for Ford to follow in Ramsey's footsteps and play at UK, it looked like it would take a bit of a miracle.

Eddie Sutton was the coach at Kentucky, and he already had his son, Sean, as well as high school legend Richie Farmer on the team. It looked a bit crowded. Ford would have to go elsewhere.

That turned out to be Missouri, where Ford was named the Big 8 Freshman of the Year. Ford always loved to watch Kyle Macy and Rex Chapman, but his game was different from theirs. First off, Ford was 5'8"—not ideal for big-time basketball. But he could shoot the lights out, regularly hitting 50 percent or better from behind the three-point line.

By the time Ford was ready to transfer, Sutton was out of Lexington and Rick Pitino had arrived. Pitino's wide-open style was perfect for Ford, and a talented roster gave the little guard a chance to make a Final Four. Turns out Ford made a good choice. In 1993, the Cats reached the Final Four, led by Ford and Jamal Mashburn.

During his career Ford won a regional Most Outstanding Player Award, was the MVP of the Maui Invitational, and claimed two SEC Tournament Most Valuable Player Awards.

Ford graduated, then starred in a Disney basketball movie called *The Sixth Man*, and went into coaching where he turned around programs at Campbellsville (67–31 after three years), Eastern Kentucky (he led the Colonels to their first NCAA Tourney in 25 years), and UMass, where he coached before leaving for Oklahoma State.

He's learned from some of the best coaches in the business, including Pitino, Billy Donovan, and Tubby Smith.

"I just want to have some of the same experiences they've had," Ford said, laughing. Like championships. And All-American players. And NBA Draft picks.

So who will be the next great UK star from Madisonville?

You'll have to go see for yourself.

70 Watch a Game from the eRUPPtion Zone

They are there at the beginning of every home game, sometimes hours before tip-off. Clever, crude, but never cruel, they take many shapes and forms.

There's Bearded Guy and The Referee, who seem to be the leaders. There's the blue Spider-Men, two students from Ohio who have gotten so popular they've been on national TV multiple times and even made the cover collage of the *Sports Illustrated* NCAA preview edition.

Sometimes you might even see Ashley Judd there, too.

It's the eRUPPtion Zone, the home of UK's student body at Rupp Arena. If you're a fan, you need to watch a game from this crowd. Located in the lower bowl area behind one goal, the zone is standing-room only. And if you're there, it's best to be loud.

After years of criticism because students were placed high in the rafters of the 23,000-plus capacity arena (students would cheer but could not be heard because they were too far away from the court, while those seated closest to the court rarely cheered), university officials decided to make one side behind the goal for students—and they held a contest to see who could name the new section.

That was won by Andrew Acker, a freshman at UK at the time who was—interestingly enough—from North Carolina. His submission was chosen from nearly 200 entries.

Now, with thousands of screaming kids at least on one side, the UK team is able to have some kind of home-court advantage.

"This is just the best place to be—right next to the band," said one of the Kentucky Spider-Men. "Around Christmas time they give us blue Santa hats. It's an amazing atmosphere."

"There's nothing like it," the other Spider-Man added.

In recent seasons, those fans in the zone have been tasked with helping to wave a giant blue flag before the game starts. It reads, simply: "Kentucky Basketball Never Stops." It's impressive to see.

The zone is where Dick Vitale always mingles before games, signing dozens of autographs and posing for countless pictures.

"Can you believe this environment?" Vitale said before an SEC game this season. "There are only a few places like this in all of college basketball. This is one of the best places to do a game!"

In January 2012, the eRUPPtion Zone was a finalist for the Best Student Section in the country, an award given by the Naismith Foundation.

And you don't necessarily have to be a student to stand in the zone. Look for discounted tickets to games for these areas when kids are off on Christmas break.

Then you, too, can be in the zone.

71 The Walk-Ons

In virtually every town and city across the Commonwealth of Kentucky and the nation at large, there are untold thousands upon thousands of young boys who dream of being offered a basketball scholarship at the University of Kentucky. Of course, for almost all of the dreamers, the dream ends in rejection. Except for some, the rejection isn't the end of the dream.

Outside the golden façade of scholarship college basketball players lies the land of the walk-ons. Walk-on is the common name for a non-scholarship player. Often unknown and unappreciated, not given either the acclaim or many of the perks that their teammates receive, walk-ons are frequently an afterthought to all but the most knowledgeable fans. Despite the odds against them, many walk-on players have a substantial place in the lore of Kentucky basketball. Here is a sort of UK walk-on All-Star Team of those few players who beat the odds.

Cameron Mills (1994–98) Mills, whose father, Terry, played under Adolph Rupp, walked on at UK under Rick Pitino. After 2½ seasons of playing only sparingly (31 total points during that time), in January 1997 Mills was suddenly forced to play major minutes after Derek Anderson's knee injury. He ended his career with 365 total points, shooting 47 percent from three-point range and being an integral part of two teams that played in the NCAA title game.

Ravi Moss (2002–06) Moss walked on under Tubby Smith, and in his last two seasons he displayed great defensive intensity and a knack for hitting big shots. Moss finished with 376 career points and shot better than 37 percent behind the three-point arc.

Junior Braddy (1989–1993) Braddy was a UK baseball player who joined Pitino's depth-challenged first squad. Much like Moss, Braddy was always a crowd favorite for hustle and three-point shooting. Braddy scored 327 points in his four seasons and played in the 1993 Final Four. He also played parts of six seasons of minor league baseball.

Todd Svoboda (1992–93) Svoboda was a senior walk-on transfer from Northern Kentucky. His single-season highlights included outscoring Tennessee All-American Allan Houston in UK's 101–40 embarrassment of the Vols and draining his only three-point attempt in the Elite Eight against Florida State.

Mark Coury (2006–08) Coury was a sometime starter for Billy Gillispie's first squad, averaging less than two points per game. He managed a double-double (13 points, 10 rebounds) in Gillispie's first game. He also transferred to Cornell after the season.

Anthony Epps (1994–97) Epps was actually not a walk-on, but this was a matter of circumstance. He initially agreed to walk on during the 1994–95 season, but after Rick Pitino struck out on several other recruits, Epps was given the last scholarship. Of course, all Epps did was land himself at second on UK's all-time assist list, score 881 points, and lead the 1995–96 and 1996–97 squads to the national title game.

Coach Tubby Smith gives guard Ravi Moss an in-game tutorial during the second half of Kentucky's exhibition game against Georgetown College on Wednesday, November 9, 2005, in Lexington, Kentucky. (AP Photo/Ed Reinke)

Marquis Estill (2000–03) Estill, on the other hand, was a scholarship player who gave up his scholarship for the 2001–02 season when Tubby Smith had more players than scholarships. Estill averaged almost nine points per game that season and totaled 936 in his three-year career. Quite a walk-on!

Saul Smith (1997–2001) Tubby's middle son, Saul, walked on for his father and was a back-up on the 1997–98 title team. While he was a polarizing figure, Saul always played hard. He finished with 730 points and 364 assists, good for tenth on UK's career list.

JV Teams

The best UK team you never heard of was probably the 1971–72 Super Kittens. In the days before freshman eligibility, UK fielded a junior varsity squad mainly to give the freshmen, who were ineligible for varsity competition, some experience and to provide a glorified try-out for the varsity. Joe B Hall led that 1971–72 squad to a 22–0 record. The team's average score? 100–68! Of course, the group of freshmen would be the core of Hall's 1975 NCAA runner-up squad (Kevin Grevey, Jimmy Dan Conner, Mike Flynn, etc.).

UK had a long and illustrious JV history before the Super Kittens. In the 1949–51 seasons, Rupp's right hand man, Harry Lancaster, led the JV squad to 43 wins and one loss. The JV history seemed to end in 1977. However, it had a brief revival in 1995–96 when Rick Pitino re-instituted the program. That squad went 9–4, but more important, Nazr Mohammed sweated off pounds and Cameron Mills found his shooting range, with both actually seeing playing time outside the varsity roster of almost-certain pro prospects. Without the 1995–96 JV team, the 1996–97 NCAA runner-up team and the 1997–98 NCAA Championship team probably wouldn't have happened.

72 Take in a Barnstorming Tour

I (Ryan Clark) once saw Patrick Sparks get more than 70 points in a game. Then again, I once saw Ramel Bradley get 100. It's almost an annual rite of spring, when outgoing senior Kentucky basketball players go on a barnstorming tour across the state to meet the fans and make a little dough.

As a fan you must go out and see these exhibitions if you can, if not for the athleticism then for the sheer absurdity of it all. Sometimes the UK players will be matched up against a group of regional All-Stars, which means a player like Gerald Fitch could face off against one of the eighth region's best guards. Yeah, probably a 17-year-old.

It's no contest. The Kentucky player wins. Always.

Other times these games could involve a group of Kentucky All-Stars, maybe a team featuring someone like former Georgetown College star Collier Mills (brother of Cameron).

These games can be competitive. But UK still wins.

In the summer of 2011, there were some added thrills because due to an impending NBA lockout, UK players like Brandon Knight, DeAndre Liggins, and Josh Harrellson all played extended Barnstorming Tour seasons. The difference here was their team would feature surprise guests who were normally just working out at UK during the lockout. Guests included Tayshaun Prince, Rajon Rondo and DeMarcus Cousins.

And per tradition, the players would stay afterward and sign all autographs. No fans go away unhappy. And you never know who you may see.

In Maysville in the summer of 2011, I watched the barnstorming group practicing before a game against some local All-Stars at

Mason County High. The place was packed—thousands of fans, many of them little kids, screaming for their favorite players.

As the players held their own half-court shooting contest (Josh Harrellson outdueled Brandon Knight in a surprise) a voice came over the loudspeaker, "Deron Feldhaus, you are needed in the lobby. Deron Feldhaus."

The crowd cheered like crazy at just the mention of one of their hometown heroes. Later that day I also saw Jeff Sheppard, who helped organize the event. Everyone had fun, proving that sometimes these kinds of fan events can be better than any real game.

73 UK and UNC Rivalry

It seems like every time they meet it comes down to a last-second play.

But when you play for two of the greatest programs in the history of college basketball, it figures that each team will give its all to win. It's the Kentucky and North Carolina rivalry—and as fans we've seen some of their best games in recent years. As a UK fan, you must know this rivalry. And you should probably come to hate that pale blue Carolina color.

In 2009, John Wall and Patrick Patterson led Kentucky to a 68–66 victory in Lexington. It stopped a streak of five straight wins for Carolina in the series—and it meant more to Wall, a Carolina native.

A season later, Brandon Knight, Doron Lamb, and Terrence Jones led a young UK squad into Chapel Hill for a rematch. Late free throws gave the Tar Heels a two-point lead, and a desperate heave by Lamb at half court at the buzzer fell short. UNC prevailed 75–73.

Later that season, the pair met again in the NCAA Tournament—in the regional finals with a Final Four berth on the line. The two teams were not ranked the highest in the land (Carolina was ranked No. 7, UK was No. 11), but it could be argued that no teams were playing better than the pair.

With superstars all over the court (UK had Lamb, Knight, Jones, and future NBA picks DeAndre Liggins and Josh Harrellson, while UNC chipped in Harrison Barnes, Tyler Zeller, and John Henson), the game was marketed as a pseudo championship game. It lived up to the hype. Down 11 in the second half, UNC came all the way back to tie. But Knight hit a three to regain the lead, and with 37 seconds remaining and Kentucky up one, Liggins hit another three to put the game away. UK won 76–69.

The next season Carolina had revenge on its mind. After losing out on a place in the Final Four, the Tar Heels brought back Zeller, Henson, and Barnes, plus their point guard, Kendall Marshall, who had also become a star. They came in to Rupp Arena to find some familiar faces (Lamb and Jones) and some new ones (Anthony Davis and Michael Kidd-Gilchrist). It was a matchup of No. 1 UK versus No. 5 UNC, and it was the first game played on CBS that season.

It did not disappoint. Both teams flexed their muscles early, and Carolina looked to be the better team in the first half, leading by five. But Kentucky shot 56 percent in the second, and with less than a minute to play, the Cats had a one-point lead and a one-and-one at the line by point guard Marquis Teague.

He missed, setting up Marshall and the Tar Heels to play out the clock with one last try. Marshall found Zeller down low, but the pass was bobbled. As the seconds ticked off, the ball found its way out to 6'11" John Henson on the baseline. Henson squared up

A Revered Rivalry

Date	Teams / Location	W/L	Score
12/3/2011	(No. 5) North Carolina at (No. 1) Kentucky	W	73–72
3/27/2011	(No. 11) Kentucky vs. (No. 7) North Carolina NCAA East Regional Finals (at Newark, NJ)	W	76–69
12/4/2010	(No. 10) Kentucky at North Carolina	L	73–75
12/5/2009	(No. 10) North Carolina at (No. 5) Kentucky	W	68–66
11/18/2008	Kentucky at (No. 1) North Carolina	L	58–77
12/1/2007	(No. 1) North Carolina at Kentucky	L	77–86
12/2/2006	Kentucky at (No. 7) North Carolina	L	63–75
12/3/2005	North Carolina at (No. 10) Kentucky	L	79–83
12/4/2004	(No. 8) Kentucky at (No. 9) North Carolina	L	78–91
1/3/2004	(No. 9) North Carolina at (No. 8) Kentucky	W	61–56
12/7/2002	(No. 18) Kentucky at (No. 12) North Carolina	W	98–81
12/8/2001	North Carolina at (No. 11) Kentucky	W	79–59
12/2/2000	Kentucky at (No. 6) North Carolina	W	93–76
3/25/1995	(No. 2) Kentucky vs. (No. 4) North Carolina NCAA Southeast Regional Finals (at Birmingham, AL)	L	61–74
12/10/1990	(No. 25) Kentucky at (No. 10) North Carolina	L	81–84
12/27/1989	Kentucky vs. (No. 24) North Carolina (at Louisville, KY)	L	110–121
12/26/1981	(No. 2) Kentucky vs. (No. 1) North Carolina (at East Rutherford, NJ)	L	69–82
3/19/1977	(No. 3) Kentucky vs. (No. 5) North Carolina NCAA East Regional Finals (at College Park, MD)	L	72–79
12/8/1975	(No. 7) Kentucky vs. (No. 4) North Carolina (at Charlotte, NC)	L	77–90

for a shot he'd already hit once in the game. This attempt would either win or lose the game.

But he never got the chance. Instead, Kentucky's 6'10" center Anthony Davis left the man he was guarding (Zeller) and ran out to challenge the Henson shot. He stretched and jumped as high and as far as he could. And he got his fingertips on the ball, tipping it up into the air, where he was able to reach up and snag it. Davis then found Teague racing upcourt and threw him the ball. The Cats ran out the clock. It was UK by one 73–72.

"Let's make it best of seven," *Lexington Herald-Leader*'s John Clay asked after the most recent edition of the rivalry.

Date	Teams / Location	W/L	Score
12/9/1974	(No. 15) Kentucky vs. (No. 9) North Carolina (at Louisville, KY)	W	90–78
12/10/1973	(No. 10) Kentucky vs. (No. 5) North Carolina (at Greensboro, NC)	L	84–101
12/11/1972	(No. 8) Kentucky vs. (No. 13) North Carolina (at Louisville, KY)	L	70–78
12/8/1969	(No. 2) Kentucky vs. (No. 7) North Carolina (at Charlotte, NC)	W	94–87
12/7/1968	(No. 2) North Carolina at (No. 3) Kentucky	L	77–87
12/12/1967	(No. 9) Kentucky vs. (No. 5) North Carolina (at Greensboro, NC)	L	77–84
12/13/1966	(No. 8) North Carolina at (No. 3) Kentucky	L	55–64
12/7/1964	(No. 11) Kentucky vs. (No. 13) North Carolina (at Charlotte, NC)	L	67–82
12/9/1963	North Carolina at (No. 9) Kentucky	W	100–80
12/17/1962	North Carolina at Kentucky	L	66–68
12/13/1960	Kentucky vs. (No. 5) North Carolina (at Greensboro, NC)	W	70–65
12/18/1959	North Carolina at Kentucky UKIT	W	76–70
1/9/1950	North Carolina at (No. 2) Kentucky	W	83–44
2/27/1932	Kentucky vs. North Carolina Southern Conference Tournament (at Atlanta, GA)	L	42–43
1/4/1929	North Carolina at Kentucky	L	15–26
2/29/1924	Kentucky vs. North Carolina Southern Conference Tournament (at Atlanta, GA)	L	20–41

But the same could be asked after most of the games the two storied traditions have played. The two teams either lead or are found in the top three of all the most important statistical basketball categories, including all-time wins, most championships won, and most NCAA Tournament games won.

The rivalry began in 1924 when North Carolina defeated UK 41–20 on a neutral site in Atlanta. The Tar Heels lead the overall series 22–13, but the Cats are gaining ground.

74 Surf on Over to Jon Scott's UK Website

On a sleepless night, what if you suddenly find yourself wondering who the top scoring Wildcat with a last name starting with Z was? Or which Wildcats hailed from Texas? Or how many UK freshmen have scored 30 points in a single game? What if you would like a list of the 40 McDonald's All-Americans who have played at Kentucky?

Or maybe you're more interested in thoughtful, careful analysis than numbers or lists. Maybe you'd like to know about the charges of racism that some people level at Adolph Rupp. Or about flaws in the RPI system, which is often cited in NCAA Tournament seedings. Fortunately, you're in luck. Superfan Jon Scott has not only done all the work, he has posted it on the Internet, on his Kentucky Wildcat basketball page. At press time, the site was located at http://www.bigbluehistory.net/bb/wildcats.html. That said, Internet providers are constantly changing, but a quick search should turn up Scott's site.

Jon Scott's Kentucky Wildcat basketball page has been present on the Internet for around two decades and has received more than 700,000 visitors. As for the Wizard behind the cyberspace haven, he's fairly quiet, content to let his work speak for itself. Scott did not attend UK, and in fact, he has never lived in Kentucky. He advised the *Lexington Herald-Leader* that he obtained degrees with the University of Illinois and North Carolina State. Scott, an early 40-something trained to become a chemical engineer, said that his father was a big Kentucky fan and that he himself became a fan after attending UK's basketball camp in the early 1980s.

Scott began his site as merely a UK fan site, albeit one dedicated to correcting misconceptions about the UK program. Scott admitted, "As someone who has always lived outside of Kentucky, I think I have a better understanding of how UK basketball is looked at and portrayed by the national media than people who live in Kentucky." Two early sections, "Misconceptions" and "Detractors" helped Scott utilize his objectivity and knowledge to right a few wrongs about the Big Blue Nation. Both sections are essential reading.

In the late 1990s, Scott began expanding the site to include exhaustive statistical information. From there, he later added box scores for individual games and has since begun adding biographical information for a great number of players. In essence, when it comes to dates, names, or verifiable facts, if Scott doesn't have it, it's a safe conclusion that no one does.

Scott does still solicit information from anyone who can add anything to his Internet warehouse of information. Be advised, though, that the last box score Scott deems as "critical" in terms of missing information is from 1922.

Numbers, names, and facts aside, Scott's written analysis is stunning. Whether systematically taking on some of Kentucky's historical detractors and picking apart their misstatements and inaccuracies or preparing historical summaries of some of Kentucky's greatest roundball rivalries, Scott is sharp-witted, entertaining, and always accurate. His work is so authoritative that in October 2011, the *Lexington Herald-Leader* published Scott's commentary on UK's ancient rivalry with cross-town foe Transylvania University.

Despite that dalliance with mainstream media status, Scott is often at his finest when taking the so-called major media to task. Specifically, his stinging rebuke of some of the modern "yellow journalism" that has surrounded UK in the Calipari era should shame a great number of so-called major national publications. Scott himself prefers to stay a bit less controversial. He humbly explained, "The thing I find the most rewarding is researching early players and filling in the history of the early eras of the program."

By the way, in case you are still wondering, Karl Zerfoss (133 points) was the top scoring Z-named Cat. Pitino protégé Jeff Brassow and Rupp's All-American center Bob Burrow are UK's two Texans, and four UK freshmen (Terrence Jones, Doron Lamb, Jamal Mashburn, and Brandon Knight) have scored 30 in a game. All of that information, and so much more, was available at the click of a button, thanks entirely to Jon Scott.

Cotton Nash

Cotton Nash had seen a large portion of the country by the time he graduated high school. His father moved around a lot due to his job, so Nash had seen New Jersey, Indiana, and Louisiana.

Luckily for Nash, he was a gifted athlete, one who could easily play professional basketball or baseball. He could always fit in on a new team. In the early 1960s, Nash's family settled in Louisiana.

The 6'5" talent had honed his basketball game so that he could do it all. He could be a tall guard able to hit the outside jumper, or he could utilize his quickness against bigger foes. But he could also go to work down low, as he had a great post game to take on smaller opponents who dared to guard him on the blocks.

By the time Nash graduated from Lake Charles High in Louisiana, he was a Parade All-American, one who could choose between any number of basketball powerhouses. Much of the basketball world was centered on Ohio at the time, since Ohio State and Cincinnati had dominated the most recent NCAA championship games.

But one school was still legendary for winning. And they still had a legendary coach.

Nash knew where he wanted to go to school.

"I wanted to go test myself where they played the best basketball," Nash said. "I knew about Coach Rupp, and I thought the best basketball was being played in the SEC. And I wanted to go to the best in the SEC."

So Nash became a Wildcat. Some recruits can single-handedly save a program for a year or so. Patrick Patterson did that, keeping UK relevant until other athletes could come and help. Nash may have been the first to serve in that role.

Nash's first season was amazing: 23–3 and a share of the conference title. The only setback was a tourney loss to No. 1 Ohio State.

Then things got rough.

His junior year, Nash did just about everything, taking on the scoring load to average more than 20 points per game. By sheer force of will, Nash carried the team to a 16–9 record. (Even Cawood Ledford conceded, saying the school should build a monument in Nash's honor.)

Help arrived in Nash's senior year, when players like Larry Conley and Tommy put on the Blue and White. *Now this could be a team*, Nash thought.

He was right.

The Cats started off 10–0 and reached No. 1 in the country with a win over Duke in the Sugar Bowl Classic. Sadly, those may have been the best of times for Nash as a member of Big Blue nation. His senior-year squad was young and inconsistent, and they would drop a first-round NCAA game to unranked Ohio University.

From being a program that some had forgotten about, to beating Duke, Kentucky knew it had come back to being elite again.

Without Nash, however, Kentucky would have been lost. His career 22.7 points-per-game average is second only to Dan Issel's 25.8. Nash went on to play two seasons of pro basketball for the Los Angeles Lakers, San Francisco Warriors, and the ABA Kentucky Colonels and three seasons of Major League Baseball for the Chicago White Sox and Minnesota Twins.

He looks back fondly on his days in Lexington. "We were able to get the program back to where it was supposed to be," Nash said. "That was something I was very proud of."

76 Richie Farmer

While 20 or so years have passed, Rick Pitino can probably still hear the call-in show questions. "Coach, is Richie going to start tonight?" "Coach, how much is Richie going to play?" "Can y'all get Richie more shots, Coach?" Richie, of course, was Richie Farmer, and while there have been more prolific Wildcats, there may have been none who were more beloved.

Farmer was a legend of almost unequalled brilliance in his high school days at Clay County High in Manchester. A 6' guard, who seemed to be born with a full mustache and a deadly jump shot, Farmer led Clay County to the state title and won state tournament MVP honors as a high school junior in 1986–87. In his senior season, he led the Tigers back to the title game. Farmer's squad lost to Allan Houston and Louisville Ballard 88–79, but Farmer was again named MVP, as he made nine threes and scored 51 points in the loss. Farmer won Kentucky's Mr. Basketball award following the season.

UK was reluctant to offer Farmer a scholarship, extending an offer only after LSU's Dale Brown nearly stole Richie for his Tigers. However, Coach Eddie Sutton, under intense public pressure from the Eastern part of the Commonwealth, eventually brought Farmer to UK. Richie's pure shooting did not earn him an abundance of time in Sutton's sluggish system; he played less than 10 minutes per game in UK's morbid 13–19 season in 1988–89.

Farmer's sweet shooting touch would eventually flourish under Rick Pitino. That said, relations between the two were not always cheerful. Farmer, feeling bullied by Pitino and strength coach Rock Oliver's incredibly rigorous off-season training program, nearly left the UK team before his sophomore season. Pitino cajoled Farmer back and was rewarded with Richie's deadeye shooting touch, his penchant for making big plays, and his incredibly vocal cheering section. Farmer canned 147 three-point shots at UK, still in the school's top 20 in that category, and he shot better than 80 percent at the foul line in each of his four seasons. Richie averaged 10.1 points per game as a junior in 1990–91 and 9.6 per game as a senior in 1991–92. He also had periodic explosive shooting streaks when the high school gunner extraordinaire would resurface and leave many eastern Kentuckians muttering, "We told them so."

Farmer the player at times seemed to take a back seat to Farmer the icon. Fans and media could not help but enjoy the witty banter between Pitino, with his thick New York accent, and Farmer, with his syrupy mountain drawl. Rarely was this more apparent than on Farmer's Senior Day in March 1992, which was not only the last home game for Farmer's senior class but for broadcaster Cawood Ledford, as well. Farmer was chosen to speak in postgame ceremonies on behalf of his teammates and the 39 years of UK players whose games had been announced by Ledford. After amusing Pitino by asking if the coach could understand him, Farmer moved the crowd by recalling growing up as a young boy in eastern Kentucky, listening to Ledford call UK basketball games, saying the venerable Ledford was one of his heroes. A hushed crowd heard Farmer admit, "He was Kentucky basketball to me." Funny enough, many Kentucky fans felt the same way about Farmer himself.

For his part, Farmer was hardly unaware of his popularity, invoking it successfully after basketball in 2003 and 2007 campaigns for the position of Kentucky's Commissioner of Agriculture and unsuccessfully in a 2011 campaign for Lieutenant Governor.

77 Visit Ted Arlinghaus and Rupp Arena North

Just across the river from Cincinnati, there's a town where a UK fan has created a little bit of Lexington in his own backyard.

"It started when I was building a gym for my family," said Ted Arlinghaus, a 61-year-old resident of Edgewood in Kenton County, Kentucky. "At first we were just building an enclosed basketball goal, you know? We have 10 children, and we wanted to give them a chance to play. But then we decided to build a full court, and then it became regulation-sized, and then we started to add more stuff."

It was 1992. Arlinghaus, a Kentucky alum, was running a successful home construction business. He was in the middle of building his gymnasium next to his expansive home. In the world of Kentucky basketball, Rick Pitino was rebuilding his new team. They were an overachieving bunch, a group that had stolen the hearts of UK fans everywhere.

So it was natural, then, for Arlinghaus to decide to just go ahead and build a regulation-sized basketball arena in his backyard and then to go ahead and paint it in the same fashion as Rupp Arena. In fact, that's sort of what he had painted on the floor—it reads, "Rupp Arena North."

"We thought, 'Why not?'" Arlinghaus said. "We've come this far. We might as well keep going. We had a family friend who could do some painting, so we had him paint it on the floor for us, just like at Rupp in Lexington."

So then they got some of their favorite UK players—John Pelphrey, Deron Feldhaus, Richie Farmer, Sean Woods and Jamal Mashburn, among others on that Unforgettable squad—to sign a shrine that would be placed on a wall in the gym.

"We just loved that team so much," Arlinghaus said. "We wanted them to be a part of all of it, too."

At any certain time, you may see one of any number of teams practicing on the court. Even now, 20 years later, area little league basketball teams, or the local high school team, or even the Arlinghaus family will be shooting hoops at Rupp Arena North.

In fact, just about anyone who wants to can call up Arlinghaus and ask to come by and shoot a few buckets.

"We allow a lot of folks to come by and play," he said.

If you can't play on the Rupp Arena court, or if you're not good enough to be a Wildcat, maybe you'll like shooting on the court of Rupp Arena North.

"It's really taken on a life of its own," Arlinghaus said laughing.

78 Louie Dampier

Louie Dampier probably thought he would die. It was 1965, and the junior guard had been hoping to improve on the previous season's disappointing 15–10 campaign. Before the 1965–66 season, Dampier was introduced to a new assistant coach named Joe B.

Louie Dampier (10) out-jumps Michigan's Jim Myers under the basket as the ball heads for the hoop during the NCAA Mideast final at Iowa City, Iowa, on March 12, 1966. (AP Photo/Larry Stoddard)

Hall. Coach Hall came from tiny Regis College and immediately introduced a rough new conditioning program to UK basketball. In the fall of 1965, Dampier, like the Energizer Bunny some decades later, was running and running and running. Larry Conley, Dampier's backcourt mate, ruefully remembered those days and told an interviewer, "I left some green beans and mashed potatoes out there." For Conley as well as Dampier and the rest of the squad, that which did not kill them certainly made them stronger.

Dampier had come to UK from Indianapolis' Southport High. The petite young guard, who was 6' and weighed in at less than 170 pounds, had been one of the most prolific scorers in Indiana high school history. Dampier was a jump shooter, although the mere statement is akin to saying, "Van Gogh was a painter" or "Shakespeare was a writer." His smooth outside shooting undoubtedly left Adolph Rupp with visions of his elusive fifth NCAA title.

As mentioned above, 1964–65 was a down season. At 15–10, UK was excluded from any postseason play. However, sophomore Dampier made a splash in his Wildcat debut in the era before freshman eligibility. Dampier scored 17 points per game on 51 percent shooting. He and fellow sophomore Pat Riley gave Kentucky the beginnings of a bright future.

Once assistant coach Hall came on board and introduced the returning players to leaner, meaner versions of themselves, UK's fortunes immediately improved. Juniors Dampier and Riley teamed with sophomore big man Thad Jaracz and seniors Conley and Tommy Kron to form the starting five. Kentucky would field a team that was short (no starter was taller than 6'5") but could outscore and outhustle virtually anyone. They were Rupp's Runts, and Dampier was one of the stars of the season.

In 1965–66, Dampier averaged 21.1 points per game, connecting on 52 percent of his shots and making a robust 83 percent of his free throws. Louie was rewarded with All-SEC and

All-American honors. In 16 of UK's 29 games, Dampier had 20 or more points. In a February game at Vanderbilt's Memorial Gymnasium, Dampier caught fire, making 18-of-29 shots and all six free throw attempts for a career high 42 points.

With Dampier's outside gunning and Pat Riley's post play leading the way, UK entered the NCAA Tournament as the top-ranked team in the nation, boasting a 24–1 record. In the Tournament, Dampier averaged 24 points and made 56 percent of his shots in leading UK to the NCAA title game.

UK was a heavy favorite in that game against Texas Western. Nobody bothered to tell the Miners, who used steady offense and an aggressive ball-hawking defense to upend the Cats 72–65. Dampier tied with Riley for UK's high-scoring honors with 19 points, but Dampier shot only 7-of-18 from the field and had six turnovers. His title dreams fell just short.

The 1966–67 season was unbefitting of two legends like Dampier and Riley. Riley was hurt, the team never clicked, and it took a victory in the season's final game to avoid giving Rupp a losing season. Dampier was again voted All-American and scored 20.7 points per game. Dampier's 1,575 points in three seasons ranked third on UK's all-time scoring list. He is still 13th and would've been higher had the three-point line existed.

Dampier's UK career led him to the helter-skelter American Basketball Association. Dampier was drafted by the Kentucky Colonels and would go on to play for the team in all nine of its ABA seasons. Dampier scored 18.9 points per game in the ABA, made 794 three-point baskets, and was an ABA All-Star seven times. Dampier was the ABA's leading career scorer and won a championship in 1975 with the Colonels. He played three seasons with the NBA's San Antonio Spurs after the ABA merger in 1976, retiring 14 years after Joe B. Hall ran him ragged back in Memorial Coliseum.

Tayshaun Prince

Reggie Miller streaked toward the basket. Seconds remained in Game 2 of the 2004 NBA Eastern Conference finals. Miller had the ball and an open path to the basket to tie the game. Indiana had won the first game, and if they could capture the second they would be well on their way to the NBA Finals. Miller, a 17-year NBA veteran and five-time NBA All-Star, was about to learn a valuable lesson—do not underestimate Tayshaun Prince. From nowhere, Prince raced up on Miller's left, materializing as if from thin air to swat Miller's layup out of bounds. One of the biggest defensive plays in NBA history had just been made. Detroit and Prince won the game, the series, and the NBA title. As for Prince, the skinny young man from Compton, California, looked more like a great bowler than a basketball superstar. But there he was— Tayshaun Prince, NBA champion, Olympic gold medal winner, and Kentucky Wildcat.

Prince came to UK for the 1998–99 season. A lanky 6'9" forward, Prince was hardly an imposing player. He rarely showed emotion on the court and often looked as if a stiff breeze might blow him into Indiana. Prince spent most of his first season deferring to his talented teammates, four of whom would also play in the NBA. He averaged 5.8 points per game but had perhaps the best game of his season in UK's season-ending Elite Eight loss to Michigan State, scoring 12 points without missing a shot.

Prince stepped up his game, scoring from the outside and off the dribble, and he was the leading scorer on UK's 1999–2000 squad with 13.3 points per game. He was named All-SEC and had a double-double with 21 points and 10 rebounds in UK's first game in the 2000s, a win over Georgia Tech. The team struggled,

Tayshaun Crushes the Heels

In December 2001, Prince and Kentucky had an early-season matchup with North Carolina in Lexington. Of course, North Carolina is another marquee school with a fine history, but Prince put the Tar Heels in their place. Prince made three-point shots on five consecutive UK possessions in the first five minutes of the game. Each shot seemed more implausible than the last, with the fifth being shot from the edge of the UK logo marked at halfcourt, around 28' from the basket. Rupp Arena may have registered on the Richter scale after the fifth trifecta from Prince.

Prince finished with 31 points, UK won by 20, and Kentucky won its 1,800[th] game ever, holding an 18-game lead over the Tar Heels, who were second. As CBS's Bill Raftery observed, Prince was a king on this date.

going 23–10, losing their first game in the SEC Tournament, and losing in the second round of the NCAA Tournament.

In 2000–01, Prince was an All-American and SEC Player of the Year. He scored 17 points per game. Highlights of the season included a February win over No. 8 Florida with Prince hitting the game-winning shot with three seconds to play. Tayshaun and the Cats won the SEC Tournament Title and were ready for an Elite Eight rematch with Duke in the NCAA Tournament—until Southern California interfered by upsetting the Cats 80–76 in the Sweet 16.

Prince placed his name in the NBA Draft but was ultimately moved to come back to Kentucky. Unfortunately, he was stuck on "Team Turmoil," an ego-driven squad with several basket cases who underachieved dramatically. Prince was the one solid rock on the team, scoring 17.5 points per game and leading the squad in rebounding. Tayshaun was held to less than double-figure scoring only four times all season, and when the chips were down, he played particularly well. In the NCAA Tournament's second round, Prince scored 41 points to lead UK past a plucky Tulsa squad. The season ended in the Sweet 16 with a loss to a Maryland team that went on to win the NCAA Tournament.

Tayshaun Prince's 1,775 career points rank eighth on UK's career scoring list. His 204 three-point baskets are the third-most in UK history. Despite his spindly nature, Prince grabbed 759 boards, 19th on UK's career list.

Prince was drafted by the NBA's Detroit Pistons. He is still active with the Pistons and was a mainstay on their 2004 NBA Championship squad. His career totals feature an average of just less than 13 points per game. Prince was a four-time NBA All-Defensive Team selection and was chosen for the 2008 U.S. Olympic team, which won a gold medal in Beijing. Prince is still skinny and unimposing, and still rarely makes grand displays of emotion. All he does is play great basketball. Underestimate him at your own risk.

80 Party at Woodlawn and Euclid

On the night Kentucky won its eighth national championship, there was a party like none other in Lexington.

Fans appeared from everywhere, from State Street and Limestone, Woodlawn and Euclid. Fans of all ages—from college students to grandparents with grandchildren in tow—danced in the streets to a cacophony of honking horns and howls.

It was joyous. And if a fan can't be with the UK team as it wins a title, the next best place to be is in Lexington. Fireworks shot off from every direction as fraternity boys climbed lamp posts and street signs. Sorority girls hopped on the shoulders of their boyfriends and held posters that read "Celebr8!" People littered the streets with the latest editions of the campus and city newspapers, all proclaiming UK the champions of the college basketball world.

A chant of "C-A-T-S, Cats! Cats! Cats!" broke out, and the crowd danced and sang together.

There were no fights, no violence. However, some still felt the need (perhaps it's tradition) to burn a ratty couch and dance around the bonfire like *Lord of the Flies*. Maybe it harkens back to our more primitive days in the caves.

No matter. No one was hurt. The smell of burning embers floated through the air as people drank their beverages of choice and reveled in Kentucky being No. 1 again after so long.

From the Two Keys Bar and Joe Bologna's to Hugh Jass Burgers and deSha's, the joy was felt in every eatery and bar. And many fans gathered around Rupp Arena, taking pictures for proof that they were there when Kentucky won.

Of course, a day layer, it was much easier to celebrate. When Kentucky wins a title, fans welcome back their team in grand style. Thousands of fans first greet the team when they land at the airport, then they line the streets as a special blue bus delivers the team to

Wheeler's Pharmacy

If burning couches is a bit much, and your UK memories are more along the lines of Ralph Beard or Bill Spivey than John Wall or Anthony Davis, an alternative spot to visit is Wheeler's Pharmacy. Virtually every town across Kentucky has a place like Wheeler's, where the venerable and opinionated folks congregate to eat breakfast, drink coffee, and critique Kentucky basketball. But none of those places have Joe B. Hall as a regular visitor or have Coach Cal occasionally dropping in for a cup of coffee and a bit of chatting with the regulars. Owner Buddy Wheeler recalls all of UK's coaches, other than pariahs Eddie Sutton or Billy Gillispie, dropping in at some point. Wheeler's is located at 336 Romany Road in Lexington.

Rupp Arena where 20,000 screaming fans await them. In 2012, there was a 24-second standing ovation for hometown hero Darius Miller.

"You people never cease to amaze me," Calipari told the crowd. "Let's raise a banner!"

With that, the celebration hits full crazy mode, as the new championship banner, which has already been made, is unfurled from the rafters.

And that's just the day after the title. These celebrations last for weeks, as players go on autograph tours, books and other memorabilia are released, videos are made and fans do everything they can to honor and remember the season.

Thousands of fans come out to shops in places like Hazard, Kentucky, to meet their heroes.

Because UK fans know how to celebrate.

81 Eddie Sutton

Eddie Sutton came in to the UK job in 1985 right in the middle of an NCAA investigation. He left in the exact same way. While the first investigation concerned Joe B. Hall, the second investigation was under Sutton's watch and was, according to the *University of Kentucky Basketball Encyclopedia*, the "lowest point in Wildcats history."

But Sutton looked to be a slam-dunk hire. He'd been to the Final Four with Arkansas. He even won at Creighton. His coaching tree traced back to the great Hank Iba. And Sutton wanted the UK job badly.

Sutton's first season was an amazing run. Kenny Walker and Roger Harden, then seniors, led their Cats to a 32–4 record, something no one truly expected. While they were upset in the NCAA

Tournament, their efforts were appreciated. The following two years brought the arrival of Rex Chapman, and even though there was excitement and talent, there were no Final Fours.

And the possible judgment of the NCAA loomed heavy over the program for years.

Of course, there were memorable moments: Chapman's 26-point outburst as a freshman against Louisville; a comeback for the ages against Tennessee where, down 10 with 1:13 to go, the Cats forced overtime and won; and Chapman becoming the first freshman since Alex Groza to lead the team in scoring.

But Sutton had his own demons, too. Many talked of Sutton drinking too much, and when he and Chapman began feuding, it was obvious to many in the media. It was said that Sutton wanted Chapman to play more slow and steady, while Chapman—and the fans—wanted to see his flair for the dramatic, going full-speed, shooting threes, and dunking the ball at the rim.

The 1987–88 season again saw a talented UK squad (Chapman and Ed Davender in the backcourt, Rob Lock, Winston Bennett, and Eric Manuel in the front court) come up short in the NCAAs.

After losing some important seniors (Davender and Bennett), everyone wanted to know if the frustrated Chapman would leave UK and turn pro. His decision was made a bit easier when in April, the infamous Emery package addressed to recruit Chris Mills popped open, revealing $1,000 in cash.

The NCAA had what it needed. Rex left, and Eddie Sutton was left with what everyone called "The Young and the Rexless." Most of the talent would eventually transfer, and it was a team that just was not very good. The final record was 13–19, the first losing record since before Adolph Rupp was coach.

Along the way, Cliff Hagan, then the athletic director, resigned. Dick Vitale made his opinion known on national television. He said Sutton should resign "for the good of the UK program."

Weeks after the season ended, Sutton did just that. His style was never quite embraced by the fanbase or his star players. He never quite won the big game. And he coached under the worst of circumstances. He really needed a change of scenery.

But all would turn out better for Sutton. He sought treatment for his personal demons, and he resurfaced at Oklahoma State where he would lead the Cowboys to the Final Four.

Maybe all he needed was to get out of Kentucky.

82 Derek Anderson and Ron Mercer—Thunder and Lightning

Derek Anderson and Ron Mercer were called Thunder and Lightning. But really, who was who? Both Derek Anderson and Ron Mercer could throw down hellacious dunks. Both were quicker than most of the other players in the country. So who was Thunder, and who, exactly, was Lightning?

I'm not sure the players themselves even knew. But together they were the two parts of a truly special team, one that could have gone on to win a national championship.

First, we must start at the beginning.

Derek Anderson

Out of high school, Derek Anderson knew where he wanted to go to college. He'd been a Louisville fan his entire life. Although Anderson was a top prospect out of Louisville Doss High, one widely regarded for his athleticism and jumping ability, Cards Coach Denny Crum did not want the 6'5" Anderson. Crum recruited other players instead.

So Anderson looked elsewhere, too. He liked the idea of playing at Ohio State and in the Big Ten, so he chose to be a Buckeye. After two seasons, he scored 554 points and had become a star. But after an unhappy two seasons in Columbus, Anderson decided to transfer, and this time, Louisville came calling. It was Anderson's turn to say no.

"At that time, Kentucky was the place to be, and it came down to UK or UCLA," Anderson said. "I just really liked the guys at UK, so that's where I went."

It was a good decision. Anderson sat out the 1994–95 season and watched the Wildcats get upset in the regional finals by North Carolina. He knew he could make an immediate impact as a junior. He was right, as he helped lead the Wildcats win the 1996 National Championship.

In the title game, with the Wildcats playing far from their best, Anderson scored a much-needed 11 points. But who was the big player who stepped up in the clutch when least expected to? It was a freshman named Ron Mercer.

Ron Mercer

At 6'7" and with the ability to slash to the hoop and step back and shoot, it was no wonder Mercer was the No. 1 recruit coming out of high school in 1995. A Nashville native, Mercer was already being called the next Michael Jordan. There were heavy expectations. And he wanted to ball with his friends at Vanderbilt.

Huh? The No. 1 player in the country wanted to play at Vandy?

It was true. Mercer sent off his paperwork. The only problem was his academic records would not be worthy of Vandy. His records would be fine at Kentucky.

Going against a player like Derek Anderson in practice everyday, as well as playing his freshman year with him, only made Ron Mercer better. He learned the speed of the college game, and when he was needed in the national title game, he stepped up to score those 20 points. No one was more confident than Mercer was before the 1996–97 season.

Well, maybe one person.

Thunder and Lightning

Anderson had been saying it since just minutes after the 1996 championship. "Repeat," he'd told the *Courier-Journal*.

Few paid attention or thought Anderson was anything close to a prophet. But he was close. When Anderson and Mercer both hit the court to defend the national title, few could beat them. There was a 34-point win over No. 12 Syracuse, another 34-point win over No. 8 Indiana, and a 20-point win over No. 16 Louisville. Mercer averaged a little more than 18 points per game, Anderson a little more than 17. They were roommates. And Anderson said they were like brothers.

Rapidly, many saw UK as a real threat to win another national title.

It would not last. On January 18 against Auburn that season, Anderson went down with a torn ACL in his knee. We enjoyed Thunder and Lightning for exactly one half of a season.

Afterward, Mercer was pressed to grow up quickly and he did, leading his team to a 35–5 record, an SEC Tournament championship, and a return trip to the Final Four and the national title game. UK played together, with role players like Scott Padgett and Cameron Mills stepping up to play much better than anyone ever thought they could.

Anderson actually was ready to play by the time the Final Four rolled around, but Coach Rick Pitino repeatedly said he would not risk further injury to Anderson and play him. Pitino said the only way Anderson would appear was if there was a technical foul and he needed someone to shoot free throws. In the semifinal game against

Minnesota, Coach Clem Haskins got a technical. Anderson was up in a hurry—he buried the two shots.

UK lost to Arizona in overtime in the title game. When asked if things would have been different if Anderson was in, the player smiled. "Man, I was ready to go," he said. "I could play. I think I should have been in there."

Both Anderson and Mercer entered the NBA Draft that year. Anderson was drafted in the first round by the Cleveland Cavaliers. He went on to an 11-year pro career and won a world championship in 2006 with the Miami Heat. Mercer was drafted in the first round by the Boston Celtics and enjoyed an eight-year pro career.

Kevin Grevey

In 1975, everything Kevin Grevey had worked for—everything he'd ever dreamed of—was right there for the taking.

He was a senior, and his University of Kentucky Wildcats had advanced to the national championship against UCLA. The Bruins defeated Louisville in the Final Four, putting an end to any talk of UK and U of L playing for a title. Instead, the Cats faced the Bruins, a team the Cats felt confident they could defeat.

"Yes, we thought we could beat them," Grevey said in an interview from a bar he owns just outside Washington D.C. "Then of course their coach had to open his mouth."

That would be John Wooden, the most successful coach in the history of college basketball. To that point in history Wooden had won nine national titles. Could they win a 10th? Wooden was going to try everything he could to ensure it happened.

On 1978

All told, 1978 was a pretty good year for Kevin Grevey. That year he watched his former teammates at Kentucky win the NCAA Championship with a victory over Duke.

He also participated in—and won—the NBA World Championship as a member of the Washington Bullets.

And finally, he met the woman he would marry in 1978.

Still, to this day, if he finds something with 78 written on it, he will buy it, he said.

"Sometimes you have horrible disappointments in life," Grevey said in *Game of My Life: Kentucky*. "Was the loss in the title game a tragedy? No, it was just a failure. But you can learn from these things. You become resilient."

Grevey was a sweet-shooting guard from Cincinnati who was productive in his first season. In fact, his freshman team went undefeated 22–0 and were known as the Super Kittens. A national championship as seniors seemed to be their birthright.

Then history occurred. On the day before the title game, Wooden held a press conference. He announced he was retiring after the title game. As if it weren't enough that UK had to face UCLA, now they had to beat the ghost of a legend, too. Coach Joe B. Hall told his team it would make no difference. He was wrong.

Grevey led the way with 34 points but didn't get much help, and UCLA's big front line muscled UK around. "It took me a full summer to get over that loss," Grevey said in the book, *Game of My Life: Kentucky*.

But Grevey couldn't hang his head. He averaged 23.6 points as a senior and led his team as far as it could go.

Later that year he was drafted by the Washington Bullets, and two years later he was starting for them, averaging 16 points per game. One year after that, he finally became a champion.

Chuck Hayes

If there was a typical Tubby Smith recruit, Chuck Hayes would be it.

Listed at 6'6" but probably really 6'5", Hayes was not glamorous. He was not a McDonald's All-American. He was not a great shooter. He did not blind you with great speed.

But as the song goes, all he did was win. He was a Parade All-American and Mr. Basketball in the state of California, and he chose Kentucky over Kansas.

A fan favorite from the start because of a toughness and willingness to rebound, the Modesto, California, native broke into the starting lineup early and was a member of some amazing teams. Paired alongside center Erik Daniels from Cincinnati, the two developed a second sense of where the other would be on the court. They became one of the best interior passing tandems that fans had seen in years.

Over Hayes' sophomore, junior, and senior seasons, UK went 87–15, finishing with rankings of first, second, and seventh in the nation. As a senior, Hayes was named the 2005 SEC Defensive Player of the Year.

The real sadness is that a winner like Hayes was unable to play in a Final Four. In 2003, Dwyane Wade and Marquette upset No. 1 UK in the regional finals. In 2004, Kentucky (again No. 1 in the nation) was upset by Alabama-Birmingham in the round of 32. In 2005, Kentucky lost a double-overtime thriller to Michigan State in the regional finals.

So close. But Hayes would find a place in the hearts of UK fans everywhere, as he finished seventh all-time in rebounds, eighth in

Chuck Hayes (44) shoots the winning shot in overtime with just seconds remaining to beat Louisiana State University 79–78 in their semifinal game of the Southeastern Conference tournament at the Georgia Dome in Atlanta on Saturday, March 12, 2005. Hayes was defended by LSU's Glen Davis.
(AP Photo/Bill Haber)

From D-League to Millionaire

Despite being the MVP of the Portsmouth pre-draft camp, Chuck Hayes was not drafted by an NBA team. Instead, he was signed as a free agent by the Houston Rockets and played in several preseason games before being cut. Then he was drafted by the Albuquerque Thunderbirds of the NBA Developmental League. During that season he led the league in rebounding with 12.2 per game.

In 2006, Houston experienced a multitude of injuries. They gave Hayes a 10-day contract, and in his second game he nabbed a double-double: 12 points and 13 rebounds in a double overtime win over Chicago. Houston signed Hayes for the rest of the season. After a productive year, Houston picked up the option on Hayes' contract, keeping him for the following season.

Hayes was a starter for most of the 2006–07 season. He signed an endorsement deal with Chinese athletic apparel company Li Ning for $5 million, upped his contract with the Rockets to an incentive-laden deal worth $8 million over four years, and by 2009 was co-captain of the team with Shane Battier.

As a free agent in 2011, Hayes got his big payday—a 4-year, $22 million deal from the Sacramento Kings, where he still plays.

That's how you go from the D-League to being a millionaire.

steals, 13th in blocked shots, and 40th in points. He also tied Alex Groza for most consecutive starts with 110.

And perhaps Hayes' best times were ahead of him—when he would become a longtime NBA veteran.

85 Go to YouTube and Check Out UKCAT8FAN's Videos

Check out UKCAT8FAN's videos on YouTube. Most Big Blue fans know him—they just don't really know him.

I try to read as much as I can about Kentucky on the Internet and in the newspapers, so when someone finds something cool online it's normally posted somewhere. Eventually, I'll see it. This is the case with the one they call UKCAT8FAN. An amateur videographer, he makes the most interesting and inspiring videos about UK basketball I've ever seen. Normally set to great music, we see highlights spliced between interviews and sound bytes.

We caught up with UKCAT8FAN one day around breakfast and, at long last, everyone in Big Blue country—meet Tim Matthews.

Your Name: Tim Matthews

Your Age: 33

Where you're from: I grew up in Grayson, Kentucky, but am now living in Pikeville.

What you do for a living: I'm a metallurgical analyst at Mineral Labs Inc.

How you got to be a Cats fan in the first place: I'm basically a self-made Cats fan. I really had nobody else in my family who shared my love for basketball. I started watching the Cats at around 11 years old during the Unforgettables season. That team stole my heart, and I've been a die-hard Cats fan ever since.

What was the first video you made: The very first Kentucky video I made was actually of Jodie Meeks' 54-point game (at Tennessee), but the first video I made that got some attention was one called, "They're Baaaacck!" I made it shortly after Calipari arrived and signed his first class.

How you get inspiration: Good question. I don't think there's any one thing that inspires me; it's basically just my love for Kentucky basketball as a whole. I see special moments happen throughout the season, and I instantly start to piece together videos in my mind. I can pretty much envision my entire video before I ever begin work on it. The challenge is bringing that vision to life just the way I pictured it.

Your favorite team of all time: Even though the Unforgettables are the ones that stole my heart, and this past season's team was truly special as well, my favorite team is still the 1996 champs. I was totally obsessed with that team all season long. They were the first championship team I ever witnessed, so they remain at the top of my list.

Your Favorite Player: I'm not sure I can pick just one, but my all-time starting five would be Jamal Mashburn, Tony Delk, Anthony Davis, Jodie Meeks, and Tayshaun Prince.

Anything else we need to include: Maybe include which videos are my personal favorites. I would have to say "The Pursuit for No. 8," "Round 2," and "This is Our Time" are my top three. Even though I made them, I still watch them occasionally as just a fan like everyone else.

Find these videos and more at youtube.com, www.ukcat8fan. blogspot.com, twitter.com/ukcat8fan, or www.facebook.com/ UKCAT8FAN.

86 Jeff Sheppard

Legend has it that in elementary school, when the teacher asked the children to write reports on what they wanted to do when they grew up, Jeff Sheppard wrote about how he wanted to play basketball for the University of Kentucky.

His hero was Rex Chapman, and as Sheppard grew, he modeled his game after his hero. An outstanding leaper, Sheppard also wanted to develop into a better shooter and leader.

By the time Sheppard left UK, he was both.

Sheppard came into UK in the mid-1990s as a shooter, and as Rick Pitino tended to do, he played Sheppard out of position and then recruited over him. For a year Pitino tried to make Sheppard a point guard, which did not work. In 1996, Pitino had Ron Mercer, Derek Anderson, and Allen Edwards as swingmen, along with Cameron Mills off the bench. Tony Delk was the starting shooting guard. Sheppard played sparingly, but the team won a title.

With everyone but Delk returning, Pitino convinced Sheppard to redshirt. (As it turns out, Pitino really needed Sheppard that year when Anderson got hurt, but who can see the future, right?) Anyway, Sheppard sat out the 1997 season and came back ready for his senior year.

But of course, Pitino left, and Tubby Smith arrived, and he and the team had to get acquainted. Looking back, Kentucky was loaded with talent. Included on that team were Sheppard, Scott Padgett, Wayne Turner, Jamaal Magloire, Nazr Mohammed, Heshimu Evans, Allen Edwards, Cameron Mills, and Michael Bradley, among others.

It took about one regular season for Kentucky and Tubby to get on the same page. Luckily, it was just the regular season, and they still had a full postseason to go. That's when things, as they say, got real.

The Cats won the SEC Tourney and earned a No. 2 seed going into the NCAA Tournament. The top seed? Duke. The teams met in the regional finals in another epic game. Sheppard scored 17 in the comeback win over Duke, sending Kentucky to its third consecutive Final Four. And Sheppard only got better.

Turning into a great clutch player in big moments, Sheppard dropped a career-high 27 points in UK's 86–85 semifinal overtime win over Stanford, then he scored another 16 points in the national championship game over Utah. Down 64–63 with less than five minutes remaining in the game, Sheppard's baseline jumper put the Cats up for good on the way to the title.

"Shep," as they call him, was named Most Outstanding Player of the tournament.

He went on to play a year for the Atlanta Hawks and then played overseas. Now he runs an athletic apparel company.

"I am just so blessed," Sheppard said in the book, *Game of My Life: Kentucky.* "Very few people get to live out their dreams."

87 1997: Almost a Three-Peat

Four players had left for the NBA. The top remaining scorer was lost to injury. The next season's top scorer was redshirting and could not play. Two players who had scored a combined 43 points during the previous season were pivotal parts of the playing rotation, as was another reserve who had scored all of 28 points in his last season before he flunked out of school. If the team had been placed in a Hollywood movie, the 1996–97 Wildcats would have won the NCAA title, and the movie would have bombed because it was unbelievable. In real life, the team almost did win the title, and it was indeed unbelievable.

The top three scorers from the 1995–96 title team—Delk, Walker, and McCarty—were in the NBA when the 1997 season began, as was solid veteran Mark Pope, who was sixth on that team in scoring. Another solid contributor from the previous year, senior Jeff Sheppard, would redshirt in 1996–97 and thus also be unavailable. UK returned Derek Anderson (9.4 points per game in 1995–96), Ron Mercer (8 PPG), Anthony Epps (6.7 PPG), Wayne

Turner (4.5 PPG), and a few other reserves from the end of the long 1995–96 bench.

The 1996–97 squad began the season ranked No. 3, and promptly lost the season opener to Clemson. UK regrouped, as Mercer and Anderson developed a Michael Jordan and Scottie Pippen–like rapport as UK's "Air Pair." Memorably, the two combined for 56 points in a 34-point thumping of Bob Knight's Indiana Hoosiers. With the talented duo leading the way, UK was No. 5 in the nation and had a 16–2 record after a January 18 win against Auburn. However, Anderson, who was leading the SEC at 18.6 points per game, blew out his knee in that game and was shut down for the season.

Displaying amazing resiliency, UK just refashioned itself in midseason. Mercer would have to take on the star mantle alone, though he was aided by rock-steady guards Turner and Epps, as well as sophomore Scott Padgett, and a low post attack of senior Jared Prickett, a vastly improving Mohammed, and freshman Jamaal Magloire. Also, junior Cameron Mills, who had scored 31 points in 2½ seasons, suddenly turned into Larry Bird. Mills finished the season shooting a sizzling 53 percent from three-point range, and the young man who had never scored in double figures at UK before Anderson's injury averaged double-figure scoring in both the SEC and NCAA Tournaments.

UK lost only twice more in the 1996–97 regular season, both times against South Carolina. After winning three games in the SEC Tournament by 42, 18, and 27 points, UK was seeded No. 1 in the West region. After surviving a tough second-round game against Iowa, UK beat St. Joseph's and Utah by 15 and 13 points, respectively, to earn a second consecutive Final Four trip. Mills shot 13-of-18 (72 percent) from three-point range during the first four NCAA games, and Mercer and Turner scored in double figures in each game.

UK played Minnesota in the Final Four. UK won 78–69, with the greatest highlight being a technical foul on Minnesota coach Clem Haskins, resulting in Derek Anderson—torn knee and all—checking in to drain two free throws. Mercer had 19 points with the eternally solid Epps adding 13 and Mills netting 10 as UK returned to the national title game.

In the final, Arizona and its talented guard Miles Simon camped out at the free throw line (41 Arizona attempts to 17 for UK) and won in overtime 84–79. Bad luck may have finally caught up with UK. Mohammed, a 54-percent free throw shooter coming in, was 0-for-6 at the line. Odds of this occurring were roughly 1:109. After beating the odds so many times in 1996–97, maybe it was inevitable that in the final game the odds beat UK. There would be no Hollywood ending. But if the ending was not up to par, the reality of the 1996–97 season was still little short of miraculous.

88 Jodie Meeks

While Jodie Meeks may not have been Tubby Smith's best recruit (think: Tayshaun Prince, Keith Bogans, Rajon Rondo), Meeks definitely deserves to be in the conversation. At a time when Smith was on the tail end of his career at UK, there were more notable misses than hits in the Smith recruiting regime.

But Meeks was a find—and he was a big hit from Day 1 on the UK campus. A star out of Norcross, Georgia, the 6'4" guard was heavily recruited (he chose the Wildcats over Florida), but he was not a McDonald's All-American. He did lead his team to the state championship, however, and he was named the Atlanta Player of the Year by various local newspapers.

Jodie Meeks (23) drives around Georgia's Corey Butler during the first half of their game at Stegeman Coliseum on Saturday, January 18, 2009, in Athens, Georgia. (AP Photo/John Curry)

His freshman year at UK (the 2006–07 season) showed flashes of brilliance. In Meeks' first game, an exhibition against Lindsey Wilson College, he came off the bench to score 17 points, grab four rebounds, and dish five assists. What the fans loved most about the freshman was his pure shooting stroke. It was as if every time he let one fly, you just knew it was going in. But his true coming-out party came later that season against Louisville in Freedom Hall. That day Meeks scored a career-high 18 points and led UK to victory.

In three separate weeks he was honored as the SEC Freshman of the Week, and Meeks was named to several conference and freshman All-American teams. His future looked bright. But things got strange.

Coach Tubby Smith decided he was finished in Lexington and left for the head coaching position at Minnesota. The school hired a new coach named Billy Gillispie—and Meeks' fortunes would be forever changed.

The 2007–08 season, his sophomore year, was a bust. He came out on fire, scorching Pikeville College for 34 points, and things looked to be big for Meeks that year. Sadly, injuries (including a sports hernia) limited Meeks to only 11 games as a sophomore. And after the season, a disappointing one by UK standards, Meeks was healed and ready to lead his team the next season.

There was only one problem: he and Gillispie seemed to be at odds all the time.

In the season opener against the Virginia Military Institute, Meeks scored 39 points—but UK lost 111–103. He dropped 37 on Kansas State that same year in the Findlay Tournament in Las Vegas, which Kentucky would go on to win. Maybe things were turning around. On December 20, Meeks scored 46 against Appalachian State in Freedom Hall. He hit nine three-pointers in the game that tied the school record held by Tony Delk.

Then he scored a UK record 54 points in a 90–72 win at Tennessee. It was a magical night, in a nationally televised game on

The 54-Point Game

Meeks said he knew early on that he was "feeling it" in his legendary 54-point game against Tennessee on January 13, 2009.

He scored in any number of ways, from three-pointers and free throws to layups and putbacks. In the game, Meeks hit 10-of-15 three-pointers, breaking the record of nine three-pointers in a game, which he shared with Tony Delk. He also went 14–14 from the free throw line.

Dan Issel formerly held the scoring record for UK, which was 53 points in a 120–85 win against Ole Miss on February 7, 1970. Of course, back then there was no three-point line.

And just like Issel's father back in the day, Meeks' dad was in the crowd that night to see it happen.

"To be in the same sentence as guys like Dan Issel and other Kentucky legends, it means a lot," Meeks told ESPN that night. "It's kind of mind-boggling to me."

ESPN, but even it was marred by controversy as word leaked out afterword that Gillispie had told Meeks to stop being so selfish and get his teammates more involved. As Gillispie famously said, "We are not the University of Jodie Meeks."

Meeks continued to have an All-American–type season and still feuded with his coach. Against Florida in Rupp Arena, Meeks hit the game-winning three-pointer; he scored 45 in a win at Arkansas; and he set the UK season record for three-pointers made in a season with 117.

But the season was a disappointment, as Kentucky finished just 20–13 overall and 8–8 in the SEC. The team did not make it to the NCAA Tournament, breaking a streak of 17 years of earning a bid. UK accepted a bid to the National Invitational Tournament, where they won two games before being knocked out in the third round by Notre Dame 77–67.

Meeks was named to the All-SEC first team as well as a second-team All-American.

Even when Gillispie was fired after that season and John Calipari was brought in to coach the team, Meeks felt his time in Lexington was done. He decided to put his name in the NBA Draft, where he was selected No. 41 overall in the second round by the Milwaukee Bucks. Now with the Philadelphia 76ers, Meeks has been in the league for three years and has made two playoff appearances.

89 Wayne Turner: The Ultimate Winner

When Wayne Turner arrived in Lexington as a freshman in the fall of 1995, some wondered just how much he would accomplish. Turner was small (generously listed at 6'2"), rail thin (equally generously weighed at 190 pounds as a senior), was a poor foul shooter (less than 63 percent for his career), and had an awkward, corkscrew jump shot. However, by the time he graduated four years later, Wayne Turner was the all-time Wildcats leader in one pivotal category—wins.

Turner played in 151 of the 152 games UK played in his four seasons, posting a career record of 131–20 in those games. As the NCAA does not list a record for most wins for a player, it is not entirely clear whether Turner would hold such a record. It appears that Turner's record was tied by Duke's Shane Battier, who also won 131 games. Three Memphis players won 134 games under John Calipari in the 2000s, but one season's worth of those wins were vacated by the NCAA due to no fault of those players.

In Turner's case, his career got off to a memorable start with an NCAA title in his freshman year in 1996. Turner backed up Anthony Epps at point guard, starting only one game. He played

13 minutes per game and scored 4.5 points per game. Turner played in every game that season, except the last one, UK's title win over Syracuse at the Meadowlands.

In 1996–97, Turner helped UK return to the title game. He played with Epps again, this time averaging 23 minutes, 6.6 points, and three assists per game. Turner was named to the All-NCAA region team, showing the clutch scoring skills that would become his calling card as he increased his production to 12.7 points per game in the NCAA Tournament. The Cats lost the All-Wildcat championship game to Arizona, but Turner's stock was on the rise.

The following season, in 1997–98, Turner finished the job, leading UK to its seventh NCAA title as the starting point guard. Taking the reins of Coach Tubby Smith's first Kentucky squad, Turner was MVP of the SEC Tournament and was chosen as Most Outstanding Player of the East region of the NCAA Tournament. Turner averaged just better than nine points and four assists per game for the season, and he again upped his production in the crucial moments. He scored 16 points and had eight assists in UK's regional final revenge win over Duke. It is that image of Turner that sticks with UK fans—rallying UK from a 17-point deficit by breaking down Duke's defense (especially Duke's Steve Wojciechowski) again and again, driving and scoring or driving and dishing to open teammates. Two games later, Turner and the Cats celebrated in San Antonio as they cut down the Utah Utes and then the championship nets.

As a senior in 1998–99, Turner's attempt to return for a fourth time to the Final Four was denied when Michigan State rallied to oust the Cats in the NCAA regional final. Turner averaged more than 10 points per game and raised himself to fourth on the UK career assists list with 494. Turner ended his career with 1,170 career points and is still UK's career steals leader with 238, a full 37 steals more than Tony Delk, who is second.

Turner pursued a professional career after his time at UK, playing very briefly for Rick Pitino with the NBA's Boston Celtics. Turner returned to UK for the 2010–11 season, helping out as a member of the UK basketball staff while he completed his undergraduate degree. As Turner had been away from college for eleven years, it was probably a difficult transition back to life as a student. But as any UK fan had long since learned, whatever it looked like, Wayne Turner would find a way to win. Turner graduated in May 2011.

90 Pitino's 1989–90 UK Coaching Staff

The 1989–90 Kentucky squad battled to a 14–14 season. The team on the court was lacking in depth (eight scholarship players), height (no player taller than 6'7"), and experience (only two players with substantial prior college playing time). The coaching Cats were a veritable Murderers' Row.

Little needs to be said of then-UK maestro Rick Pitino's coaching abilities. Having taken Providence and Louisville to the Final Four, as well as making three such trips with UK, Pitino has won 627 NCAA games as of the beginning of the 2012–13 season, and has made 17 NCAA tournament appearances, as well as two NBA playoff appearances.

Ralph Willard was the associate head coach on the 1989–90 team. He parlayed that season into the Western Kentucky University head coaching job in 1990–91. Willard won 336 games as a head coach at WKU, Pittsburgh, and Holy Cross before returning to the Pitino coaching tree as an assistant with Louisville. Willard coached six NCAA Tournament teams and enjoyed a Sweet 16 run at WKU in 1993.

Assistant coach Tubby Smith, while not a household name at the time, has gone on to win 490 NCAA games himself, including his 1998 NCAA title at UK. Tubby has made 16 NCAA tourney appearances, including nine trips to the NCAA's Sweet 16. Tubby was promoted to associate coach after the 1989–90 season and left for his first head coaching job at Tulsa after 1990–91. From Tulsa, Smith has gone on to coach at Georgia, UK, and Minnesota.

Assistant Herb Sendek was often ribbed by Pitino for being an honors graduate of Carnegie Mellon University. Sendek had to be pretty smart to be part of this amazing coaching staff. He would stay at UK for four seasons with Pitino before taking the head coaching job at Miami of Ohio. Sendek has since coached at North Carolina State and Arizona State. In total, he has won 352 games through 2011–12. His assistant coaches have included current Arizona head coach Sean Miller and Ohio State coach Thad Matta. Sendek has coached in seven NCAA tournaments, including a Sweet 16 run at NC State in 2005.

Rookie coach Billy Donovan was 24 years old and one year removed from playing for Pitino with the New York Knicks when he was added to the UK staff. Donovan was noted for participating in many UK practices, as the team was short on numbers. While his jump shot may have been ahead of his coaching in 1989, the ensuing years have been rather kind. Including a brief tenure at Marshall, Donovan has won 421 games and has bettered Pitino with two NCAA titles of his own as the head coach of the Florida Gators. Donovan has made a dozen NCAA Tournament appearances, including three trips to the national title game. At only age 47, Donovan has a fine chance to end up as the winningest coach on this staff, which is no mean feat.

Possibly the most important coaching hire that Pitino made was strength and conditioning coach Ray "Rock" Oliver. Oliver, who had worked at the University of Pittsburgh, was talked into the UK job under Pitino by his friend, John Calipari. Oliver trained the 1989–90 squad in grueling and backbreaking fashion. The high speed and constant tenacity of the team had as much to do with Rock's training as Rick's coaching. Oliver went on to coach in the NFL and NBA before returning to UK.

The grand total among Pitino and his 1989–90 assistant coaches: 2,226 collegiate victories, 58 NCAA Tournament appearances, ten Final Four appearances, and four NCAA titles. To put that in perspective, no university has amassed that many wins or tournament appearances, and only six schools (including UK) have amassed ten Final Four appearances. While Pitino might not have yet brought in Jamal Mashburn, Tony Delk, or Ron Mercer, his first UK dream team of coaches was every bit as amazing as the players who would follow.

91 The Comeback Against Kansas

The 1978–79 season figured to be a tough one for Coach Joe B. Hall. All-Americans Jack Givens and Rick Robey had moved on to the NBA. Starting center Mike Phillips and sixth man extraordinaire James Lee had also exhausted their eligibility. The 1978–79 Cats figured to feature guard Kyle Macy, a cast of former reserves, and talented but inexperienced youngsters.

In the third game of the season, on December 9, 1978, UK faced a marquee matchup with No. 5 Kansas. The Cats were ranked 10th in the nation, and the two schools were the top two in all-time NCAA hoops victories. Kansas featured All-American Darnell Valentine, and even ardent UK fans realized this would be a tough match-up.

Kansas opened up a seven-point halftime advantage 35–28. Kentucky fought back bravely to a 56–56 count at the end of regulation. However, in the extra five minutes of overtime, Valentine and the Jayhawks took control of the game. Valentine, who scored 27 points to lead all scorers, knocked down two free throws with 31 seconds left, boosting Kansas to a 66–60 advantage. UK starting guard Truman Claytor and top reserve Jay Shidler had each fouled out, and in an era before the three-point shot, it was a foregone conclusion that UK had suffered its first loss of the young season.

However, no one bothered to tell Kentucky. Freshman guard Dwight Anderson had only played 10 minutes in the game and had not scored. However, with the Cats in desperation mode, Anderson drove the lane and dropped in a basket to cut the Kansas advantage to 66–62 with 22 seconds left. Still, the clock continued to run and Kansas was in the bonus and would shoot free throws on a UK foul. The Jayhawks were not alarmed.

Kentucky was in a defensive press, denying any inbounds pass for Kansas. With 16 seconds left, a frustrated Valentine, trying to get open before a five-second violation would be called, shoved UK's Anderson in the back and was immediately whistled for a foul. The clock stopped, and Anderson went to the foul line with a chance to cut further into the Kansas lead. Anderson did not make matters any easier when he missed the front of a one-and-one. UK missed a shot on the rebound, but Anderson eventually corralled the loose ball and was fouled in the act of shooting with 10 seconds on the clock.

This time, Anderson made good on both free throws, cutting the Kansas lead to 66–64 with 10 seconds remaining. Still, if Kansas could merely inbound the ball, the game was virtually over.

Kansas could not. Anderson, living up to his nickname of "The Blur," sprinted into the corner, saving an errant KU pass all the way across court to Macy on the left wing. The All-American canned a

15' jump shot to tie the score at 66 with four ticks on the clock. In the pandemonium, Kansas signaled for a timeout. They had none.

A technical foul was properly assessed, and Macy, always a cool customer at the charity stripe, rolled home the winning shot. UK connected on an inbounds pass, and to the delight and amazement of the Rupp Arena partisans, a 7–0 run in the last 22 seconds of overtime left Kentucky with an improbable victory over a formidable, if now shell-shocked, Kansas squad.

Of course, in basketball miracle endings are the exception rather than the rule. The 1978–79 Wildcats struggled without the veterans of the previous year's squad. In fact, the team ended the season by losing in the first round of the NIT. Anderson, who showed worlds of potential as a freshman, would play only a year and a half as a Wildcat before transferring to Southern California. However, on one memorable December night in Lexington, Dwight "The Blur" Anderson and the never-say-die Cats shocked everyone.

92 Meet UK Elvis: Rick Cothern

Most of the time you can see him at important home games or on the road at the SEC and NCAA Tournaments. With those sunglasses, those sideburns, and that jumpsuit it's easy to see that Rick Cothern of Bowling Green, Kentucky, is a great Elvis impersonator.

Every UK fan should go up and get a picture with him. "Why shur," he'll say, before smiling for your camera.

Cothern, a professional Elvis impersonator, has been following the Cats for years, but you can also see him dressed for Tennessee Titans games in Nashville, too.

Kentucky fan and Elvis impersonator Rick Cothern (left) of Bowling Green, Kentucky, cheers for the Kentucky Wildcats as they arrive on court for the championship game of the Southeastern Conference basketball tournament at the Georgia Dome in Atlanta on Sunday, March 13, 2005. Kentucky was about to face the Florida Gators. (AP Photo/John Bazemore)

"I'd rent some of the Elvis movies and try to pick up some of his facial expressions and some of the little lines he said," Cothern told the *Bowling Green Daily News* in 2000. "I haven't really perfected the singing part yet."

He's been known to take his stepsons, Dakota and Tyler Jopes, with him when they were younger and dress them like Elvis, too. Cothern says he likes dressing up because he keeps getting on national television and *Monday Night Football*. Plus, people keep high-fiving him and asking him to be in pictures. He said he likes to make fans happy.

"When I was young I watched all these crazy characters that helped create the ambiance," he told the paper. "I never thought I'd be one of those crazy characters."

Well, he had some idea. When he began in the mid-1990s, he would go to games wearing crazy masks, like those of Richard Nixon or Ronald Reagan or Jimmy Carter. But they got too hot. He needed a character that could be iconic yet not make him sweat through his costume.

"He's a true fan," said Nick Wilkins, a friend who got Cothern his first jumpsuit and still supplies the faux Elvis with a wig every year. "He's very energetic and works the crowd. He's an icon."

And when the SEC Tournament was being held in Memphis, Cothern decided to show up in the character Memphis loves the most—Elvis. So he got a wig. He got some blue suede shoes. He got some sunglasses, and he was good to go.

He was an instant success. When he's there, you can easily find him in the crowd, and chances are, if the national TV cameras are there, he will be, too.

Just mosey on over and say hello. But don't you dare step on his blue suede shoes.

93 UK and Arkansas Rivalry

Hogs vs. Cats. It used to be prime-time television scheduled right before the Super Bowl—Nolan Richardson's Arkansas Razorbacks versus Rick Pitino's Kentucky Wildcats. Both teams liked to run and gun. Arkansas wanted to pressure you like hell for 40 minutes. Kentucky wanted to unleash its full-court press and see if your point guard could survive.

For the majority of the games, both teams were ranked in the top 10, sometimes the top five. And you could bet the teams would

The 1995 SEC Tourney Comeback

No game stands out more in this rivalry than the amazing comeback(s) of the 1995 SEC Tournament game. It was No. 3 UK versus No. 5 Arkansas. The Hogs were the defending National Champs and brought back much of that same squad. In the first half, UK could hit nothing. Arkansas, however, couldn't miss. The score was 35–16 with just more than nine minutes to go in the first frame. But the Cats started to mount a comeback with better defense and improved shooting. At the half it was the Hogs by six, 50–44. Arkansas came out in the second half like it did in the first, rebuilding its lead. But again UK stormed back, tying the game at 80, and with just less than six seconds left, Rodrick Rhodes stole the ball and was fouled. He had two shots to win the game with 1.3 seconds remaining. He missed both shots. Rhodes, in tears on the bench, then watched as UK went down 91–82 in the overtime only to again come back. This time, the Hogs missed 4-of-6 free throws, and Tony Delk hit a three to cut the score to 93–90 with 39 seconds left. An Antoine Walker steal and layup cut the lead to one, and an Anthony Epps steal and two free throws gave UK a 94–93 lead. Scotty Thurman's long three missed, and Tony Delk rebounded and was fouled. He made 1-of-2 to close out UK's remarkable 95–93 overtime victory and the SEC Tournament title.

match up again in the SEC Tournament later in the year. It was great theater.

It all started when Arkansas first joined the SEC from the old Southwest Conference in the 1991–92 season. The Razorbacks were scheduled to come into Rupp that year and play Pitino's highly ranked Wildcats squad.

"They had no clue what kind of team we had," former Arkansas head coach Nolan Richardson told the *Herald-Leader* in 2012. "We had played teams like Alabama, Vanderbilt, a couple [others] in the SEC. And to me, they weren't that good. So we went into the [SEC] thinking, 'They're not as good as we are.' I thought Big O [Oliver Miller] and [Todd] Day and [Lee] Mayberry, no way they thought Kentucky was as good as we were."

The Razorbacks came into that first game with no fear—and they demolished Kentucky 105–88, sending a message to the Wildcats: we're here, deal with it.

For the better part of the next decade, the two teams fought absolute wars. More often than not, Arkansas would win the regular season game and Kentucky would take the matchup in the SEC Tourney.

"That was always a classic," Richardson told the newspaper. "You had the two flagship teams…Kentucky and Arkansas. We dominated the television rights back in those times. That made it a huge game every year whether you played it at Rupp Arena or played at our place."

And of course, it made it even better that each team was a threat to make the Final Four, with Arkansas wining the title in 1994, then making it back to the title game in 1995, and Kentucky making it to the next three title games, winning in 1996 and 1998.

While the two teams met up for some important games before 1992 (like a memorable Final Four showdown in 1978, won by UK by five points on the road to its fifth national title), the spice really started with the arrival of Arkansas in the SEC. Since the departure of Nolan Richardson, the Arkansas teams have been lackluster, but with new coach—former Richardson assistant Mike Anderson at the helm for the Razorbacks, the excitement is back in Fayetteville, and the rivalry is expected to be fun again very soon.

Date	Home Team	Visiting Team	Location	SEC Tournament
2012/01/17	Kentucky 86	Arkansas 63	Rupp Arena	
2011/02/23	Arkansas 77	Kentucky 76	Bud Walton Arena	
2010/01/23	Kentucky 101	Arkansas 70	Rupp Arena	
2009/02/14	Arkansas 63	Kentucky 79	Bud Walton Arena	
2008/02/23	Kentucky 63	Arkansas 58	Rupp Arena	
2007/02/03	Arkansas 74	Kentucky 82	Bud Walton Arena	
2006/01/29	Kentucky 78	Arkansas 76	Rupp Arena	
2005/01/29	Arkansas 67	Kentucky 68	Bud Walton Arena	
2004/02/18	Kentucky 73	Arkansas 56	Rupp Arena	
2003/02/19	Arkansas 50	Kentucky 66	Bud Walton Arena	
2002/02/23	Kentucky 71	Arkansas 58	Rupp Arena	
2001/03/10	Kentucky 87	Arkansas 78	Gaylord Entertainment Center	Yes
2001/02/25	Arkansas 82	Kentucky 78	Bud Walton Arena	
2000/03/10	Kentucky 72	Arkansas 86	Georgia Dome	Yes
2000/02/26	Kentucky 60	Arkansas 55	Rupp Arena	
1999/03/07	Arkansas 63	Kentucky 76	Stegeman Coliseum	Yes
1999/02/20	Arkansas 74	Kentucky 70	Bud Walton Arena	
1998/03/07	Kentucky 99	Arkansas 74	Georgia Dome	Yes
1998/01/17	Kentucky 80	Arkansas 77	Rupp Arena	
1997/01/26	Arkansas 73	Kentucky 83	Bud Walton Arena	
1996/03/09	Kentucky 95	Arkansas 75	New Orleans Superdome	Yes
1996/02/11	Kentucky 88	Arkansas 73	Rupp Arena	
1995/03/12	Kentucky 95	Arkansas 93	Georgia Dome	Yes
1995/01/29	Arkansas 94	Kentucky 92	Bud Walton Arena	
1994/03/12	Kentucky 90	Arkansas 78	The Pyramid, Memphis	Yes
1994/02/09	Kentucky 82	Arkansas 90	Rupp Arena	
1993/03/13	Kentucky 92	Arkansas 81	Rupp Arena	Yes
1993/02/10	Arkansas 101	Kentucky 94	Barnhill Arena	
1992/01/25	Kentucky 88	Arkansas 105	Rupp Arena	

94 Brandon Knight

It could be said that Brandon Knight's one and only season in a UK uniform produced two of the biggest game-winning shots in one season since Patrick Sparks hit three free throws to beat Louisville, then came back to hit a bouncing, roll-around-the-rim three at the buzzer to send the 2005 regional final against Michigan State into overtime.

Did Knight's shots mean more? Probably—they got UK back to the Final Four and, in doing so, made the young point guard from Florida a Kentucky folk hero.

But we'll get to all of that in a second.

Knight chose to come to Kentucky over Kansas, Connecticut, and his home state school of Florida because he wanted to be the next in line of the great Calipari point guards. First there was Derrick Rose, who was NCAA Player of the Year, a No. 1 NBA Draft pick, NBA Rookie of the Year, and the NBA's Most Valuable Player. In college, Rose took his team to the Final Four and almost won a national title.

Secondly, there was Tyreke Evans, who took his college team to the Sweet 16 and went on to become another lottery pick who won NBA Rookie of the Year. John Wall followed Evans, and Wall took his team to an Elite Eight, won the Rupp National Player of the Year Award, and also became the No. 1 pick in the NBA Draft.

Say what you will about Calipari, but he knows how to develop young talent.

Brandon Knight, a super scorer and McDonald's All-American who twice won the Gatorade Player of the Year Award, was ready to be next in line of the great point guards. Kentucky fans had to get used to a new system and a new point guard—with new talents.

Brandon Knight drives past Vanderbilt's Brad Tinsley during the second half of their game in Lexington, Kentucky, on Tuesday, March 1, 2011. Knight had 17 points in the 68–66 Kentucky win. (AP Photo/Ed Reinke)

Knight was a deadeye shooter, and even if he'd had a bad night, he still believed the next shot was going in. He was much more of a scoring point guard, while Wall preferred to dish. And because of his skills, Kentucky could run many more pick-and-roll plays with Knight and the forwards.

But Brandon was more than a basketball player. He was a 4.0 student who loved to read Shakespeare. One of his favorite school subjects was math, and he came to UK with almost a year's worth of college credits under his belt.

On the court, Knight came into the 2010–11 season with—again—a No. 1 recruiting class of himself, shooter Doron Lamb, power forward Terrence Jones, center Enes Kanter, and forward Stacey Poole. While most agreed the class was not as powerful as the previous season's of Cousins, Wall, and Bledsoe, Brandon Knight's team was going to be very exciting.

Even when the NCAA ruled Kanter ineligible early in the season, backup center Josh Harrellson stepped up to fill the role admirably, combining with Jones to make one of the most efficient front lines in the country.

But it took a while for this team to come around. Going into the 28th game of the season, Kentucky was ranked No. 22 in the land. It was 19–8, 7–6 in the SEC, and all its conference losses had come on the road. Fans were wondering if this team would come around.

It did, and according to Knight, it started that night when UK played No. 13 Florida at Rupp Arena on February 26, 2011. Led by Lamb, Knight, and junior Darius Miller's 24 points, UK beat Florida 76–68. A three by Miller with four minutes to play gave the Cats an 11-point lead, and they never looked back.

They won 10 games in a row, defeating Florida again in the SEC Tourney final and chugging right along to the Final Four.

Knight saved his best (and you could say some of his worst) for last. Let's explain. Kentucky, a No. 4 seed in the region, faced

Princeton in the first round of the 2011 NCAA Tournament. At 25–6, the champs of the Ivy League always seemed to be a formidable foe in the NCAAs. They proved it once again. By double-teaming Knight the entire game, the freshman was forced to take bad shots, and he had zero points for the first 39 minutes of the game. Still, Kentucky was up by a bucket when Princeton hit a step-back shot to tie the game with a little more than 36 seconds to play.

The previous day, UK Coach John Calipari told the media, "You can't count on freshmen." Apparently that didn't apply to Knight, the holder of UK's freshman scoring record of 657 points.

Naturally, Calipari put the ball in the hands of his star freshman (who had scored zero points) and told him to make a play. Off the inbound, Knight shimmied, drove to the right of the hoop, and scooped up a shot that went in and provided the difference in the game.

Survive and advance, right?

In the second round, UK faced the team that knocked it out of the tournament the previous year—West Virginia. This time the story for UK, and for Knight, would be different. The freshman scored a career-high 30 points to help defeat the Mountaineers and get Kentucky back into the Sweet 16. Knight came out on fire, scoring 14 of his team's first 21 points.

That's when the real fun began. In a made-for-TV matchup if there ever was one, Kentucky faced No. 1 Ohio State for a spot in the Elite Eight. Many Kentucky fans thought they were already playing with house money. *Bring on the No. 1 team*, they thought.

The game was an instant classic, with a lead often switching hands, and it went back-and-forth until the final horn. Harrellson held his own against the Buckeyes' All-American center Jared Sullinger, and six Kentucky players scored at least six points or more. Kentucky led by three until Ohio State tied it on a three with 21 seconds to go.

Calipari elected not to take a time out and instead let Knight, who this time had just seven total points, do his thing. After bringing the ball up court on the right side, Knight again shimmied his defender, but this time he got some space and rose up from 15' for the jumper. He drained it.

The Buckeyes could only muster an off-balance three at the end and it missed, sending the UK players into a frenzy.

The Cats then went on to beat North Carolina 76–69 for a spot in the Final Four. Knight led the way with 22 points, seven rebounds, and four assists. It would be the first Final Four appearance for UK in 13 years.

Kentucky's magical run came to an end with a loss in the Final Four to eventual champ Connecticut 56–55. Knight scored 17 points on 6-of-23 from the field. It wasn't a great shooting night for anyone.

After the season, Knight was selected eighth overall in the NBA Draft by the Detroit Pistons. But Knight's two shots will go down in UK history, and they will always be remembered.

95 Patrick Patterson

May 16, 2007, was probably one of the least productive work days in many offices across Kentucky. New UK coach Billy Gillispie was involved in a heated recruiting battle over Huntington, West Virginia, big man Patrick Patterson. In the severe talent drought of the times, Patterson was like a gallon of water for a desert full of parched UK fans. Add in the fact that Patterson's other two finalists were Duke and Florida, and there was no mistaking the fact that UK had to get Patterson.

On the afternoon of the press conference, a link briefly circulated of an Internet version of the Huntington newspaper column breaking the story that Patterson had committed to the Gators at his press conference. Apparently, the paper had prepared a draft story for each school because Patterson had done no such thing. He did choose UK that day, but Kentucky cardiologists' billing rates probably spiked for a few minutes when the false article link was circulated.

Patterson was recruited initially by Tubby Smith, was signed by Gillispie, and in 2009–10 finally ended his career on a John Calipari team that befitted a player of his talent and grace. It was a long, strange trip for P-Pat, and Kentucky fans are unlikely to forget him anytime soon.

Patterson was a freshman on Gillispie's first UK squad, the 2007–08 team. Patterson teamed with seniors Ramel Bradley and Joe Crawford to provide the team's firepower. The trio totaled more than 50 points per game, and each was chosen All-SEC. Patterson averaged 16.4 points per game on 57 percent shooting. He led the team in rebounding and was second in blocked shots. Patterson had 23 points and 12 boards in a memorable double-overtime win over Vanderbilt. Patterson sustained a stress fracture in his foot against Ole Miss late in the season, and he missed the remainder of the year.

The 2008–09 season proved to be strange for all involved. It began with a home loss to VMI, and ended in the NIT. In the middle, Billy Gillispie lost his marbles and his team, and for most of the season, Kentucky was reduced to the Jodie Meeks and Patrick Patterson Show. The unflappable Patterson upped his numbers to 17.9 points and 9.3 rebounds per game. He shot better than 60 percent from the field and was again named All-SEC. But Kentucky was 22–14, and Patterson had enough of mediocre basketball. Pat entered his name in the NBA Draft.

And with some help from John Calipari and UK's top-ranked recruiting class in 2009, he took his name back out. Patterson

Huntington High School power forward Patrick Patterson signs to play basketball for the University of Kentucky during a signing ceremony at Huntington High School on Wednesday, May 16, 2007, in Huntington, West Virginia. Patterson announced that he chose Kentucky over Florida because he wanted to be close to his family. Four other programs courted Patterson: Duke, Virginia, Wake Forest, and West Virginia. (AP Photo/The Herald-Dispatch, Lori Wolfe)

became the elder statesman on the 2009–10 UK team. He provided leadership for John Wall, DeMarcus Cousins, and the other new Cats. While Patterson's scoring dropped to 14.3 points per game and his rebounding fell to 7.4 boards per game, he led the team by shooting 57 percent from the field. Patterson also extended his game. In his first two seasons, he was 0-for-4 on three-point shots. In 2009–10, he made 24 threes, shooting a respectable 35 percent from long distance.

While Patterson finally enjoyed team success with SEC regular season and SEC Tournament championships in 2010, his season ended one game shy of the Final Four with a tough loss to West Virginia. For the second straight season, SEC coaches chose him as first team All-Conference. Patterson finished his UK career with 1,564 points, 13th on UK's career scoring list. His 791 rebounds also place him at 13th on that UK career list, as well.

With all of the criticism regarding John Calipari's high-voltage recruits and their transition to the NBA, many missed the fact that Patterson, in addition to his numerous on-court achievements, graduated from UK in three years. After his junior year, Patterson was chosen 14th in the 2010 NBA Draft by the Houston Rockets. In two years with the Rockets, Patterson has seen his role on the team gradually increase. Seems he was worth all the fuss on that May day back in 2007.

96 John Wooden's Last Game

The 1974–75 Kentucky Wildcats were primed to win the school's fifth NCAA championship and Coach Joe B. Hall's first title. They had overcome the unbeaten Indiana juggernaut in the Elite Eight and thumped Syracuse in the national semifinal by 16 points. In the other semifinal, Denny Crum and Louisville were outlasted by UCLA and John Wooden by a single point. Kentucky seemed like a solid bet to down the Bruins and bring the championship hardware back home to Lexington.

But a funny thing happened on the way to the winner's circle. UCLA head coach John Wooden, with his nine previous NCAA championships, had an announcement after the Louisville win. The 64-year-old Wooden revealed that the title game would be his final game as head coach. Suddenly, the UCLA players had one more giant incentive to win the title, and UK was understandably thrown off-kilter.

The 1974–75 Wildcats were a talented and deep squad, well worthy of the national title. All-American Kevin Grevey was the star of the group, averaging 23.6 points per game and shooting better than 51 percent in doing so. Fellow senior Jimmy Dan Conner was a tough clutch player who scored 12.4 points per game.

Freshmen Rick Robey (10.4 points per game) and Jack Givens (9.4 PPG) helped round out the team. The 1974–75 squad's freshman class also featured Mike Phillips and James Lee, two tough reserves who would go on to contribute even greater things in UK's future. Seniors Mike Flynn and Bob Guyette rounded out the playing rotation.

UK was 26–4 heading into the NCAA title game. UK averaged more than 92 points per game and could score with anybody. UCLA lacked Kentucky's depth but was a tough, veteran squad—and now it wanted to send out the legendary Coach Wooden with a bang.

Kentucky struck first, surging to a six-point lead early in the first half mostly on the strength of the Cats' talented front court. UCLA answered, eventually taking a 43–40 lead into the halftime locker room.

Jimmy Dan Conner sank the first basket of the second half, cutting UCLA's lead to one. The game then see-sawed back and forth with UCLA jumping back to an eight-point lead with just more than 12 minutes to play.

Kevin Grevey did his utmost to keep Kentucky in the game. The left hander would finish with 34 points in his final UK appearance. Led by his scoring touch, UK trimmed the UCLA lead to a single point again around the five-minute mark. UCLA, however, would have the last run and the victory.

UCLA beat Kentucky in shooting accuracy (49 percent to 38 percent), rebounding (55 to 49), and, not shockingly, in fouls (UK was whistled for 28 fouls compared to 19 for UCLA). The game's officials certainly seemed a bit intimidated by calling John Wooden's last game, and UCLA certainly got its fair share of breaks on close calls.

At the end, Wooden had his 10th NCAA title in 12 years, and UK was stuck on its fourth of all time. While UCLA's goodbye gift to Wooden was a feel-good story for much of the nation, it wasn't for UK fans. Kevin Grevey has acknowledged his true feelings, noting in *Game of My Life: Kentucky*, "[Wooden's] retirement was a selfish thing, I think. He took the spotlight and put it on him before his team played in the championship, and that's not what I was taught. You don't call attention to yourself. Wooden's teachings were so eloquent, but this seemed to go against them."

Whatever the situation, UCLA made one last trip to the winner's circle. It is interesting that aside from Wooden's 10 titles in 12 years, the Bruins have won exactly one other NCAA title ever. Meanwhile, UK's title dreams were not so much defeated, as deferred. The super freshmen of the 1975 squad—Givens, Robey, Phillips, and Lee—would have another chance three years later and would provide a very different result.

97 Get Your Maker's Mark Bottle Signed

Let me introduce you to the Samuels family—they have been making whiskey since Robert Samuels came to Kentucky in 1784. "After their distilleries were shut down during Prohibition and World War II, Bill Samuels Sr. and his wife, Margie, decided to get back into the business in 1951 with a new recipe," their website reads.

That's how Maker's Mark began.

Maker's Mark, the bourbon made in Loretto, Kentucky, is famous for a little more in Kentucky than its great bourbon. In certain years, always in the spring, Maker's Mark chooses to honor certain Kentucky sports luminaries, most of the time associated with the men's basketball team. Those who know the normal Maker's Mark bottles may be quick to note that the top of the bottle is closed with melted wax—red melted wax.

Visit John Carpenter of Firebrick

Sure, John Carpenter has Adolph Rupp's autograph. A guy from Illinois mailed it to him. And he's got every other UK coach's autograph, too—all except one. "Coach Calipari," he said. "I really need to get Coach Calipari's autograph."

And when he says he needs to, he means it—because 52-year-old John Carpenter, who lives in tiny Firebrick in Lewis County, Kentucky, has the largest private collection of sports memorabilia in the world. While some may argue, Carpenter's collection has been verified as the largest private collection by *Ripley's Believe It or Not.* And while there are a lot of non-UK items in the collection, Carpenter says he has a lot of UK stuff, too. After all, that's his favorite basketball team.

Of course, he's also been featured on ESPN, had his own bobblehead made for him, and he's appeared on a limited edition Wheaties box. And for someone who has the world's largest collection of memorabilia, he really needs the official signature of the most current UK coach on a UK picture. (He has Cal's autograph on a UMass photo.).

Carpenter will not sell any part of his collection, and anyone interested in seeing his more than 6,000 pieces of memorabilia (from signed pictures to a baseball hit by Babe Ruth to a shoe worn by Jim Thorpe) is encouraged to drop on by.

"We enjoy having people over," he said.

Just remember—bring gifts.

However, for the Kentucky bottles, the wax is blue—and each special bottle has a different design.

The bottles are limited-release specials, and when they come out, you can find collectors (mostly Kentucky fans) standing in lines at their local liquor stores that stretch outside and around corners until the owner puts out the bottles for sale. Then, when the Keeneland race track in Lexington opens in the spring, those featured on the bottle will come out to sign it for free.

The first UK bottle was sold in 1993, just after the Wildcats had made a run to the Final Four. When Kentucky won the 1996 National Championship, the bourbon bottle was colored denim to match the unusual color of the UK jerseys that season. Other special bottles included:

2001: Wildcat mascot

2002: Bill Keightley

2006: Rupp's Runts

2007: The Unforgettables

2008: Joe B. Hall

2009: Rich Brooks

2010: John Calipari

2012: Tim Couch

Maker's estimated a profit of about $300,000 on the 24,000 Calipari bottles. Proceeds from the sales went to the UK Symphony Orchestra Outreach Program. The Tim Couch bottles—numbered at about 20,000—were predicted to make about $200,000 for the Gil Heart Institute, which wants to grow its practice and create quality heart healthcare for rural Eastern Kentuckians.

We can all drink to that.

98 Josh Harrellson and His Jorts

How different the UK universe might have been had Josh Harrellson worn long pants on his official recruiting visit. Of course, the big man was seen sporting jean shorts, a not entirely pleasant fashion memory of anyone who had to live through the 1980s. Photos of Harrellson in his "jorts" immediately began circulating on the Internet. When the obscure big man from Southwestern Illinois Junior College enrolled at UK, he was immediately dubbed "Jorts."

Harrellson may have been the most random of Billy Gillispie's otherworldly compilation of recruits. Jorts originally signed a letter of intent after high school with Western Illinois. He changed his mind and went the junior college route. After a season at Southwestern Illinois, Harrellson decided to transfer into Division I. Gillispie outrecruited the St. Louis Billikens and signed Harrellson.

Harrellson was a rugged post player at 6'10". He was not blessed with an abundance of physical skills, but he played hard and possessed solid outside shooting ability. He arrived at UK in 2008–09 in time for one of the weirdest seasons ever. Billy Gillispie was in the process of getting himself fired in his second year at UK. Jorts reached double-figure scoring in six games but ended the season with just 3.6 points and 2.5 rebounds per game. Even more notably, Harrellson was allegedly shut in a bathroom stall at halftime of a loss at Vanderbilt by an irate Gillispie. Other rumors indicated that Harrellson once had to ride back from a game in the equipment van rather than the team bus.

Fortunately for everyone involved, the insanity of Billy G. gave way to the calm of John Calipari in 2009–10. Returning players were often shuttled to new destinations if they did not fit into Calipari's system. Harrellson was on the border of such a demotion but was ultimately encouraged to stay. In 2009–10, Harrellson played 88 minutes the entire season. He averaged 1.3 points and 1.2 boards per game and seemed destined to finish his career in obscurity.

This destiny was emphasized when highly rated recruit Enes Kanter signed with UK. However, Harrellson didn't give up,

Josh Harrellson answers a question during a news conference in Lexington, Kentucky, on Tuesday, March 29, 2011. Harrellson's teammates call him "Jorts." Opposing coaches have called him everything from "mother hen" to the most underrated big man in the country. (AP Photo/Ed Reinke)

and the issue of Kanter's eligibility dragged on and on, eventually resulting in Kanter being denied the chance to ever play for the Cats. Meanwhile, Harrellson grabbed 26 rebounds in a Blue-White scrimmage. Calipari commented, "Either we are the worst offensive rebounding team in America or he's gotten better." When Harrellson posted a reply on his Twitter account, expressing disdain for the lack of any credit from his coach, Calipari was furious. Harrellson's Twitter account was dropped, and he spent extra time doing conditioning drills as punishment.

And somewhere along the way, the end-of-the-bench substitute became the rock in the middle of Kentucky's team. Against Louisville on December 31, 2010, Harrellson made Rick Pitino pay for not paying him enough attention, logging 23 points and 14 rebounds in a thumping of the Cardinals. Harrelson became a tenacious rebounder and a capable scorer. He managed eight double-doubles on the season and averaged 7.6 points and 8.7 boards per contest.

In the NCAA Tournament, Harrellson shone. In the Sweet 16, he found himself battling Ohio State and Player of the Year candidate Jared Sullinger. Early in the game, Harrellson tried to save a loose ball and fired a Nolan Ryan–ish fastball into Sullinger's chest. The ball thudded hard and fell out of bounds off Ohio State. Harrellson gave Sullinger all he wanted, scoring 17 points and grabbing 10 rebounds, including tipping the last Ohio State miss safely away from danger, as UK prevailed 62–60.

While the season ended in the Final Four for Harrellson, his career did not. The player who nobody had wanted was suddenly drafted by the New Orleans Hornets and immediately traded to the New York Knicks. He made the roster and in the fourth game of his NBA career and found himself starting against DeMarcus Cousins and the Sacramento Kings. Harrellson had 14 points and 12 rebounds as the Knicks rolled to victory. Logic fails to explain the rapid improvement of Harrellson. Simply put, it had to be the jorts.

99 Listen to the Joe B. and Denny Show

Five days a week, the two old enemies go toe to toe—two College Hall of Fame coaches with a combined three NCAA championships and nine Final Four appearances. Once again, it's the friendly Kentucky country boy who played under Rupp and then succeeded him versus the California import who put Louisville basketball on the map. Somewhere along the way, in the course of trying to outrecruit, outscheme, and outwin the other, the relationship changed. These days, instead of battling each other for supremacy, Joe B. Hall and Denny Crum are, well, friends. More specifically, they are friends who talk about sports on the radio.

How in the world did this happen? Some of the credit has to go to two other legendary rivals who, after retirement, found each other's company much more favorable. Former Alabama coach Wimp Sanderson and former Auburn coach Sonny Smith had a similar radio show in Alabama for some time. Joe B. Hall was a guest on that show via telephone one morning, just after having breakfast in Wheeler's Pharmacy in Lexington. Hall was sitting with a friend, Lexington sports agent Dick Robinson. Suddenly, in mid-interview, Robinson had an idea. He slid a napkin over to Hall, who was still on the air. *"The Joe B. and Denny Show?"* Robinson had scribbled.

For his part, Crum, recently retired from Louisville, was ready to go. In March 2004, the *Joe B. and Denny Show* went on the air. Dick Robinson produced the show until 2011 when he suffered a fatal bicycle accident. As for the two main attractions, they are both still going strong. Around 20 stations run the *Joe B. and Denny Show* on weekdays.

The show is simply a delight. Crum, who is 75, is still very much on his toes. The razor sharp two-time NCAA title winning coach never hides far beneath the surface. Hall is 83, and his health is not quite as good, but he remains the consummate man of the people. A great many calls seem to result in Joe B. recalling some long-ago interaction with a caller with picture-perfect accuracy. Hall is folksy and likeable, while Crum is smooth and knowledgeable. Tony Cruise is the latest third man on the team. The conversation rarely lags.

Of course, working together has fostered a tighter relationship for the two legendary headliners. Crum told Lostlettermen.com that he had been to visit Hall at Lake Barkley in Western Kentucky and that the two had been bass fishing. He also reported that Hall had returned the favor by visiting Crum in Idaho for some extended trout fishing.

The off-court ties did lead to one surprising on-court union of Crum and Hall. In August 2011, John Calipari was coaching the Dominican Republic national team. With the NBA locked out, Calipari set up an exhibition game in Lexington, and then another in Louisville, pitting the Dominicans against the Kentucky Pros, a team of former UK players who were now in the NBA. Calipari coached the Dominicans and, in keeping with his respect for Kentucky tradition, tapped Hall to coach the Pros in Lexington.

When the second game in Louisville approached, Hall added Denny Crum as his co-coach of the Pros. The games led to a series of odd sights—Calipari imploring Dominicans Edgar Sosa and Francisco Garcia, both Louisville products, to outplay John Wall; a blue-filled Yum! Center; and Joe B. and Denny side by side not in a radio studio but on the court. Add one more odd sight to the list—Joe B. and Denny going down in defeat. The Dominicans edged the Pros 91–86.

Exiled back to retirement, Joe B. and Denny still have their radio show and their fishing trips. Calipari recently joked that perhaps he and Rick Pitino would co-host a radio show someday. If so, they should be prepared to take second place in the radio ratings and perhaps in the hearts of listeners across Kentucky. Joe B and Denny were formidable as opponents, but as a team they're unbeatable.

Billy Gillispie

Kentucky was 5–0 in the SEC and led Ole Miss on the road by two points at halftime. Kentucky entered the game at No. 24 in the country, which was the first time UK had been ranked in almost two seasons. The ESPN broadcast swung to courtside reporter Jeannine Edwards, who awaited a few monosyllables of irrelevant coach speak. She asked the UK coach a question about making adjustments for UK's top scorer, Jodie Meeks, who had been held to six points in the half. Unfortunately, Billy Gillispie apparently missed the day in coach's school when dealing with halftime interviews was taught.

A cranky Gillispie protested that Kentucky was not a one-man team, then smirked and berated Edwards, saying, "What difference does it make? That's really a bad question." It was an ugly moment that suddenly gave the Big Blue Nation and the ESPN audience a look at the other side of Billy Gillispie.

The successful side of Billy Gillispie was the hard-working Texan who had taken UTEP and Texas A&M each up a few notches on the basketball food chain. In 2007, when Tubby Smith bolted Lexington and Billy Donovan apparently turned down the job, Gillispie was smart enough to be busy beating Louisville in Rupp Arena with Texas A&M. Desperation and circumstance led Mitch Barnhart to hire Gillispie as UK's next head coach.

Where Is He Now?

After his UK tenure, Gillispie apparently spent a period in a rehab center, trying to conquer his personal demons. While the stint seemed successful, his basketball demons have been perhaps a tougher foe. In 2011–12, Gillispie was hired for the Texas Tech head coaching job. The Red Raiders were 8–23 with a miserable 1–17 record in the Big 12 Conference. Even if Billy G. has cleaned up his personal life, he's still facing quite a challenge in Lubbock.

Up until the January 2009 tussle with Jeannine Edwards, Billy Gillispie's time at UK was going fairly well. Gillispie was 34–17 at UK at that moment. The 2007–08 team had fought through incredibly limited talent and depth to make the NCAA Tournament. Gillispie was considered an old-school coach, a tough guy who broke down his players to build them back up. Joe Crawford and Ramel Bradley were mature enough players to make things seem that way.

The 2008–09 Cats were 16–4 on the night that the future of UK basketball began to twist. They would limp home at 8–10 for the rest of the season. A Senior Day loss to a Georgia team that had previously fired its head coach was perhaps the most puzzling defeat, although a loss to a thoroughly mediocre South Carolina team by 18 points warrants dishonorable mention.

More than the W's and L's, Gillispie lost control of his team. To this day, bizarre and nearly unfathomable rumors circulate as to his behavior. One of the most common rumors, which was apparently true, is that Gillispie shut Josh Harrellson in a bathroom stall at halftime of one game. A few more stories, which may or may not be entirely accurate, include Gillispie forcing a particularly thin player to eat a large amount of food and then run for punishment, Gillispie ordering players to ride in an equipment van rather than on the team bus, or kicking players off the bus with instructions to walk back to the team hotel. He allegedly once ordered the team's departure for a road game with exactly five players. Another popular rumor is that Gillispie attempted to kick All-American Jodie Meeks off his 2008–09 NIT squad at halftime of Meeks' last UK game.

Hindsight suggests that more issues than bad behavior might have been in play. Gillispie was arrested for DUI shortly after the end of his UK tenure, and this was not his first such issue. In any case, Billy Gillispie never seemed to warm to the constant scrutiny and attention that the UK coaching job draws. He was ill at ease with fans and the media. After his January dispute with Jeannine Edwards, in February he had another dust up with her. Fielding a question from Edwards about stopping Florida guard Nick Calathes he again smirked at her, saying, "You seem to know more about that than me."

While Gillispie's odd social behavior drew headlines, his recruiting might have been even more damaging. While at UK, Gillispie took verbal commitments from players like Dakotah Euton, Vinny Zollo, and KC Ross-Miller. Nice kids, but they were all recruited in the ninth grade, and none of the bunch developed into UK–caliber talent. Taking a commitment from eighth grader Michael Avery might have been crazier than arguing with Jeannine Edwards or allegedly abusing his own players.

On March 27, 2009, Gillispie was relieved of his UK coaching duties. He had somehow never signed a contract with the university, which became the subject of a lengthy litigation battle. Gillispie's last act in Lexington was being chased into his office by local TV reporter Alan Cutler in a surreal scene. While the balm of hiring John Calipari has eased the sting of Gillispie, Billy Clyde's tenure was still a remarkably surreal chapter in the history of UK basketball.

Sources

Books

Clark, Ryan. *Game of My Life: Kentucky, Memorable Stories of Wildcat Basketball* Champaign, IL: Sports Publishing, LLC, 2007.

Doyel, Gregg. *Kentucky Wildcats: Where Have You Gone?* Champaign, IL: Sports Publishing, 2005.

Ledford, Cawood, with Billy Reed. *Hello Everybody, This Is Cawood Ledford*. Lexington, KY: Host Communications, 1992.

Ledford, Cawood. *Six Roads to Glory*, Lexington, KY: Host Communications, 1997.

Pitino, Rick, with Dick Weiss. *Full-Court Pressure: A Year in Kentucky Basketball*. New York, NY: Hyperion Books, 1993.

Rice, Russell. *Kentucky Basketball's Big Blue Machine*, Huntsville, AL: Strode Publishers 1976.

Rice, Russell. *The Wildcats—A Story of Kentucky Football*. Huntsville, AL: Strode Publishers, 1975.

Trease, Denny. *Tales From the Kentucky Hardwood—A Collection of the Greatest Basketball Stories Ever Told!* Champaign, IL: Sports Publishing LLC, 2002.

Wallace, Tom, and Kyle Macy. *The University of Kentucky Basketball Encyclopedia*. Champaign, IL: Sports Publishing, 2012.

Wheeler, Lonnie. *Blue Yonder*, Wilmington, Ohio: Orange Frazer Press, 1998.

Wojciechowski, Gene. *The Last Great Game: Duke vs. Kentucky and the 2.1 Seconds That Changed Basketball*. New York, NY: Blue Rider Press, 2012.

Ukathletics.com and Kentucky Media Guides from 2010-11 and 2009-10.

Newspapers

The Lexington Herald-Leader
The Courier-Journal
The New York Times
The Philadelphia Inquirer
The Chicago Sun-Times

Websites

Tom Leach's website—www.tomleachky.com
Jon Scott's website—www.bigbluehistoryu.net/bb/wildcats.html
John Calipari's website—www.coachcal.com

Other Sources

Personal interviews conducted over the course of the last five years.
Other articles noted in chapters.